Natural Language Processing with Java

Second Edition

Techniques for building machine learning and neural network models for NLP

Richard M. Reese
AshishSingh Bhatia

BIRMINGHAM - MUMBAI

Natural Language Processing with Java
Second Edition

Copyright © 2018 Packt Publishing

Commissioning Editor: Pravin Dhandre
Acquisition Editor: Divya Poojari
Content Development Editor: Eisha Dsouza
Technical Editor: Jovita Alva
Copy Editor: Safis Editing
Project Coordinator: Nidhi Joshi
Proofreader: Safis Editing
Indexer: Tejal Daruwale Soni
Graphics: Jisha Chirayil
Production Coordinator: Shraddha Falebhai

First published: March 2015
Second edition: July 2018

Production reference: 1300718

Published by Packt Publishing Ltd.
Livery Place
35 Livery Street
Birmingham
B3 2PB, UK.

ISBN 978-1-78899-349-4

www.packtpub.com

`mapt.io`

Mapt is an online digital library that gives you full access to over 5,000 books and videos, as well as industry leading tools to help you plan your personal development and advance your career. For more information, please visit our website.

Why subscribe?

- Spend less time learning and more time coding with practical eBooks and Videos from over 4,000 industry professionals

- Improve your learning with Skill Plans built especially for you

- Get a free eBook or video every month

- Mapt is fully searchable

- Copy and paste, print, and bookmark content

PacktPub.com

Did you know that Packt offers eBook versions of every book published, with PDF and ePub files available? You can upgrade to the eBook version at `www.PacktPub.com` and as a print book customer, you are entitled to a discount on the eBook copy. Get in touch with us at `service@packtpub.com` for more details.

At `www.PacktPub.com`, you can also read a collection of free technical articles, sign up for a range of free newsletters, and receive exclusive discounts and offers on Packt books and eBooks.

About the authors

Richard M. Reese has worked in both industry and academia. For 17 years, he worked in the telephone and aerospace industries, serving in several capacities, including research and development, software development, supervision, and training. He currently teaches at Tarleton State University. Richard has written several Java books and a C Pointer book. He uses a concise and easy-to-follow approach to teaching about topics. His Java books have addressed EJB 3.1, updates to Java 7 and 8, certification, functional programming, jMonkeyEngine, and natural language processing.

AshishSingh Bhatia is a learner, reader, seeker, and developer at core. He has over 10 years of IT experience in different domains, including banking, ERP, and education. He is persistently passionate about Python, Java, R, and web and mobile development. He is always ready to explore new technologies.

I would like to first and foremost thank my loving parents and friends for their continued support, patience, and encouragement.

About the reviewers

Doug Ortiz is an experienced enterprise cloud, big data, data analytics, and solutions architect who has designed, developed, re-engineered, and integrated enterprise solutions. His other expertise is in Amazon Web Services, Azure, Google Cloud, business intelligence, Hadoop, Spark, NoSQL databases, and SharePoint, to mention just a few.

He is the founder of Illustris, LLC, and is reachable at dougortiz@illustris.org.

Huge thanks to my wonderful wife, Milla, as well as Maria, Nikolay, and our children for all their support.

Paraskevas V. Lekeas received his PhD and MS in CS from the NTUA, Greece, where he conducted his postdoc on algorithmic engineering, and he also holds degrees in math and physics from the University of Athens. He was a professor at the TEI of Athens and the University of Crete before taking an internship at the University of Chicago. He has extensive experience in knowledge discovery and engineering, having addressed many challenges for startups and for corporations using a diverse arsenal of tools and technologies. He is leading the data group at H5, helping H5 advancing in innovative knowledge discovery.

Packt is searching for authors like you

If you're interested in becoming an author for Packt, please visit authors.packtpub.com and apply today. We have worked with thousands of developers and tech professionals, just like you, to help them share their insight with the global tech community. You can make a general application, apply for a specific hot topic that we are recruiting an author for, or submit your own idea.

Table of Contents

Preface

Natural Language Processing (NLP) allows you to take any sentence and identify patterns, special names, company names, and more. The second edition of *Natural Language Processing with Java* teaches you how to perform language analysis with the help of Java libraries, while constantly gaining insights from the outcomes.

You'll start by understanding how NLP and its various concepts work. Having got to grips with the basics, you'll explore important tools and libraries in Java for NLP, such as CoreNLP, OpenNLP, Neuroph, Mallet, and more. You'll then start performing NLP on different inputs and tasks, such as tokenization, model training, parts of speech, parsing trees, and more. You'll learn about statistical machine translation, summarization, dialog systems, complex searches, supervised and unsupervised NLP, and other things. By the end of this book, you'll have learned more about NLP, neural networks, and various other trained models in Java for enhancing the performance of NLP applications.

Who this book is for

Natural Language Processing with Java is for you if you are a data analyst, data scientist, or machine learning engineer who wants to extract information from a language using Java. Knowledge of Java programming is needed, while a basic understanding of statistics will be useful, but is not mandatory.

What this book covers

Chapter 1, *Introduction to NLP*, explains the importance and uses of NLP. The NLP techniques used in this chapter are explained with simple examples illustrating their use.

Chapter 2, *Finding Parts of Text*, focuses primarily on tokenization. This is the first step in more advanced NLP tasks. Both core Java and Java NLP tokenization APIs are illustrated.

Chapter 3, *Finding Sentences*, proves that sentence boundary disambiguation is an important NLP task. This step is a precursor for many other downstream NLP tasks in which text elements should not be split across sentence boundaries. This includes ensuring that all phrases are in one sentence and supporting Parts-of-Speech analysis.

Chapter 4, *Finding People and Things*, covers what is commonly referred to as **Named Entity Recognition** (**NER**). This task is concerned with identifying people, places, and similar entities in text. This technique is a preliminary step for processing queries and searches.

Chapter 5, *Detecting Parts of Speech*, shows you how to detect Parts-of -Speech, which are grammatical elements of text, such as nouns and verbs. Identifying these elements is a significant step in determining the meaning of text and detecting relationships within text.

Chapter 6, *Representing Text with Features*, explains how text is presented using N-grams and outlines role they play in revealing the context.

Chapter 7, *Information Retrieval*, deals with processing the huge amount of data uncovered in information retrieval and finding the relevant information using various approaches, such as Boolean retrieval, dictionaries, and tolerant retrieval.

Chapter 8, *Classifying Texts and Documents*, proves that classifying text is useful for tasks such as spam detection and sentiment analysis. The NLP techniques that support this process are investigated and illustrated.

Chapter 9, *Topic Modeling*, discusses the basics of topic modeling using a document that contains some text.

Chapter 10, *Using Parsers to Extract Relationships*, demonstrates parse trees. A parse tree is used for many purposes, including information extraction. It holds information regarding the relationships between these elements. An example implementing a simple query is presented to illustrate this process.

Chapter 11, *Combined Pipeline*, addresses several issues surrounding the use of combinations of techniques that solve NLP problems.

Chapter 12, *Creating a ChatBot*, looks at different types of chatbot, and we will be developing a simple appointment-booking chatbot too.

To get the most out of this book

Java SDK 8 is used to illustrate the NLP techniques. Various NLP APIs are needed and can be readily downloaded. An IDE is not required but is desirable.

Download the example code files

You can download the example code files for this book from your account at `www.packtpub.com`. If you purchased this book elsewhere, you can visit `www.packtpub.com/support` and register to have the files emailed directly to you.

You can download the code files by following these steps:

1. Log in or register at `www.packtpub.com`.
2. Select the **SUPPORT** tab.
3. Click on **Code Downloads & Errata**.
4. Enter the name of the book in the **Search** box and follow the onscreen instructions.

Once the file is downloaded, please make sure that you unzip or extract the folder using the latest version of:

- WinRAR/7-Zip for Windows
- Zipeg/iZip/UnRarX for Mac
- 7-Zip/PeaZip for Linux

The code bundle for the book is also hosted on GitHub at `https://github.com/PacktPublishing/Natural-Language-Processing-with-Java-Second-Edition`. In case there's an update to the code, it will be updated on the existing GitHub repository.

We also have other code bundles from our rich catalog of books and videos available at `https://github.com/PacktPublishing/`. Check them out!

Download the color images

We also provide a PDF file that has color images of the screenshots/diagrams used in this book. You can download it here: `http://www.packtpub.com/sites/default/files/downloads/NaturalLanguageProcessingwithJavaSecondEdition_ColorImages.pdf`.

Conventions used

There are a number of text conventions used throughout this book.

`CodeInText`: Indicates code words in text, database table names, folder names, filenames, file extensions, pathnames, dummy URLs, user input, and Twitter handles. Here is an example: "To process the text, we will use the `theSentence` variable as input to `Annotator`."

A block of code is set as follows:

```
System.out.println(tagger.tagString("AFAIK she H8 cth!"));
System.out.println(tagger.tagString(
    "BTW had a GR8 tym at the party BBIAM."));
```

Any command-line input or output is written as follows:

```
mallet-2.0.6$ bin/mallet import-dir --input sample-data/web/en --output
tutorial.mallet --keep-sequence --remove-stopwords
```

Bold: Indicates a new term, an important word, or words that you see onscreen. For example, words in menus or dialog boxes appear in the text like this. Here is an example: "Select **System info** from the **Administration** panel."

Warnings or important notes appear like this.

Tips and tricks appear like this.

Get in touch

Feedback from our readers is always welcome.

General feedback: Email `feedback@packtpub.com` and mention the book title in the subject of your message. If you have questions about any aspect of this book, please email us at `questions@packtpub.com`.

Errata: Although we have taken every care to ensure the accuracy of our content, mistakes do happen. If you have found a mistake in this book, we would be grateful if you would report this to us. Please visit www.packtpub.com/submit-errata, selecting your book, clicking on the Errata Submission Form link, and entering the details.

Piracy: If you come across any illegal copies of our works in any form on the Internet, we would be grateful if you would provide us with the location address or website name. Please contact us at copyright@packtpub.com with a link to the material.

If you are interested in becoming an author: If there is a topic that you have expertise in and you are interested in either writing or contributing to a book, please visit authors.packtpub.com.

Reviews

Please leave a review. Once you have read and used this book, why not leave a review on the site that you purchased it from? Potential readers can then see and use your unbiased opinion to make purchase decisions, we at Packt can understand what you think about our products, and our authors can see your feedback on their book. Thank you!

For more information about Packt, please visit packtpub.com.

Introduction to NLP 1

Natural Language Processing (NLP) is a broad topic focused on the use of computers to analyze natural languages. It addresses areas such as speech processing, relationship extraction, document categorization, and summation of text. However, these types of analyses are based on a set of fundamental techniques, such as tokenization, sentence detection, classification, and extracting relationships. These basic techniques are the focus of this book. We will start with a detailed discussion of NLP, investigate why it is important, and identify application areas.

There are many tools available that support NLP tasks. We will focus on the Java language and how various Java **Application Programmer Interfaces (APIs)** support NLP. In this chapter, we will briefly identify the major APIs, including Apache's OpenNLP, Stanford NLP libraries, LingPipe, and GATE.

This is followed by a discussion of the basic NLP techniques illustrated in this book. The nature and use of these techniques is presented and illustrated using one of the NLP APIs. Many of these techniques will use models. Models are similar to a set of rules that are used to perform a task such as tokenizing text. They are typically represented by a class that is instantiated from a file. We'll round off the chapter with a brief discussion on how data can be prepared to support NLP tasks.

NLP is not easy. While some problems can be solved relatively easily, there are many others that require the use of sophisticated techniques. We will strive to provide a foundation for NLP-processing so that you will be able to better understand which techniques are available for and applicable to a given problem.

NLP is a large and complex field. In this book, we will only be able to address a small part of it. We will focus on core NLP tasks that can be implemented using Java. Throughout this book, we will demonstrate a number of NLP techniques using both the Java SE SDK and other libraries, such as OpenNLP and Stanford NLP. To use these libraries, there are specific API JAR files that need to be associated with the project in which they are being used. A discussion of these libraries is found in the *Survey of NLP tools* section and contains download links to the libraries. The examples in this book were developed using NetBeans 8.0.2. These projects require the API JAR files to be added to the **Libraries** category of the **Projects Properties** dialog box.

In this chapter, we will learn about the following topics:

- What is NLP?
- Why use NLP?
- Why is NLP so hard?
- Survey of NLP tools
- Deep learning for Java
- Overview of text-processing tasks
- Understanding NLP models
- Preparing data

What is NLP?

A formal definition of NLP frequently includes wording to the effect that it is a field of study using computer science, **Artificial Intelligence (AI)**, and formal linguistics concepts to analyze natural language. A less formal definition suggests that it is a set of tools used to derive meaningful and useful information from natural language sources, such as web pages and text documents.

Meaningful and useful implies that it has some commercial value, though it is frequently used for academic problems. This can readily be seen in its support of search engines. A user query is processed using NLP techniques in order to generate a result page that a user can use. Modern search engines have been very successful in this regard. NLP techniques have also found use in automated help systems and in support of complex query systems, as typified by IBM's Watson project.

When we work with a language, the terms syntax and semantics are frequently encountered. The syntax of a language refers to the rules that control a valid sentence structure. For example, a common sentence structure in English starts with a subject followed by a verb and then an object, such as "Tim hit the ball." We are not used to unusual sentence orders, such as "Hit ball Tim." Although the rule of syntax for English is not as rigorous as that for computer languages, we still expect a sentence to follow basic syntax rules.

The semantics of a sentence is its meaning. As English speakers, we understand the meaning of the sentence, "Tim hit the ball." However, English, and other natural languages, can be ambiguous at times and a sentence's meaning may only be determined from its context. As we will see, various machine learning techniques can be used to attempt to derive the meaning of a text.

As we progress with our discussions, we will introduce many linguistic terms that will help us better understand natural languages and provide us with a common vocabulary to explain the various NLP techniques. We will see how the text can be split into individual elements and how these elements can be classified.

In general, these approaches are used to enhance applications, thus making them more valuable to their users. The uses of NLP can range from relatively simple uses to those that are pushing what is possible today. In this book, we will show examples that illustrate simple approaches, which may be all that is required for some problems, to the more advanced libraries and classes available to address sophisticated needs.

Why use NLP?

NLP is used in a wide variety of disciplines to solve many different types of problems. Text analysis is performed on text that ranges from a few words of user input for an internet query to multiple documents that need to be summarized. We have seen a large growth in the amount and availability of unstructured data in recent years. This has taken forms such as blogs, tweets, and various other social media. NLP is ideal for analyzing this type of information.

Machine learning and text analysis are used frequently to enhance an application's utility. A brief list of application areas follow:

- **Searching**: This identifies specific elements of text. It can be as simple as finding the occurrence of a name in a document or might involve the use of synonyms and alternate spellings/misspellings to find entries that are close to the original search string.

- **Machine translation**: This typically involves the translation of one natural language into another.
- **Summation**: Paragraphs, articles, documents, or collections of documents may need to be summarized. NLP has been used successfully for this purpose.
- **Named-Entity Recognition** (**NER**): This involves extracting names of locations, people, and things from text. Typically, this is used in conjunction with other NLP tasks, such as processing queries.
- **Information grouping**: This is an important activity that takes textual data and creates a set of categories that reflect the content of the document. You have probably encountered numerous websites that organize data based on your needs and have categories listed on the left-hand side of the website.
- **Parts-of-Speech tagging** (**POS**): In this task, text is split up into different grammatical elements, such as nouns and verbs. This is useful for analyzing the text further.
- **Sentiment analysis**: People's feelings and attitudes regarding movies, books, and other products can be determined using this technique. This is useful in providing automated feedback with regards to how well a product is perceived.
- **Answering queries**: This type of processing was illustrated when IBM's Watson successfully won a Jeopardy competition. However, its use is not restricted to winning gameshows and has been used in a number of other fields, including medicine.
- **Speech-recognition**: Human speech is difficult to analyze. Many of the advances that have been made in this field are the result of NLP efforts.
- **Natural-Language Generation** (**NLG**): This is the process of generating text from a data or knowledge source, such as a database. It can automate the reporting of information, such as weather reports, or summarize medical reports.

NLP tasks frequently use different machine learning techniques. A common approach starts with training a model to perform a task, verifying that the model is correct, and then applying the model to a problem. We will examine this process further in the *Understanding NLP models* section.

Why is NLP so hard?

NLP is not easy. There are several factors that make this process hard. For example, there are hundreds of natural languages, each of which has different syntax rules. Words can be ambiguous where their meaning is dependent on their context. Here, we will examine a few of the more significant problem areas.

At the character level, there are several factors that need to be considered. For example, the encoding scheme used for a document needs to be considered. Text can be encoded using schemes such as ASCII, UTF-8, UTF-16, or Latin-1. Other factors, such as whether the text should be treated as case-sensitive or not, may need to be considered. Punctuation and numbers may require special processing. We sometimes need to consider the use of emoticons (character combinations and special character images), hyperlinks, repeated punctuation (... or ---), file extensions, and usernames with embedded periods. Many of these are handled by preprocessing text, as we will discuss in the *Preparing data* section.

When we **tokenize** text, it usually means we are breaking up the text into a sequence of words. These words are called **tokens**. The process is referred to as **tokenization**. When a language uses whitespace characters to delineate words, this process is not too difficult. With a language such as Chinese, it can be quite difficult since it uses unique symbols for words.

Words and morphemes may need to be assigned a **Part-of-Speech** (POS) label, identifying what type of unit it is. A **morpheme** is the smallest division of text that has meaning. Prefixes and suffixes are examples of morphemes. Often, we need to consider synonyms, abbreviation, acronyms, and spellings when we work with words.

Stemming is another task that may need to be applied. **Stemming** is the process of finding the word stem of a word. For example, words such as *walking*, *walked*, or *walks* have the word stem *walk*. Search engines often use stemming to assist in asking a query.

Closely related to stemming is the process of **lemmatization**. This process determines the base form of a word, called its **lemma**. For example, for the word *operating*, its stem is *oper* but its lemma is *operate*. Lemmatization is a more refined process than stemming, and uses vocabulary and morphological techniques to find a lemma. This can result in more precise analysis in some situations.

Words are combined into phrases and sentences. Sentence detection can be problematic and is not as simple as looking for the periods at the end of a sentence. Periods are found in many places, including abbreviations such as Ms., and in numbers such as 12.834.

We often need to understand which words in a sentence are nouns and which are verbs. We are often concerned with the relationship between words. For example, **coreferences resolution** determines the relationship between certain words in one or more sentences. Consider the following sentence:

"The city is large but beautiful. It fills the entire valley."

The word *it* is the coreference to city. When a word has multiple meanings, we might need to perform **word-sense disambiguation (WSD)** to determine the intended meaning. This can be difficult to do at times. For example, "John went back home." Does the home refer to a house, a city, or some other unit? Its meaning can sometimes be inferred from the context in which it is used. For example, "John went back home. It was situated at the end of a cul-de-sac."

Despite these difficulties, NLP is able to perform these tasks reasonably well in most situations and provide added value to many problem domains. For example, sentiment analysis can be performed on customer tweets, resulting in possible free product offers for dissatisfied customers. Medical documents can be readily summarized to highlight the relevant topics and improved productivity.

Summarization is the process of producing a short description of different units. These units can include multiple sentences, paragraphs, a document, or multiple documents. The intent may be to identify those sentences that convey the meaning of the unit, determine the prerequisites for understanding a unit, or to find items within these units. Frequently, the context of the text is important in accomplishing this task.

Survey of NLP tools

There are many tools available that support NLP. Some of these are available with the Java SE SDK but are limited in their utility for all but the simplest types of problems. Other libraries, such as Apache's OpenNLP and LingPipe, provide extensive and sophisticated support for NLP problems.

Low-level Java support includes string libraries, such as `String`, `StringBuilder`, and `StringBuffer`. These classes possess methods that perform searching, matching, and text-replacement. **Regular expressions** use special encoding to match substrings. Java provides a rich set of techniques to use regular expressions.

As discussed earlier, tokenizers are used to split text into individual elements. Java provides supports for tokenizers with:

- The `String` class' `split` method
- The `StreamTokenizer` class
- The `StringTokenizer` class

There also exist a number of NLP libraries/APIs for Java. A partial list of Java-based NLP APIs can be found in the following table. Most of these are open source. In addition, there are a number of commercial APIs available. We will focus on the open source APIs:

API	URL
Apertium	`http://www.apertium.org/`
General Architecture for Text Engineering	`http://gate.ac.uk/`
Learning Based Java	`https://github.com/CogComp/lbjava`
LingPipe	`http://alias-i.com/lingpipe/`
MALLET	`http://mallet.cs.umass.edu/`
MontyLingua	`http://web.media.mit.edu/~hugo/montylingua/`
Apache OpenNLP	`http://opennlp.apache.org/`
UIMA	`http://uima.apache.org/`
Stanford Parser	`http://nlp.stanford.edu/software`
Apache Lucene Core	`https://lucene.apache.org/core/`
Snowball	`http://snowballstem.org/`

Many of these NLP tasks are combined to form a **pipeline**. A pipeline consists of various NLP tasks, which are integrated into a series of steps to achieve a processing goal. Examples of frameworks that support pipelines are **General Architecture for Text Engineering (GATE)** and Apache UIMA.

In the next section, we will cover several NLP APIs in more depth. A brief overview of their capabilities will be presented along with a list of useful links for each API.

Apache OpenNLP

The Apache OpenNLP project is a machine-learning-based tool kit for processing natural-language text; it addresses common NLP tasks and will be used throughout this book. It consists of several components that perform specific tasks, permit models to be trained, and support for testing the models. The general approach, used by OpenNLP, is to instantiate a model that supports the task from a file and then executes methods against the model to perform a task.

For example, in the following sequence, we will tokenize a simple string. For this code to execute properly, it must handle the `FileNotFoundException` and `IOException` exceptions. We use a try-with-resource block to open a `FileInputStream` instance using the `en-token.bin` file. This file contains a model that has been trained using English text:

```
try (InputStream is = new FileInputStream(
        new File(getModelDir(), "en-token.bin"))){
    // Insert code to tokenize the text
} catch (FileNotFoundException ex) {
    ...
} catch (IOException ex) {
    ...
}
```

An instance of the `TokenizerModel` class is then created using this file inside the `try` block. Next, we create an instance of the `Tokenizer` class, as shown here:

```
TokenizerModel model = new TokenizerModel(is);
Tokenizer tokenizer = new TokenizerME(model);
```

The `tokenize` method is then applied, whose argument is the text to be tokenized. The method returns an array of `String` objects:

```
String tokens[] = tokenizer.tokenize("He lives at 1511 W."
    + "Randolph.");
```

A for-each statement displays the tokens, as shown here. The open and closed brackets are used to clearly identify the tokens:

```
for (String a : tokens) {
    System.out.print("[" + a + "] ");
}
System.out.println();
```

When we execute this, we will get the following output:

```
[He] [lives] [at] [1511] [W.] [Randolph] [.]
```

In this case, the tokenizer recognized that `W.` was an abbreviation and that the last period was a separate token demarking the end of the sentence.

We will use the OpenNLP API for many of the examples in this book. OpenNLP links are listed in the following table:

OpenNLP	Website
Home	https://opennlp.apache.org/
Documentation	https://opennlp.apache.org/docs/
Javadoc	http://nlp.stanford.edu/nlp/javadoc/javanlp/index.html
Download	https://opennlp.apache.org/cgi-bin/download.cgi
Wiki	https://cwiki.apache.org/confluence/display/OPENNLP/Index%3bjsessionid=32B408C73729ACCCDD071D9EC354FC54

Stanford NLP

The Stanford NLP Group conducts NLP research and provides tools for NLP tasks. The Stanford CoreNLP is one of these toolsets. In addition, there are other toolsets, such as the Stanford Parser, Stanford POS tagger, and the Stanford Classifier. The Stanford tools support English and Chinese languages and basic NLP tasks, including tokenization and name-entity recognition.

These tools are released under the full GPL, but it does not allow them to be used in commercial applications, though a commercial license is available. The API is well-organized and supports the core NLP functionality.

There are several tokenization approaches supported by the Stanford group. We will use the `PTBTokenizer` class to illustrate the use of this NLP library. The constructor demonstrated here uses a `Reader` object, a `LexedTokenFactory<T>` argument, and a string to specify which of the several options is to be used.

`LexedTokenFactory` is an interface that is implemented by the `CoreLabelTokenFactory` and `WordTokenFactory` classes. The former class supports the retention of the beginning and ending character positions of a token, whereas the latter class simply returns a token as a string without any positional information. The `WordTokenFactory` class is used by default.

The `CoreLabelTokenFactory` class is used in the following example. A `StringReader` is created using a string. The last argument is used for the option parameter, which is `null` for this example. The `Iterator` interface is implemented by the `PTBTokenizer` class, allowing us to use the `hasNext` and `next` methods to display the tokens:

```
PTBTokenizer ptb = new PTBTokenizer(
```

```
new StringReader("He lives at 1511 W. Randolph."),
new CoreLabelTokenFactory(), null);
while (ptb.hasNext()) {
  System.out.println(ptb.next());
}
```

The output is as follows:

```
He
lives
at
1511
W.
Randolph
.
```

We will use the Stanford NLP library extensively in this book. A list of Stanford links is found in the following table. Documentation and download links are found in each of the distributions:

Stanford NLP	Website
Home	http://nlp.stanford.edu/index.shtml
CoreNLP	http://nlp.stanford.edu/software/corenlp.shtml#Download
Parser	http://nlp.stanford.edu/software/lex-parser.shtml
POS Tagger	http://nlp.stanford.edu/software/tagger.shtml
java-nlp-user mailing list	https://mailman.stanford.edu/mailman/listinfo/java-nlp-user

LingPipe

LingPipe consists of a set of tools to perform common NLP tasks. It supports model training and testing. There are both royalty-free and licensed versions of the tool. The production use of the free version is limited.

To demonstrate the use of LingPipe, we will illustrate how it can be used to tokenize text using the `Tokenizer` class. Start by declaring two lists, one to hold the tokens and a second to hold the whitespace:

```
List<String> tokenList = new ArrayList<>();
List<String> whiteList = new ArrayList<>();
```

 You can download the example code files for all Packt books you have purchased from your account at http://www.packtpub.com. If you purchased this book elsewhere, you can visit http://www.packtpub.com/support and register to have the files emailed directly to you.

Next, declare a string to hold the text to be tokenized:

```
String text = "A sample sentence processed \nby \tthe " +
    "LingPipe tokenizer.";
```

Now, create an instance of the `Tokenizer` class. As shown in the following code block, a static `tokenizer` method is used to create an instance of the `Tokenizer` class based on an `Indo-European factory` class:

```
Tokenizer tokenizer = IndoEuropeanTokenizerFactory.INSTANCE.
tokenizer(text.toCharArray(), 0, text.length());
```

The `tokenize` method of this class is then used to populate the two lists:

```
tokenizer.tokenize(tokenList, whiteList);
```

Use a for-each statement to display the tokens:

```
for(String element : tokenList) {
   System.out.print(element + " ");
}
System.out.println();
```

The output of this example is shown here:

```
A sample sentence processed by the LingPipe tokenizer
```

A list of LingPipe links can be found in the following table:

LingPipe	Website
Home	http://alias-i.com/lingpipe/index.html
Tutorials	http://alias-i.com/lingpipe/demos/tutorial/read-me.html
JavaDocs	http://alias-i.com/lingpipe/docs/api/index.html
Download	http://alias-i.com/lingpipe/web/install.html
Core	http://alias-i.com/lingpipe/web/download.html
Models	http://alias-i.com/lingpipe/web/models.html

GATE

GATE is a set of tools written in Java and developed at the University of Sheffield in England. It supports many NLP tasks and languages. It can also be used as a pipeline for NLP-processing. It supports an API along with GATE Developer, a document viewer that displays text along with annotations. This is useful for examining a document using highlighted annotations. GATE Mimir, a tool for indexing and searching text generated by various sources, is also available. Using GATE for many NLP tasks involves a bit of code. GATE Embedded is used to embed GATE functionality directly in the code. Useful GATE links are listed in the following table:

Gate	Website
Home	https://gate.ac.uk/
Documentation	https://gate.ac.uk/documentation.html
JavaDocs	http://jenkins.gate.ac.uk/job/GATE-Nightly/javadoc/

Download	https://gate.ac.uk/download/
Wiki	http://gatewiki.sf.net/

TwitIE is an open source GATE pipeline for information-extraction over tweets. It contains the following:

- Social media data-language identification
- Twitter tokenizer for handling smileys, username, URLs, and so on
- POS tagger
- Text-normalization

It is available as part of the GATE Twitter plugin. The following table lists the required links:

TwitIE	Website
Home	https://gate.ac.uk/wiki/twitie.html
Documentation	https://gate.ac.uk/sale/ranlp2013/twitie/twitie-ranlp2013.pdf?m=1

UIMA

The **Organization for the Advancement of Structured Information Standards (OASIS)** is a consortium focused on information-oriented business technologies. It developed the **Unstructured Information Management Architecture (UIMA)** standard as a framework for NLP pipelines. It is supported by Apache UIMA.

Although it supports pipeline creation, it also describes a series of design patterns, data representations, and user roles for the analysis of text. UIMA links are listed in the following table:

Apache UIMA	Website
Home	https://uima.apache.org/
Documentation	https://uima.apache.org/documentation.html

JavaDocs	`https://uima.apache.org/d/uimaj-2.6.0/apidocs/index.html`
Download	`https://uima.apache.org/downloads.cgi`
Wiki	`https://cwiki.apache.org/confluence/display/UIMA/Index`

Apache Lucene Core

Apache Lucene Core is an open source library for full-featured text search engines written in Java. It uses tokenization for breaking text into small chunks for indexing elements. It also provide pre- and post-tokenization options for analysis purposes. It supports stemming, filtering, text-normalization, and synonym-expansion after tokenization. When used, it creates a directory and index files, and can be used to search the contents. It cannot be taken as an NLP toolkit, but it provides powerful tools for working with text and advanced string-manipulation with tokenization. It provides a free search engine. The following table list the important links for Apache Lucene:

Apache Lucene	Website
Home	`http://lucene.apache.org/`
Documentation	`http://lucene.apache.org/core/documentation.html`
JavaDocs	`http://lucene.apache.org/core/7_3_0/core/index.html`
Download	`http://lucene.apache.org/core/mirrors-core-latest-redir.html?`

Deep learning for Java

Deep learning is a part of machine learning that is a subset of AI. Deep learning is inspired by the functioning of the human brain in its biological form. It uses terms such as neurons in creating neural networks, which can be part of supervised or unsupervised learning. Deep learning concepts are widely applied in fields of computer vision, speech recognition, NLP, social network analysis and filtering, fraud detection, predictions, and so on. Deep learning proved itself in the field of image processing in 2010 when it outperformed all others in an image net competition, and now it has started to show promising results in NLP. Some of the areas where deep learning has performed very well include **Named Entity Recognition** (**NER**), sentiment analysis, POS tagging, machine translation, text-classification, caption-generation, and question-answering.

This excellent read can be found in Goldbergs work at `https://arxiv.org/abs/1510.00726`. There are various tools and libraries available for deep learning. The following is a list of libraries to get you started:

- **Deeplearning4J** (`https://deeplearning4j.org/`): It is an open source, distributed, deep learning library for JVM.
- **Weka** (`https://www.cs.waikato.ac.nz/ml/weka/index.html`): It is known as a data-mining software in Java and has a collection of machine learning algorithms that support preprocessing, prediction, regression, clustering, association rules, and visualization.
- **Massive Online Analysis** (**MOA**) (`https://moa.cms.waikato.ac.nz/`): Used on realtime streams. Supports machine learning and data mining.
- **Environment for Developing KDD-Applications Supported by Index Structures** (**ELKI**) (`https://elki-project.github.io/`): It is a data-mining software that focuses on research algorithms, with an emphasis on unsupervised methods in cluster-analysis and outlier-detection.
- **Neuroph** (`http://neuroph.sourceforge.net/index.html`): It is a lightweight Java neural network framework used to develop neural network architectures licensed under Apache Licensee 2.0. It also supports GUI tools for creating and training data sets.
- **Aerosolve** (`http://airbnb.io/aerosolve/`): It is a machine learning package for humans, as seen on the web. It is developed by Airbnb and is more inclined toward machine learning.

You can find approximately 366 repositories on GitHub (`https://github.com/search?l=Javaamp;q=deep+learningamp;type=Repositoriesamp;utf8=%E2%9C%93`) for deep learning and Java.

Overview of text-processing tasks

Although there are numerous NLP tasks that can be performed, we will focus only on a subset of these tasks. A brief overview of these tasks is presented here, which is also reflected in the following chapters:

- `Chapter 2`, *Finding Parts of Text*
- `Chapter 3`, *Finding Sentences*
- `Chapter 4`, *Finding People and Things*
- `Chapter 5`, *Detecting Parts-of-Speech*
- `Chapter 8`, *Classifying Text and Documents*

- Chapter 10, *Using Parsers to Extract Relationships*
- Chapter 11, *Combined Approaches*

Many of these tasks are used together with other tasks to achieve an objective. We will see this as we progress through the book. For example, tokenization is frequently used as an initial step in many of the other tasks. It is a fundamental and basic step.

Finding parts of text

Text can be decomposed into a number of different types of elements, such as words, sentences, and paragraphs. There are several ways of classifying these elements. When we refer to parts of text in this book, we are referring to words, sometimes called tokens. **Morphology** is the study of the structure of words. We will use a number of morphology terms in our exploration of NLP. However, there are many ways to classify words, including the following:

- **Simple words**: These are the common connotations of what a word means, including the 17 words in this sentence.
- **Morphemes**: This are the smallest unit of a word that is meaningful. For example, in the word bounded, *bound* is considered to be a morpheme. Morphemes also include parts such as the suffix, *ed*.
- **Prefix/suffix**: This precedes or follows the root of a word. For example, in the word graduation, the *ation* is a suffix based on the word *graduate*.
- **Synonyms**: This is a word that has the same meaning as another word. Words such as small and tiny can be recognized as synonyms. Addressing this issue requires word-sense disambiguation.
- **Abbreviations**: These shorten the use of a word. Instead of using Mister Smith, we use Mr. Smith.
- **Acronyms**: These are used extensively in many fields, including computer science. They use a combination of letters for phrases such as FORmula TRANslation for FORTRAN. They can be recursive, such as GNU. Of course, the one we will continue to use is NLP.
- **Contractions**: We'll find these useful for commonly used combinations of words, such as the first word of this sentence.
- **Numbers**: A specialized word that normally uses only digits. However, more complex versions can include a period and a special character to reflect scientific notation or numbers of a specific base.

Identifying these parts is useful for other NLP tasks. For example, to determine the boundaries of a sentence, it is necessary to break it apart and determine which elements terminate a sentence.

The process of breaking text apart is called tokenization. The result is a stream of tokens. The elements of the text that determine where elements should be split are called **delimiters**. For most English text, whitespace is used as a delimiter. This type of a delimiter typically includes blanks, tabs, and new line characters.

Tokenization can be simple or complex. Here, we will demonstrate a simple tokenization using the `String` class' `split` method. First, declare a string to hold the text that is to be tokenized:

```
String text = "Mr. Smith went to 123 Washington avenue.";
```

The `split` method uses a regular expression argument to specify how the text should be split. In the following code sequence, its argument is the `\\s+` string. This specifies that one or more whitespaces will be used as the delimiter:

```
String tokens[] = text.split("\\s+");
```

A for-each statement is used to display the resulting tokens:

```
for(String token : tokens) {
    System.out.println(token);
}
```

When executed, the output will appear as shown here:

```
Mr.
Smith
went
to
123
Washington
avenue.
```

In `Chapter 2`, *Finding Parts of Text*, we will explore the tokenization process in depth.

Finding sentences

We tend to think of the process of identifying sentences as simple. In English, we look for termination characters, such as a period, question mark, or exclamation mark. However, as we will see in Chapter 3, *Finding Sentences*, this is not always that simple. Factors that make it more difficult to find the end of sentences include the use of embedded periods in such phrases as *Dr. Smith* or *204 SW. Park Street*.

This process is also called **sentence boundary disambiguation (SBD)**. This is a more significant problem in English than it is in languages such as Chinese or Japanese, which have unambiguous sentence delimiters.

Identifying sentences is useful for a number of reasons. Some NLP tasks, such as POS tagging and entity-extraction, work on individual sentences. Question-answering applications also need to identify individual sentences. For these processes to work correctly, sentence boundaries must be determined correctly.

The following example demonstrates how sentences can be found using the Stanford DocumentPreprocessor class. This class will generate a list of sentences based on either simple text or an XML document. The class implements the Iterable interface, allowing it to be easily used in a for-each statement.

Start by declaring a string containing the following sentences:

```
String paragraph = "The first sentence. The second sentence.";
```

Create a StringReader object based on the string. This class supports simple read type methods and is used as the argument of the DocumentPreprocessor constructor:

```
Reader reader = new StringReader(paragraph);
DocumentPreprocessor documentPreprocessor =
new DocumentPreprocessor(reader);
```

The DocumentPreprocessor object will now hold the sentences of the paragraph. In the following statement, a list of strings is created and is used to hold the sentences found:

```
List<String> sentenceList = new LinkedList<String>();
```

Each element of the documentPreprocessor object is then processed and consists of a list of the HasWord objects, as shown in the following block of code. The HasWord elements are objects that represent a word. An instance of StringBuilder is used to construct the sentence with each element of the hasWordList element being added to the list. When the sentence has been built, it is added to the sentenceList list:

```
for (List<HasWord> element : documentPreprocessor) {
```

```
StringBuilder sentence = new StringBuilder();
List<HasWord> hasWordList = element;
for (HasWord token : hasWordList) {
    sentence.append(token).append(" ");
}
sentenceList.add(sentence.toString());
}
```

A for-each statement is then used to display the sentences:

```
for (String sentence : sentenceList) {
  System.out.println(sentence);
}
```

The output will appear as shown here:

```
The first sentence .
The second sentence .
```

The SBD process is covered in depth in `Chapter 3`, *Finding Sentences*.

Feature-engineering

Feature-engineering plays an essential role in developing NLP applications; it is very important for machine learning, especially in prediction-based models. It is the process of transferring the raw data into features, using domain knowledge, so that machine learning algorithms work. Features give us a more focused view of the raw data. Once the features are identified, feature-selection is done to reduce the dimension of data. When raw data is processed, the patterns or features are detected, but it may not be enough to enhance the training dataset. Engineered features enhance training by providing relevant information that helps in differentiating the patterns in the data. The new feature may not be captured or apparent in original dataset or extracted features. Hence, feature-engineering is an art and requires domain expertise. It is still a human craft, something machines are not yet good at.

`Chapter 6`, *Representing Text with Features*, will show how text documents can be presented as traditional features that do not work on text documents.

Finding people and things

Search engines do a pretty good job of meeting the needs of most users. People frequently use search engines to find the address of a business or movie showtimes. A word-processor can perform a simple search to locate a specific word or phrase in a text. However, this task can get more complicated when we need to consider other factors, such as whether synonyms should be used or whether we are interested in finding things closely related to a topic.

For example, let's say we visit a website because we are interested in buying a new laptop. After all, who doesn't need a new laptop? When you go to the site, a search engine will be used to find laptops that possess the features you are looking for. The search is frequently conducted based on a previous analysis of vendor information. This analysis often requires text to be processed in order to derive useful information that can eventually be presented to a customer.

The presentation may be in the form of facets. These are normally displayed on the left-hand side of a web page. For example, the facets for laptops might include categories such as **Ultrabook**, **Chromebook**, or **Hard Disk Size**. This is illustrated in the following screenshot, which is part of an Amazon web page:

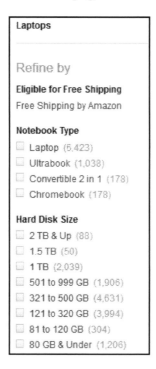

Some searches can be very simple. For example, the `String` class and related classes have methods, such as the `indexOf` and `lastIndexOf` methods, that can find the occurrence of a `String` class. In the simple example that follows, the index of the occurrence of the target string is returned by the `indexOf` method:

```
String text = "Mr. Smith went to 123 Washington avenue.";
String target = "Washington";
int index = text.indexOf(target);
System.out.println(index);
```

The output of this sequence is shown here:

```
22
```

This approach is useful for only the simplest problems.

When text is searched, a common technique is to use a data structure called an inverted index. This process involves tokenizing the text and identifying terms of interest in the text along with their position. The terms and their positions are then stored in the inverted index. When a search is made for the term, it is looked up in the inverted index and the positional information is retrieved. This is faster than searching for the term in the document each time it is needed. This data structure is used frequently in databases, information-retrieval systems, and search engines.

More sophisticated searches might involve responding to queries such as: "What are some good restaurants in Boston?" To answer this query, we might need to perform entity-recognition/resolution to identify the significant terms in the query, perform semantic analysis to determine the meaning of the query, search, and then rank the candidate responses.

To illustrate the process of finding names, we use a combination of a tokenizer and the OpenNLP `TokenNameFinderModel` class to find names in a text. Since this technique may throw `IOException`, we will use a `try...catch` block to handle it. Declare this block and an array of strings holding the sentences, as shown here:

```
try {
    String[] sentences = {
        "Tim was a good neighbor. Perhaps not as good a Bob " +
        "Haywood, but still pretty good. Of course Mr. Adam " +
        "took the cake!"};
    // Insert code to find the names here
} catch (IOException ex) {
    ex.printStackTrace();
}
```

Before the sentences can be processed, we need to tokenize the text. Set up the tokenizer using the `Tokenizer` class, as shown here:

```
Tokenizer tokenizer = SimpleTokenizer.INSTANCE;
```

We will need to use a model to detect sentences. This is needed to avoid grouping terms that may span sentence boundaries. We will use the `TokenNameFinderModel` class based on the model found in the `en-ner-person.bin` file. An instance of `TokenNameFinderModel` is created from this file as follows:

```
TokenNameFinderModel model = new TokenNameFinderModel(
new File("C:\\OpenNLP Models", "en-ner-person.bin"));
```

The `NameFinderME` class will perform the actual task of finding the name. An instance of this class is created using the `TokenNameFinderModel` instance, as shown here:

```
NameFinderME finder = new NameFinderME(model);
```

Use a for-each statement to process each sentence, as shown in the following code sequence. The `tokenize` method will split the sentence into tokens and the `find` method returns an array of `Span` objects. These objects store the starting and ending indexes for the names identified by the `find` method:

```
for (String sentence : sentences) {
    String[] tokens = tokenizer.tokenize(sentence);
    Span[] nameSpans = finder.find(tokens);
    System.out.println(Arrays.toString(
    Span.spansToStrings(nameSpans, tokens)));
}
```

When executed, it will generate the following output:

```
[Tim, Bob Haywood, Adam]
```

The primary focus of `Chapter 4`, *Finding People and Things*, is name recognition.

Detecting parts of speech

Another way of classifying the parts of text is at the sentence level. A sentence can be decomposed into individual words or combinations of words according to categories, such as nouns, verbs, adverbs, and prepositions. Most of us learned how to do this in school. We also learned not to end a sentence with a preposition, contrary to what we did in the second sentence of this paragraph.

Detecting the POS is useful in other tasks, such as extracting relationships and determining the meaning of text. Determining these relationships is called parsing. POS processing is useful for enhancing the quality of data sent to other elements of a pipeline.

The internals of a POS process can be complex. Fortunately, most of the complexity is hidden from us and encapsulated in classes and methods. We will use a couple of OpenNLP classes to illustrate this process. We will need a model to detect the POS. The POSModel class will be used and instanced using the model found in the en-pos-maxent.bin file, as shown here:

```
POSModel model = new POSModelLoader().load(
    new File("../OpenNLP Models/" "en-pos-maxent.bin"));
```

The POSTaggerME class is used to perform the actual tagging. Create an instance of this class based on the previous model, as shown here:

```
POSTaggerME tagger = new POSTaggerME(model);
```

Next, declare a string containing the text to be processed:

```
String sentence = "POS processing is useful for enhancing the "
    + "quality of data sent to other elements of a pipeline.";
```

Here, we will use WhitespaceTokenizer to tokenize the text:

```
String tokens[] = WhitespaceTokenizer.INSTANCE.tokenize(sentence);
```

The tag method is then used to find those parts of speech that stored the results in an array of strings:

```
String[] tags = tagger.tag(tokens);
```

The tokens and their corresponding tags are then displayed:

```
for(int i=0; i<tokens.length; i++) {
    System.out.print(tokens[i] + "[" + tags[i] + "] ");
}
```

When executed, the following output will be produced:

```
POS[NNP] processing[NN] is[VBZ] useful[JJ] for[IN] enhancing[VBG]
the[DT] quality[NN] of[IN] data[NNS] sent[VBN] to[TO] other[JJ]
elements[NNS] of[IN] a[DT] pipeline.[NN]
```

Each token is followed by an abbreviation, contained within brackets, for its POS. For example, NNP means that it is a proper noun. These abbreviations will be covered in Chapter 5, *Detecting Parts-of-Speech*, which is devoted to exploring this topic in depth.

Classifying text and documents

Classification is concerned with assigning labels to information found in text or documents. These labels may or may not be known when the process occurs. When labels are known, the process is called **classification**. When the labels are unknown, the process is called **clustering**.

Also of interest in NLP is the process of categorization. This is the process of assigning some text element into one of several possible groups. For example, military aircrafts can be categorized as either fighter, bomber, surveillance, transport, or rescue.

Classifiers can be organized by the type of output they produce. This can be binary, which results in a yes/no output. This type is often used to support spam filters. Other types will result in multiple possible categories.

Classification is more of a process than many of the other NLP tasks. It involves the steps that we will discuss in the *Understanding NLP models* section. Due to the length of this process, we will not illustrate it here. In Chapter 8, *Classifying Text and Documents*, we will investigate the classification process and provide a detailed example.

Extracting relationships

Relationship-extraction identifies relationships that exist in text. For example, with the sentence, "The meaning and purpose of life is plain to see," we know that the topic of the sentence is "The meaning and purpose of life." It is related to the last phrase that suggests that it is "plain to see."

Humans can do a pretty good job of determining how things are related to each other, at least at a high level. Determining deep relationships can be more difficult. Using a computer to extract relationships can also be challenging. However, computers can process large datasets to find relationships that would not be obvious to a human or that could not be done in a reasonable period of time.

Numerous relationships are possible. These include relationships such as where something is located, how two people are related to each other, the parts of a system, and who is in charge. Relationship-extraction is useful for a number of tasks, including building knowledge bases, performing trend-analysis, gathering intelligence, and performing product searches. Finding relationships is sometimes called **text analytics**.

There are several techniques that we can use to perform relationship-extractions. These are covered in more detail in `Chapter 10`, *Using Parser to Extract Relationships*. Here, we will illustrate one technique to identify relationships within a sentence using the Stanford NLP `StanfordCoreNLP` class. This class supports a pipeline where annotators are specified and applied to text. **Annotators** can be thought of as operations to be performed. When an instance of the class is created, the annotators are added using a `Properties` object found in the `java.util` package.

First, create an instance of the `Properties` class. Then, assign the annotators as follows:

```
Properties properties = new Properties();
properties.put("annotators", "tokenize, ssplit, parse");
```

We used three annotators, which specify the operations to be performed. In this case, these are the minimum required to parse the text. The first one, `tokenize`, will tokenize the text. The `ssplit` annotator splits the tokens into sentences. The last annotator, `parse`, performs the syntactic analysis, the parsing of the text.

Next, create an instance of the `StanfordCoreNLP` class using the properties' reference variable:

```
StanfordCoreNLP pipeline = new StanfordCoreNLP(properties);
```

Then, an `Annotation` instance is created, which uses the text as its argument:

```
Annotation annotation = new Annotation(
    "The meaning and purpose of life is plain to see.");
```

Apply the `annotate` method against the `pipeline` object to process the `annotation` object. Finally, use the `prettyPrint` method to display the result of the processing:

```
pipeline.annotate(annotation);
pipeline.prettyPrint(annotation, System.out);
```

The output of this code is shown as follows:

```
Sentence #1 (11 tokens):
The meaning and purpose of life is plain to see.
[Text=The CharacterOffsetBegin=0 CharacterOffsetEnd=3 PartOfSpeech=DT]
[Text=meaning CharacterOffsetBegin=4 CharacterOffsetEnd=11 PartOfSpeech=NN]
[Text=and CharacterOffsetBegin=12 CharacterOffsetEnd=15 PartOfSpeech=CC]
[Text=purpose CharacterOffsetBegin=16 CharacterOffsetEnd=23
PartOfSpeech=NN] [Text=of CharacterOffsetBegin=24 CharacterOffsetEnd=26
PartOfSpeech=IN] [Text=life CharacterOffsetBegin=27 CharacterOffsetEnd=31
PartOfSpeech=NN] [Text=is CharacterOffsetBegin=32 CharacterOffsetEnd=34
PartOfSpeech=VBZ] [Text=plain CharacterOffsetBegin=35 CharacterOffsetEnd=40
```

```
PartOfSpeech=JJ] [Text=to CharacterOffsetBegin=41 CharacterOffsetEnd=43
PartOfSpeech=TO] [Text=see CharacterOffsetBegin=44 CharacterOffsetEnd=47
PartOfSpeech=VB] [Text=. CharacterOffsetBegin=47 CharacterOffsetEnd=48
PartOfSpeech=.]
    (ROOT
      (S
        (NP
          (NP (DT The) (NN meaning)
            (CC and)
            (NN purpose))
          (PP (IN of)
            (NP (NN life))))
        (VP (VBZ is)
          (ADJP (JJ plain)
            (S
              (VP (TO to)
                (VP (VB see))))))))
        (. .)))
    root(ROOT-0, plain-8)
    det(meaning-2, The-1)
    nsubj(plain-8, meaning-2)
    conj_and(meaning-2, purpose-4)
    prep_of(meaning-2, life-6)
    cop(plain-8, is-7)
    aux(see-10, to-9)
    xcomp(plain-8, see-10)
```

The first part of the output displays the text along with the tokens and POS. This is followed by a tree-like structure that shows the organization of the sentence. The last part shows the relationships between the elements at a grammatical level. Consider the following example:

```
prep_of(meaning-2, life-6)
```

This shows how the preposition, *of*, is used to relate the words *meaning* and *life*. This information is useful for many text-simplification tasks.

Using combined approaches

As suggested earlier, NLP problems often involve using more than one basic NLP task. These are frequently combined in a pipeline to obtain the desired results. We saw one use of a pipeline in the previous section, *Extracting relationships*.

Most NLP solutions will use pipelines. We will provide several examples of pipelines in `Chapter 11`, *Combined Pipeline*.

Understanding NLP models

Regardless of the NLP task being performed or the NLP toolset being used, there are several steps that they all have in common. In this section, we will present these steps. As you go through the chapters and techniques presented in this book, you will see these steps repeated with slight variations. Getting a good understanding of them now will ease the task of learning the techniques.

The basic steps include the following:

1. Identifying the task
2. Selecting a model
3. Building and training the model
4. Verifying the model
5. Using the model

We will discuss each of these steps in the following sections.

Identifying the task

It is important to understand the problem that needs to be solved. Based on this understanding, a solution can be devised that consists of a series of steps. Each of these steps will use an NLP task.

For example, suppose we want to answer a query such as, "Who is the mayor of Paris?" We will need to parse the query into the POS, determine the nature of the question, the qualifying elements of the question, and eventually use a repository of knowledge, created using other NLP tasks, to answer the question.

Other problems may not be quite as involved. We might only need to break apart text into components so that the text can be associated with a category. For example, a vendor's product description may be analyzed to determine the potential product categories. The analysis of the description of a car would allow it to be placed into categories such as sedan, sports car, SUV, or compact.

Once you have an idea of what NLP tasks are available, you will be better able to match them with the problem you are trying to solve.

Selecting a model

Many of the tasks that we will examine are based on models. For example, if we need to split a document into sentences, we need an algorithm to do this. However, even the best sentence-boundary-detection techniques have problems doing this correctly every time. This has resulted in the development of models that examine the elements of text and then use this information to determine where sentence breaks occur.

The right model can be dependent on the nature of the text being processed. A model that does well for determining the end of sentences for historical documents might not work well when applied to medical text.

Many models have been created that we can use for the NLP task at hand. Based on the problem that needs to be solved, we can make informed decisions as to which model is the best. In some situations, we might need to train a new model. These decisions frequently involve trade-offs between accuracy and speed. Understanding the problem domain and the required quality of results enables us to select the appropriate model.

Building and training the model

Training a model is the process of executing an algorithm against a set of data, formulating the model, and then verifying the model. We may encounter situations where the text that needs to be processed is significantly different from what we have seen and used before. For example, using models trained with journalistic text might not work well when processing tweets. This may mean that the existing models will not work well with this new data. When this situation arises, we will need to train a new model.

To train a model, we will often use data that has been marked up in such a way that we know the correct answer. For example, if we are dealing with POS tagging, the data will have POS elements (such as nouns and verbs) marked in the data. When the model is being trained, it will use this information to create the model. This dataset is called a **corpus**.

Verifying the model

Once the model has been created, we need to verify it against a sample set. The typical verification approach is to use a sample set where the correct responses are known. When the model is used with this data, we are able to compare its result to the known good results and assess the quality of the model. Often, only part of a corpus is used for training while the other part is used for verification.

Using the model

Using the model is simply applying the model to the problem at hand. The details are dependent on the model being used. This was illustrated in several of the earlier demonstrations, such as in the *Detecting parts of speech* section where we used the POS model, as contained in the `en-pos-maxent.bin` file.

Preparing data

An important step in NLP is finding and preparing the data for processing. This includes the data for training purposes and the data that needs to be processed. There are several factors that need to be considered. Here, we will focus on the support Java provides for working with characters.

We need to consider how characters are represented. Although we will deal primarily with English text, other languages present unique problems. Not only are there differences in how a character can be encoded, the order in which text is read will vary. For example, Japanese orders its text in columns going from right to left.

There are also a number of possible encodings. These include ASCII, Latin, and Unicode to mention a few. A more complete list is found in the following table. Unicode, in particular, is a complex and extensive encoding scheme:

Encoding	Description
ASCII	A character-encoding using 128 (0-127) values.
Latin	There are several Latin variations that uses 256 values. They include various combination of the umlaut, and other characters. Different versions of Latin have been introduced to address various Indo-European languages, such as Turkish and Esperanto.
Big5	A two-byte encoding to address the Chinese character set.
Unicode	There are three encodings for Unicode: UTF-8, UTF-16, and UTF-32. These use 1, 2, and 4 bytes, respectively. This encoding is able to represent all known languages in existence today, including newer languages, such as Klingon and Elvish.

Java is capable of handling these encoding schemes. The `javac` executable's `-encoding` command-line option is used to specify the encoding scheme to use. In the following command line, the `Big5` encoding scheme is specified:

```
javac -encoding Big5
```

Character-processing is supported using the primitive `char` data type, the `Character` class, and several other classes and interfaces, as summarized in the following table:

Character type	Description
char	Primitive data type.
Character	Wrapper class for `char`.
CharBuffer	This class supports a buffer of `char`, providing methods for get/put characters or a sequence of characters operations.
CharSequence	An interface implemented by `CharBuffer`, `Segment`, `String`, `StringBuffer`, and `StringBuilder`. It supports read-only access to a sequence of chars.

Java also provides a number of classes and interfaces to support strings. These are summarized in the following table. We will use these in many of our examples. The `String`, `StringBuffer`, and `StringBuilder` classes provide similar string-processing capabilities but differ in whether they can be modified and whether they are thread-safe. The `CharacterIterator` interface and the `StringCharacterIterator` class provide techniques to traverse character sequences.

The `Segment` class represents a fragment of text:

Class/interface	Description
String	An immutable string.
StringBuffer	Represents a modifiable string. It is thread-safe.
StringBuilder	Compatible with the `StringBuffer` class but is not thread-safe.
Segment	Represents a fragment of text in a character array. It provides rapid access to character data in an array.
CharacterIterator	Defines an iterator for text. It supports a bidirectional traversal of text.
StringCharacterIterator	A class that implements the `CharacterIterator` interface for a `String`.

We also need to consider the file format if we are reading from a file. Often, data is obtained from sources where the words are annotated. For example, if we use a web page as the source of text, we will find that it is marked up with HTML tags. These are not necessarily relevant to the analysis process and may need to be removed.

The **Multipurpose Internet Mail Extensions (MIME)** type is used to characterize the format used by a file. Common file types are listed in the following table. Either we need to explicitly remove or alter the markup found in a file, or use specialized software to deal with it. Some of the NLP APIs provide tools to deal with specialized file formats:

File format	MIME type	Description
Text	Plain/text	Simple text file
Office type Document	Application/MS Word application/`vnd.oasis.opendocument.text`	Microsoft Office Open Office
PDF	Application/PDF	Adobe Portable Document Format
HTML	Text/HTML	Web pages
XML	Text/XML	eXtensible Markup Language
Database	Not applicable	Data can be in a number of different formats

Many of the NLP APIs assume that the data is clean. When it is not, it needs to be cleaned, lest we get unreliable and misleading results.

Summary

In this chapter, we introduced NLP and its uses. We found that it is used in many places to solve many different types of problems, ranging from simple searches to sophisticated classification problems. The Java support for NLP in terms of core string support and advanced NLP libraries was presented. The basic NLP tasks were explained and illustrated using code. The basics of deep learning in NLP and feature-engineering were also included to show how deep learning is impacting NLP. We also examined the process of training, verifying, and using models.

In this book, we will lay the foundation for employing basic NLP tasks using both simple and more complex approaches. You may find that some problems require only simple approaches, and when that is the case, knowing how to use the simple techniques may be more than adequate. In other situations, a more sophisticated technique may be needed. In either case, you will be prepared to identify which tool is needed and be able to choose the appropriate technique for the task.

In the next chapter, `Chapter 2`, *Finding Parts of Text*, we will examine the process of tokenization and see how it can be used to find parts of text.

2
Finding Parts of Text

Finding parts of text is concerned with breaking text down into individual units, called tokens, and optionally performing additional processing on those tokens. This additional processing can include stemming, lemmatization, stopword removal, synonym expansion, and converting text to lowercase.

We will demonstrate several tokenization techniques found in the standard Java distribution. These are included because sometimes this is all you may need to do the job. There may be no need to import NLP libraries in this situation. However, these techniques are limited. This is followed by a discussion of specific tokenizers or tokenization approaches supported by NLP APIs. These examples will provide a reference for how the tokenizers are used and the type of output they produce. This is followed by a simple comparison of the differences between the approaches.

There are many specialized tokenizers. For example, the Apache Lucene project supports tokenizers for various languages and specialized documents. The `WikipediaTokenizer` class is a tokenizer that handles Wikipedia-specific documents, and the `ArabicAnalyzer` class handles Arabic text. It is not possible to illustrate all of these varying approaches here.

We will also examine how certain tokenizers can be trained to handle specialized text. This can be useful when a different form of text is encountered. It can often eliminate the need to write a new and specialized tokenizer.

Next, we will illustrate how some of these tokenizers can be used to support specific operations, such as stemming, lemmatization, and stopword removal. POS can also be considered as a special instance of parts of text. However, this topic is investigated in `Chapter 5`, *Detecting Parts of Speech*.

Therefore, we will be covering the following topics in this chapter:

- What is tokenization?
- Uses of tokenizers

- NLP tokenizer APIs
- Understanding normalization

Understanding the parts of text

There are a number of ways to categorize parts of text. For example, we may be concerned with character-level issues, such as punctuation, with a possible need to ignore or expand contractions. At the word level, we may need to perform different operations, such as the following:

- Identifying morphemes using stemming and/or lemmatization
- Expanding abbreviations and acronyms
- Isolating number units

We cannot always split words with punctuation, because the punctuation is sometimes considered to be part of the word, such as the word *can't*. We may also be concerned with grouping multiple words to form meaningful phrases. Sentence-detection can also be a factor. We do not necessarily want to group words that cross sentence boundaries.

In this chapter, we are primarily concerned with the tokenization process and a few specialized techniques, such as stemming. We will not attempt to show how they are used in other NLP tasks. Those efforts are reserved for later chapters.

What is tokenization?

Tokenization is the process of breaking text down into simpler units. For most text, we are concerned with isolating words. Tokens are split based on a set of delimiters. These delimiters are frequently whitespace characters. Whitespace in Java is defined by the `Character` class' `isWhitespace` method. These characters are listed in the following table. However, there may be a need, at times, to use a different set of delimiters. For example, different delimiters can be useful when whitespace delimiters obscure text breaks, such as paragraph boundaries, and detecting these text breaks is important:

Character	Meaning
Unicode space character	(space_separator, line_separator, or paragraph_separator)
\t	U+0009 horizontal tabulation
\n	U+000A line feed
\u000B	U+000B vertical tabulation

Character	Meaning
\f	U+000C form feed
\r	U+000D carriage return
\u001C	U+001C file separator
\u001D	U+001D group separator
\u001E	U+001E record separator
\u001F	U+001F unit separator

The tokenization process is complicated by a large number of factors, such as the following:

- **Language**: Different languages present unique challenges. Whitespace is a commonly-used delimiter, but it will not be sufficient if we need to work with Chinese, where it is not used.
- **Text format**: Text is often stored or presented using different formats. How simple text is processed versus HTML or other markup techniques will complicate the tokenization process.
- **Stopwords**: Commonly-used words might not be important for some NLP tasks, such as general searches. These common words are called stopwords. Stopwords are sometimes removed when they do not contribute to the NLP task at hand. These can include words such as *a, and*, and *she*.
- **Text-expansion**: For acronyms and abbreviations, it is sometimes desirable to expand them so that postprocesses can produce better-quality results. For example, if a search is interested in the word *machine*, knowing that IBM stands for International Business Machines can be useful.
- **Case**: The case of a word (upper or lower) may be significant in some situations. For example, the case of a word can help identify proper nouns. When identifying the parts of text, conversion to the same case can be useful in simplifying searches.
- **Stemming and lemmatization**: These processes will alter the words to get to their *roots*.

Removing stopwords can save space in an index and make the indexing process faster. However, some engines do not remove stopwords because they can be useful for certain queries. For example, when performing an exact match, removing stopwords will result in misses. Also, the NER task often depends on stopword inclusion. Recognizing that *Romeo and Juliet* is a play is dependent on the inclusion of the word *and*.

Named -entity Recognition- extracting names of locations people, things from text.

There are many lists that define stopwords. Sometimes, what constitutes a stopword is dependent on the problem domain. A list of stopwords can be found at `http://www.ranks.nl/stopwords`. It lists a few categories of English stopwords and stopwords for languages other than English. At `http://www.textfixer.com/resources/common-english-words.txt`, you will find a comma-separated formatted list of English stopwords.

The top-10 stopwords adapted from Stanford (`http://library.stanford.edu/blogs/digital-library-blog/2011/12/stopwords-searc hworks-be-or-not-be`) can be found in the following table:

Stopword	Occurrences
the	7,578
of	6,582
and	4,106
in	2,298
a	1,137
to	1,033
for	695
on	685
an	289
with	231

We will focus on the techniques used to tokenize English text. This usually involves using whitespace or other delimiters to return a list of tokens.

Parsing is closely related to tokenization. They are both concerned with identifying parts of text, but parsing is also concerned with identifying the parts of speech and their relationship to each other.

Uses of tokenizers

The output of tokenization can be used for simple tasks, such as spellcheckers and processing simple searches. It is also useful for various downstream NLP tasks, such as identifying POS, sentence-detection, and classification. Most of the chapters that follow will involve tasks that require tokenization.

Frequently, the tokenization process is just one step in a larger sequence of tasks. These steps involve the use of pipelines, as we will illustrate in the *Using a pipeline* section. This highlights the need for tokenizers that produce quality results for the downstream task. If the tokenizer does a poor job, the downstream task will be adversely affected.

There are many different tokenizers and tokenization techniques available in Java. There are several core Java classes that were designed to support tokenization. Some of these are now outdated. There are also a number of NLP APIs designed to address both simple and complex tokenization problems. The next two sections will examine these approaches. First, we will see what the Java core classes have to offer, and then we will demonstrate a number of the NLP API tokenization libraries.

Simple Java tokenizers

There are several Java classes that support simple tokenization; some of them are as follows:

- Scanner
- String
- BreakIterator
- StreamTokenizer
- StringTokenizer

Although these classes provide limited support, it is useful to understand how they can be used. For some tasks, these classes will suffice. Why use a more difficult-to-understand and less-efficient approach when a core Java class can do the job? We will cover each of these classes as they support the tokenization process.

The `StreamTokenizer` and `StringTokenizer` classes should not be used for new developments. Instead, the `String` class' `split` method is usually a better choice. They have been included here in case you come across them and wonder whether they should be used or not.

Using the Scanner class

The `Scanner` class is used to read data from a text source. This might be standard input or it could be from a file. It provides a simple-to-use technique to support tokenization.

The `Scanner` class uses whitespace as the default delimiter. An instance of the `Scanner` class can be created using a number of different constructors.

The constructor in the following sequence uses a simple string. The `next` method retrieves the next token from the input stream. The tokens are isolated from the string, stored into a list of strings, and then displayed:

```
Scanner scanner = new Scanner("Let's pause, and then "
    + " reflect.");
List<String> list = new ArrayList<>();
while(scanner.hasNext()) {
    String token = scanner.next();
    list.add(token);
}
for(String token : list) {
    System.out.println(token);
}
```

When executed, we get the following output:

```
Let's
pause,
and
then
reflect.
```

This simple implementation has several shortcomings. If we needed our contractions to be identified and possibly split, as demonstrated with the first token, this implementation fails to do it. Also, the last word of the sentence was returned with a period attached to it.

Specifying the delimiter

If we are not happy with the default delimiter, there are several methods we can use to change its behavior. Several of these methods are summarized in the following table https://docs.oracle.com/javase/7/docs/api/java/util/Scanner.html. This list is provided to give you an idea of what is possible:

Method	Effect
useLocale	Uses the locale to set the default delimiter-matching
useDelimiter	Sets the delimiters based on a string or a pattern
useRadix	Specifies the radix to use when working with numbers
skip	Skips input-matching a pattern and ignores the delimiters
findInLine	Finds the next occurrence of a pattern ignoring delimiters

Here, we will demonstrate the use of the `useDelimiter` method. If we use the following statement immediately before the `while` statement in the previous section's example, the only delimiters that will be used will be the blank space, apostrophe, and period:

```
scanner.useDelimiter("[ ,.]");
```

When executed, the following will be displayed. The blank line reflects the use of the comma delimiter. It has the undesirable effect of returning an empty string as a token in this example:

```
Let's
pause
and
then
reflect
```

This method uses a pattern as defined in a string. The open and close brackets are used to create a class of characters. This is a regular expression that matches those three characters. An explanation of Java patterns can be found at `http://docs.oracle.com/javase/8/docs/api/`. The delimiter list can be reset to whitespaces using the `reset` method.

Using the split method

We demonstrated the `String` class' `split` method in Chapter 1, *Introduction to NLP*. It is duplicated here for convenience:

```
String text = "Mr. Smith went to 123 Washington avenue.";
String tokens[] = text.split("\\s+");
for (String token : tokens) {
    System.out.println(token);
}
```

The output is as follows:

```
Mr.
Smith
went
to
123
Washington
avenue.
```

The `split` method also uses a regular expression. If we replace the text with the same string we used in the previous section (`"Let's pause, and then reflect."`), we will get the same output.

The `split` method has an overloaded version that uses an integer to specify how many times the regular expression pattern is applied to the target text. Using this parameter can stop the operation after the specified number of matches has been made.

The `Pattern` class also has a `split` method. It will split its argument based on the pattern used to create the `Pattern` object.

Using the BreakIterator class

Another approach for tokenization involves the use of the `BreakIterator` class. This class supports the location of integer boundaries for different units of text. In this section, we will illustrate how it can be used to find words.

The class has a single default constructor which is protected. We will use the static `getWordInstance` method to get an instance of the class. This method is overloaded with one version using a `Locale` object. The class possesses several methods to access boundaries, as listed in the following table. It has one field, `DONE`, that is used to indicate that the last boundary has been found:

Method	Usage
`first`	Returns the first boundary of the text
`next`	Returns the next boundary following the current one
`previous`	Returns the boundary preceding the current one
`setText`	Associates a string with the `BreakIterator` instance

To demonstrate this class, we declare an instance of the `BreakIterator` class and a string to use with it:

```
BreakIterator wordIterator = BreakIterator.getWordInstance();
String text = "Let's pause, and then reflect.";
```

The text is then assigned to the instance and the first boundary is determined:

```
wordIterator.setText(text);
int boundary = wordIterator.first();
```

The loop that follows will store the beginning and ending boundary indexes for word breaks, using the `begin` and `end` variables. The boundary values are integers. Each boundary pair and its associated text are displayed.

When the last boundary is found, the loop terminates:

```
while (boundary != BreakIterator.DONE) {
    int begin = boundary;
    System.out.print(boundary + "-");
    boundary = wordIterator.next();
    int end = boundary;
    if(end == BreakIterator.DONE) break;
    System.out.println(boundary + " ["
    + text.substring(begin, end) + "]");
}
```

The output follows where the brackets are used to clearly delineate the text:

```
0-5 [Let's]
5-6 [ ]
6-11 [pause]
11-12 [,]
12-13 [ ]
13-16 [and]
16-17 [ ]
17-21 [then]
21-22 [ ]
22-29 [reflect]
29-30 [.]
```

This technique does a fairly good job of identifying the basic tokens.

Using the StreamTokenizer class

The `StreamTokenizer` class, found in the `java.io` package, is designed to tokenize an input stream. It is an older class and is not as flexible as the `StringTokenizer` class discussed in the *Using the StringTokenizer class* section. An instance of the class is normally created based on a file and will tokenize the text found in the file. It can be constructed using a string.

The class uses a `nextToken` method to return the next token in the stream. The token returned is an integer. The value of the integer reflects the type of token returned. Based on the token type, the token can be handled in different ways.

The `StreamTokenizer` class fields are shown in the following table:

Field	Data type	Meaning
nval	double	Contains a number if the current token is a number
sval	String	Contains the token if the current token is a word token
TT_EOF	static int	A constant for the end of the stream
TT_EOL	static int	A constant for the end of the line
TT_NUMBER	static int	The number of tokens read
TT_WORD	static int	A constant indicating a word token
ttype	int	The type of token read

In this example, a tokenizer is created, followed by the declaration of the `isEOF` variable, which is used to terminate the loop. The `nextToken` method returns the token type. Based on the token type, numeric and string tokens are displayed:

```
try {
    StreamTokenizer tokenizer = new StreamTokenizer(
        newStringReader("Let's pause, and then reflect."));
    boolean isEOF = false;
    while (!isEOF) {
        int token = tokenizer.nextToken();
        switch (token) {
            case StreamTokenizer.TT_EOF:
                isEOF = true;
                break;
            case StreamTokenizer.TT_EOL:
                break;
            case StreamTokenizer.TT_WORD:
                System.out.println(tokenizer.sval);
                break;
            case StreamTokenizer.TT_NUMBER:
                System.out.println(tokenizer.nval);
                break;
            default:
                System.out.println((char) token);
        }
    }
} catch (IOException ex) {
    // Handle the exception
}
```

When executed, we get the following output:

```
Let
'
```

This is not what we would normally expect. The problem is that the tokenizer uses apostrophes (single quote character) and double quotes to denote quoted text. Since there is no corresponding match, it consumes the rest of the string.

We can use the `ordinaryChar` method to specify which characters should be treated as common characters. The single quote and comma characters are designated as ordinary characters here:

```
tokenizer.ordinaryChar('\'');
tokenizer.ordinaryChar(',');
```

When these statements are added to the previous code and executed, we get the following output:

```
Let
'
s
pause
,
and
then
reflect.
```

The apostrophe is not a problem now. These two characters are treated as delimiters and returned as tokens. There is also a `whitespaceChars` method available that specifies which characters are to be treated as whitespaces.

Using the StringTokenizer class

The `StringTokenizer` class is found in the `java.util` package. It provides more flexibility than the `StreamTokenizer` class and is designed to handle strings from any source. The class' constructor accepts the string to be tokenized as its parameter and uses the `nextToken` method to return the token. The `hasMoreTokens` method returns `true` if more tokens exist in the input stream. This is illustrated in the following sequence:

```
StringTokenizerst = new StringTokenizer("Let's pause, and "
    + "then reflect.");
while (st.hasMoreTokens()) {
    System.out.println(st.nextToken());
}
```

When executed, we get the following output:

```
Let's
pause,
and
then
reflect.
```

The constructor is overloaded, allowing the delimiters to be specified and whether the delimiters should be returned as a token.

Performance considerations with Java core tokenization

When using these core Java tokenization approaches, it is worthwhile to briefly discuss how well they perform. Measuring performance can be tricky at times due to the various factors that can impact codeexecution. With that said, an interesting comparison on the performance of several Java core tokenization techniques can be found here: http://stackoverflow.com/questions/5965767/performance-of-stringtokenizer-class-vs-split-method-in-java. For the problem they were addressing, the indexOf method was the fastest.

NLP tokenizer APIs

In this section, we will demonstrate several different tokenization techniques using the OpenNLP, Stanford, and LingPipe APIs. Although there are a number of other APIs available, we restricted the demonstration to these APIs. These examples will give you an idea of what techniques are available.

We will use a string called paragraph to illustrate these techniques. The string includes a new line break that may occur in real text in unexpected places. It is defined here:

```
private String paragraph = "Let's pause, \nand then +
    + "reflect.";
```

Using the OpenNLPTokenizer class

OpenNLP possesses a `Tokenizer` interface that is implemented by three classes: `SimpleTokenizer`, `TokenizerME`, and `WhitespaceTokenizer`. This interface supports two methods:

- `tokenize`: This is passed a string to tokenize and returns an array of tokens as strings.
- `tokenizePos`: This is passed a string and returns an array of `Span` objects. The `Span` class is used to specify the beginning and ending offsets of the tokens.

Each of these classes is demonstrated in the following sections.

Using the SimpleTokenizer class

As the name implies, the `SimpleTokenizer` class performs the simple tokenization of text. The `INSTANCE` field is used to instantiate the class, as shown in the following code sequence. The `tokenize` method is executed against the `paragraph` variable and the tokens are then displayed:

```
SimpleTokenizer simpleTokenizer = SimpleTokenizer.INSTANCE;
String tokens[] = simpleTokenizer.tokenize(paragraph);
for(String token : tokens) {
    System.out.println(token);
}
```

When executed, we get the following output:

```
Let
'
s
pause
,
and
then
reflect
.
```

Using this tokenizer, punctuation is returned as separate tokens.

Using the WhitespaceTokenizer class

As its name implies, this class uses whitespaces as delimiters. In the following code sequence, an instance of the tokenizer is created and the `tokenize` method is executed against it using `paragraph` as input. The for statement then displays the tokens:

```
String tokens[] =
  WhitespaceTokenizer.INSTANCE.tokenize(paragraph);
for (String token : tokens) {
    System.out.println(token);
}
```

The output is as follows:

```
Let's
pause,
and
then
reflect.
```

Although this does not separate contractions and similar units of text, it can be useful for some applications. The class also possesses a `tokizePos` method that returns boundaries of the tokens.

Using the TokenizerME class

The `TokenizerME` class uses models created with **Maximum Entropy (MaxEnt)** and a statistical model to perform tokenization. The MaxEnt model is used to determine the relationship between data – in our case, text. Some text sources, such as various social media, are not well-formatted and use a lot of slang and special symbols, such as emoticons. A statistical tokenizer, such as the MaxEnt model, improves the quality of the tokenization process.

 A detailed discussion of this model is not possible here due to its complexity. A good starting point for an interested reader can be found at `http://en.wikipedia.org/w/index.php?title=Multinomial_logistic _regression&redirect=no`.

A `TokenizerModel` class hides the model and is used to instantiate the tokenizer. The model must have been previously trained. In the following example, the tokenizer is instantiated using the model found in the `en-token.bin` file. This model has been trained to work with common English text.

The location of the model file is returned by the `getModelDir` method, which you will need to implement. The returned value is dependent on where the models are stored on your system. Many of these models can be found at `http://opennlp.sourceforge.net/models-1.5/`.

After the instance of a `FileInputStream` class is created, the input stream is used as the argument of the `TokenizerModel` constructor. The `tokenize` method will generate an array of strings. This is followed by code to display the tokens:

```
try {
    InputStream modelInputStream = new FileInputStream(
        new File(getModelDir(), "en-token.bin"));
    TokenizerModel model = new
        TokenizerModel(modelInputStream);
    Tokenizer tokenizer = new TokenizerME(model);
    String tokens[] = tokenizer.tokenize(paragraph);
    for (String token : tokens) {
        System.out.println(token);
    }
} catch (IOException ex) {
    // Handle the exception
}
```

The output is as follows:

```
Let
's
pause
,
and
then
reflect
.
```

Using the Stanford tokenizer

Tokenization is supported by several Stanford NLP API classes; a few of them are as follows:

- The `PTBTokenizer` class
- The `DocumentPreprocessor` class
- The `StanfordCoreNLP` class as a pipeline

Each of these examples will use the `paragraph` string, as defined earlier.

Using the PTBTokenizer class

This tokenizer mimics the **Penn Treebank 3 (PTB)** tokenizer
(http://www.cis.upenn.edu/~treebank/). It differs from PTB in terms of its options and its
support for Unicode. The PTBTokenizer class supports several older constructors;
however, it is suggested that the three-argument constructor be used. This constructor uses
a Reader object, a LexedTokenFactory<T> argument, and a string to specify which of the
several options to use.

The LexedTokenFactory interface is implemented by the CoreLabelTokenFactory and
WordTokenFactory classes. The former class supports the retention of the beginning and
ending character positions of a token, whereas the latter class simply returns a token as a
string without any positional information. The WordTokenFactory class is used by default.
We will demonstrate the use of both classes.

The CoreLabelTokenFactory class is used in the following example. A StringReader
instance is created using paragraph. The last argument is used for the options, which is
null for this example. The Iterator interface is implemented by the PTBTokenizer class,
allowing us to use the hasNext and next method to display the tokens:

```
PTBTokenizer ptb = new PTBTokenizer(
    new StringReader(paragraph), new
 CoreLabelTokenFactory(),null);
while (ptb.hasNext()) {
    System.out.println(ptb.next());
}
```

The output is as follows:

```
Let
's
pause
,
and
then
reflect
.
```

The same output can be obtained using the WordTokenFactory class, as shown here:

```
PTBTokenizerptb = new PTBTokenizer(
    new StringReader(paragraph), new WordTokenFactory(), null);
```

The power of the `CoreLabelTokenFactory` class is realized with the options parameter of the `PTBTokenizer` constructor. These options provide a means to control the behavior of the tokenizer. Options include such controls as how to handle quotes, how to map ellipses, and whether it should treat British English spellings or American English spellings. A list of options can be found at `http://nlp.stanford.edu/nlp/javadoc/javanlp/edu/stanford/nlp/process/PTBTokenizer.html`.

In the following code sequence, the `PTBTokenizer` object is created using the `CoreLabelTokenFactory` variable, `ctf`, along with an option of `"invertible=true"`. This option allows us to obtain and use a `CoreLabel` object, which will give us the beginning and ending position of each token:

```
CoreLabelTokenFactory ctf = new CoreLabelTokenFactory();
PTBTokenizer ptb = new PTBTokenizer(
    new StringReader(paragraph),ctf,"invertible=true");
while (ptb.hasNext()) {
    CoreLabel cl = (CoreLabel)ptb.next();
    System.out.println(cl.originalText() + " (" +
        cl.beginPosition() + "-" + cl.endPosition() + ")");
}
```

The output of this sequence is as follows. The numbers within the parentheses indicate the tokens' beginning and ending positions:

```
Let (0-3)
's (3-5)
pause (6-11)
, (11-12)
and (14-17)
then (18-22)
reflect (23-30)
. (30-31)
```

Using the DocumentPreprocessor class

The `DocumentPreprocessor` class tokenizes input from an input stream. In addition, it implements the `Iterable` interface, making it easy to traverse the tokenized sequence. The tokenizer supports the tokenization of simple text and XML data.

To illustrate this process, we will use an instance of the `StringReader` class, which uses the `paragraph` string, as defined here:

```
Reader reader = new StringReader(paragraph);
```

An instance of the `DocumentPreprocessor` class is then instantiated:

```
DocumentPreprocessor documentPreprocessor =
    new DocumentPreprocessor(reader);
```

The `DocumentPreprocessor` class implements the
`Iterable<java.util.List<HasWord>>` interface. The `HasWord` interface contains two
methods that deal with words: `setWord` and `word`. The latter method returns a word as a
string. In the following code sequence, the `DocumentPreprocessor` class splits the input
text into sentences that are stored as `List<HasWord>`. An `Iterator` object is used to
extract a sentence and then a for-each statement will display the tokens:

```
Iterator<List<HasWord>> it = documentPreprocessor.iterator();
while (it.hasNext()) {
    List<HasWord> sentence = it.next();
    for (HasWord token : sentence) {
        System.out.println(token);
    }
}
```

When executed, we get the following output:

```
Let
's
pause
,
and
then
reflect
.
```

Using a pipeline

Here, we will use the `StanfordCoreNLP` class, as demonstrated in `Chapter 1`, *Introduction
to NLP*. However, we use a simpler annotator string to tokenize the paragraph. As shown in
the following code, a `Properties` object is created and assigned the `tokenize` and
`ssplit` annotators.

The `tokenize` annotator specifies that tokenization will occur, and the `ssplit` annotation
results in sentences being split:

```
Properties properties = new Properties();
properties.put("annotators", "tokenize, ssplit");
```

The `StanfordCoreNLP` class and the `Annotation` classes are created next:

```
StanfordCoreNLP pipeline = new StanfordCoreNLP(properties);
Annotation annotation = new Annotation(paragraph);
```

The `annotate` method is executed to tokenize the text and then the `prettyPrint` method will display the tokens:

```
pipeline.annotate(annotation);
pipeline.prettyPrint(annotation, System.out);
```

Various statistics are displayed, followed by the tokens marked up with position information in the output, which is as follows:

```
Sentence #1 (8 tokens):
Let's pause,
and then reflect.
[Text=Let CharacterOffsetBegin=0 CharacterOffsetEnd=3] [Text='s
CharacterOffsetBegin=3 CharacterOffsetEnd=5] [Text=pause
CharacterOffsetBegin=6 CharacterOffsetEnd=11] [Text=,
CharacterOffsetBegin=11 CharacterOffsetEnd=12] [Text=and
CharacterOffsetBegin=14 CharacterOffsetEnd=17] [Text=then
CharacterOffsetBegin=18 CharacterOffsetEnd=22] [Text=reflect
CharacterOffsetBegin=23 CharacterOffsetEnd=30] [Text=.
CharacterOffsetBegin=30 CharacterOffsetEnd=31]
```

Using LingPipe tokenizers

LingPipe supports a number of tokenizers. In this section, we will illustrate the use of the `IndoEuropeanTokenizerFactory` class. In later sections, we will demonstrate other ways that LingPipe supports tokenization. Its `INSTANCE` field provides an instance of an Indo-European tokenizer. The `tokenizer` method returns an instance of a `Tokenizer` class based on the text to be processed, as shown here:

```
char text[] = paragraph.toCharArray();
TokenizerFactory tokenizerFactory =
  IndoEuropeanTokenizerFactory.INSTANCE;
Tokenizer tokenizer = tokenizerFactory.tokenizer(text, 0,
  text.length);
for (String token : tokenizer) {
    System.out.println(token);
}
```

The output is as follows:

```
Let
'
s
pause
,
and
then
reflect
.
```

These tokenizers support the tokenization of normal text. In the next section, we will demonstrate how a tokenizer can be trained to deal with unique text.

Training a tokenizer to find parts of text

Training a tokenizer is useful when we encounter text that is not handled well by standard tokenizers. Instead of writing a custom tokenizer, we can create a tokenizer model that can be used to perform the tokenization.

To demonstrate how such a model can be created, we will read training data from a file and then train a model using this data. The data is stored as a series of words separated by whitespace and <SPLIT> fields. This <SPLIT> field is used to provide further information about how tokens should be identified. They can help identify breaks between numbers, such as 23.6, and punctuation characters, such as commas. The training data we will use is stored in the training-data.train file, and is shown here:

```
These fields are used to provide further information about how tokens
should be identified<SPLIT>.
They can help identify breaks between numbers<SPLIT>, such as 23.6<SPLIT>,
punctuation characters such as commas<SPLIT>.
```

The data that we use does not represent unique text, but it does illustrate how to annotate text and the process used to train a model.

We will use the OpenNLP TokenizerME class' overloaded train method to create a model. The last two parameters require additional explanations. MaxEnt is used to determine the relationship between elements of text.

We can specify the number of features the model must address before it is included in the model. These features can be thought of as aspects of the model. Iterations refer to the number of times the training procedure will iterate when determining the model's parameters. A few of the `TokenME` class parameters are as follows:

Parameter	Usage
`String`	A code for the language used
`ObjectStream<TokenSample>`	An `ObjectStream` parameter containing the training data
`boolean`	If `true`, then alphanumeric data is ignored
`int`	Specifies how many times a feature is processed
`int`	The number of iterations used to train the MaxEnt model

In the example that follows, we start by defining a `BufferedOutputStream` object that will be used to store the new model. Several of the methods used in this example will generate exceptions, which are handled in the `catch` blocks:

```
BufferedOutputStream modelOutputStream = null;
try {
    ...
} catch (UnsupportedEncodingException ex) {
    // Handle the exception
} catch (IOException ex) {
    // Handle the exception
}
```

An instance of an `ObjectStream` class is created using the `PlainTextByLineStream` class. This uses the training file and the character-encoding scheme as its constructor arguments. This is used to create a second `ObjectStream` instance of the `TokenSample` objects. These objects are text with token-span information included:

```
ObjectStream<String> lineStream = new PlainTextByLineStream(
    new FileInputStream("training-data.train"), "UTF-8");
ObjectStream<TokenSample> sampleStream =
    new TokenSampleStream(lineStream);
```

The `train` method can now be used, as shown in the following code. English is specified as the language. Alphanumeric information is ignored. The feature and iteration values are set to `5` and `100`, respectively:

```
TokenizerModel model = TokenizerME.train(
    "en", sampleStream, true, 5, 100);
```

The parameters of the `train` method are given in detail in the following table:

Parameter	Meaning
Language code	A string specifying the natural language used
Samples	The sample text
Alphanumeric optimization	If `true`, then alphanumeric are skipped
Cutoff	The number of times a feature is processed
Iterations	The number of iterations performed to train the model

The following code sequence will create an output stream and then write the model out to the `mymodel.bin` file. The model is then ready to be used:

```
BufferedOutputStream modelOutputStream = new
 BufferedOutputStream(
    new FileOutputStream(new File("mymodel.bin")));
model.serialize(modelOutputStream);
```

The details of the output will not be discussed here. However, it essentially chronicles the training process. The output of the sequence is as follows, but the last section has been abbreviated where most of the iterations steps have been deleted to save space:

```
Indexing events using cutoff of 5
    Dropped event F:[p=2, s=3.6,, p1=2, p1_num, p2=bok, p1f1=23, f1=3,
f1_num, f2=., f2_eos, f12=3.]
    Dropped event F:[p=23, s=.6,, p1=3, p1_num, p2=2, p2_num, p21=23,
p1f1=3., f1=., f1_eos, f2=6, f2_num, f12=.6]
    Dropped event F:[p=23., s=6,, p1=., p1_eos, p2=3, p2_num, p21=3.,
p1f1=.6, f1=6, f1_num, f2=,, f12=6,]
    Computing event counts... done. 27 events
    Indexing...  done.
Sorting and merging events... done. Reduced 23 events to 4.
Done indexing.
Incorporating indexed data for training...
done.
    Number of Event Tokens: 4
        Number of Outcomes: 2
    Number of Predicates: 4
...done.
Computing model parameters ...
Performing 100 iterations.
    1:  ...loglikelihood=-15.942385152878742  0.8695652173913043
    2:  ...loglikelihood=-9.223608340603953  0.8695652173913043
    3:  ...loglikelihood=-8.222154969329086  0.8695652173913043
    4:  ...loglikelihood=-7.885816898591612  0.8695652173913043
    5:  ...loglikelihood=-7.674336804488621  0.8695652173913043
```

```
    6:  ...loglikelihood=-7.494512270303332  0.8695652173913043
   Dropped event T:[p=23.6, s=,, p1=6, p1_num, p2=., p2_eos, p21=.6,
p1f1=6,, f1=,, f2=bok]
    7:  ...loglikelihood=-7.327098298508153  0.8695652173913043
    8:  ...loglikelihood=-7.1676028756216965  0.8695652173913043
    9:  ...loglikelihood=-7.014728408489079  0.8695652173913043
   ...
   100:  ...loglikelihood=-2.3177060257465376  1.0
```

We can use the model, as shown in the following sequence. This is the same technique we used in the *Using the TokenizerME class* section. The only difference is the model used here:

```java
try {
    paragraph = "A demonstration of how to train a
 tokenizer.";
    InputStream modelIn = new FileInputStream(new File(
        ".", "mymodel.bin"));
    TokenizerModel model = new TokenizerModel(modelIn);
    Tokenizer tokenizer = new TokenizerME(model);
    String tokens[] = tokenizer.tokenize(paragraph);
    for (String token : tokens) {
        System.out.println(token);
} catch (IOException ex) {
    ex.printStackTrace();
}
```

The output is as follows:

```
A
demonstration
of
how
to
train
a
tokenizer
.
```

Comparing tokenizers

A brief comparison of the NLP API tokenizers is shown in the following table. The tokens generated are listed under the tokenizer's name. They are based on the same text: "Let's pause, and then reflect." Keep in mind that the output is based on a simple use of the classes. There may be options not included in the examples that will influence how the tokens are generated. The intent is to simply show the type of output that can be expected based on the sample code and data:

SimpleTokenizer	WhitespaceTokenizer	TokenizerME	PTBTokenizer	DocumentPreprocessor	IndoEuropeanTokenizerFactory
Let	Let's	Let	Let	Let	Let
'	pause,	's	's	's	'
s	and	pause	pause	pause	s
pause	then	,	,	,	pause
,	reflect.	and	and	and	,
and		then	then	then	and
then		reflect	reflect	reflect	then
reflect		.	.	.	reflect
.					.

Understanding normalization

Normalization is a process that converts a list of words to a more uniform sequence. This is useful in preparing text for later processing. By transforming the words into a standard format, other operations are able to work with the data and will not have to deal with issues that might compromise the process. For example, converting all words to lowercase will simplify the searching process.

The normalization process can improve text-matching. For example, there are several ways that the term *modem router* can be expressed, such as modem and router, modem & router, modem/router, and modem-router. By normalizing these words to the common form, it makes it easier to supply the right information to a shopper.

Understand that the normalization process might also compromise an NLP task. Converting to lowercase letters can decrease the reliability of searches when the case is important.

Normalization operations can include the following:

- Changing characters to lowercase
- Expanding abbreviations
- Removing stopwords
- Stemming and lemmatization

We will investigate these techniques here, except for expanding abbreviations. This technique is similar to the technique used to remove stopwords, except that the abbreviations are replaced with their expanded version.

Converting to lowercase

Converting text to lowercase is a simple process that can improve search results. We can either use Java methods, such as the `String` class' `toLowerCase` method, or use the capability found in some NLP APIs, such as LingPipe's `LowerCaseTokenizerFactory` class. The `toLowerCase` method is demonstrated here:

```
String text = "A Sample string with acronyms, IBM, and UPPER "
    + "and lowercase letters.";
String result = text.toLowerCase();
System.out.println(result);
```

The output will be as follows:

```
a sample string with acronyms, ibm, and upper and lowercase letters.
```

LingPipe's `LowerCaseTokenizerFactory` approach is illustrated in the *Normalizing using a pipeline* section.

Removing stopwords

There are several approaches to remove stopwords. A simple approach is to create a class to hold and remove stopwords. Also, several NLP APIs provide support for stopword removal. We will create a simple class called `StopWords` to demonstrate the first approach. We will then use LingPipe's `EnglishStopTokenizerFactory` class to demonstrate the second approach.

Creating a StopWords class

The process of removing stopwords involves examining a stream of tokens, comparing them to a list of stopwords, and then removing the stopwords from the stream. To illustrate this approach, we will create a simple class that supports basic operations, as defined in the following table:

Constructor/method	Usage
Default constructor	Uses a default set of stopwords

Single argument constructor	Uses stopwords stored in a file
addStopWord	Adds a new stopword to the internal list
removeStopWords	Accepts an array of words and returns a new array with the stopwords removed

Create a class, called StopWords, that declares two instance variables, as shown in the following code block. The defaultStopWords variable is an array that holds the default stopword list. The HashSet variable's stopWords list is used to hold the stopwords for processing purposes:

```
public class StopWords {

    private String[] defaultStopWords = {"i", "a", "about", "an",
        "are", "as", "at", "be", "by", "com", "for", "from", "how",
        "in", "is", "it", "of", "on", "or", "that", "the", "this",
        "to", "was", "what", "when", where", "who", "will", "with"};

    private static HashSet stopWords  = new HashSet();
    ...
}
```

Two constructors of the class follow, which populate HashSet:

```
public StopWords() {
    stopWords.addAll(Arrays.asList(defaultStopWords));
}

public StopWords(String fileName) {
    try {
        BufferedReader bufferedreader =
                new BufferedReader(new FileReader(fileName));
        while (bufferedreader.ready()) {
            stopWords.add(bufferedreader.readLine());
        }
    } catch (IOException ex) {
        ex.printStackTrace();
    }
}
```

The `addStopWord` convenience method allows additional words to be added:

```
public void addStopWord(String word) {
    stopWords.add(word);
}
```

The `removeStopWords` method is used to remove the stopwords. It creates `ArrayList` to hold the original words passed to the method. The `for` loop is used to remove stopwords from this list. The `contains` method will determine whether the word submitted is a stopword, and if so, remove it. `ArrayList` is converted into an array of strings and then returned. This is shown as follows:

```
public String[] removeStopWords(String[] words) {
    ArrayList<String> tokens =
        new ArrayList<String>(Arrays.asList(words));
    for (int i = 0; i < tokens.size(); i++) {
        if (stopWords.contains(tokens.get(i))) {
            tokens.remove(i);
        }
    }
    return (String[]) tokens.toArray(
        new String[tokens.size()]);
}
```

The following sequence illustrates how stopwords can be used. First, we declare an instance of the `StopWords` class using the default constructor. The OpenNLP `SimpleTokenizer` class is declared and the sample text is defined, as shown here:

```
StopWords stopWords = new StopWords();
SimpleTokenizer simpleTokenizer = SimpleTokenizer.INSTANCE;
paragraph = "A simple approach is to create a class "
    + "to hold and remove stopwords.";
```

The sample text is tokenized and then passed to the `removeStopWords` method. The new list is then displayed:

```
String tokens[] = simpleTokenizer.tokenize(paragraph);
String list[] = stopWords.removeStopWords(tokens);
for (String word : list) {
    System.out.println(word);
}
```

When executed, we get the following output. A is not removed because it is uppercase and the class does not perform case-conversion:

```
A
simple
approach
create
class
hold
remove
stopwords
.
```

Using LingPipe to remove stopwords

LingPipe possesses the `EnglishStopTokenizerFactory` class that we will use to identify and remove stopwords. The words in this list are found at `http://alias-i.com/lingpipe/docs/api/com/aliasi/tokenizer/EnglishStopTokeniz erFactory.html`. They include words such as a, was, but, he, and for.

The `factory` class' constructor requires a `TokenizerFactory` instance as its argument. We will use the factory's `tokenizer` method to process a list of words and remove the stopwords. We start by declaring the string to be tokenized:

```
String paragraph = "A simple approach is to create a class "
    + "to hold and remove stopwords.";
```

Next, we create an instance of a `TokenizerFactory` based on the `IndoEuropeanTokenizerFactory` class. We then use that factory as the argument to create our `EnglishStopTokenizerFactory` instance:

```
TokenizerFactory factory =
  IndoEuropeanTokenizerFactory.INSTANCE;
factory = new EnglishStopTokenizerFactory(factory);
```

Using the LingPipe `Tokenizer` class and the factory's `tokenizer` method, the text declared in the `paragraph` variable is processed. The `tokenizer` method uses an array of `char`, a starting index, and its length:

```
Tokenizer tokenizer = factory.tokenizer(paragraph.toCharArray(),
    0, paragraph.length());
```

The following for-each statement will iterate over the revised list:

```
for (String token : tokenizer) {
    System.out.println(token);
}
```

The output will be as follows:

```
A
simple
approach
create
class
hold
remove
stopwords
.
```

Notice that although the letter A is a stopword, it was not removed from the list. This is because the stopword list uses a lowercase *a* and not an uppercase *A*. As a result, it missed the word. We will correct this problem in the *Normalizing using a pipeline* section.

Using stemming

Finding the stem of a word involves removing any prefixes or suffixes, and what is left is considered to be the stem. Identifying stems is useful for tasks where finding similar words is important. For example, a search may be looking for occurrences of words such as *book*. There are many words that contain this word, including books, booked, bookings, and bookmark. It can be useful to identify stems and then look for their occurrence in a document. In many situations, this can improve the quality of a search.

A stemmer may produce a stem that is not a real word. For example, it may decide that bounties, bounty, and bountiful all have the same stem, *bounti*. This can still be useful for searches.

Similar to stemming is lemmatization. This is the process of finding its lemma, its form as found in a dictionary. This can also be useful for some searches. Stemming is frequently viewed as a more primitive technique, where the attempt to get to the *root* of a word involves cutting off parts of the beginning and/or ending of a token.

Lemmatization can be thought of as a more sophisticated approach, where effort is devoted to finding the morphological or lexical meaning of a token. For example, the word *having* has a stem of *hav* while its lemma is *have*. Also, the words *was* and *been* have different stems but the same lemma, *be*.

Lemmatization can often use more computational resources than stemming. They both have their place, and their utility is partially determined by the problem that needs to be solved.

Using the Porter Stemmer

The **Porter Stemmer** is a commonly used stemmer for English. Its home page can be found at `http://tartarus.org/martin/PorterStemmer/`. It uses five steps to stem a word. The steps are :

1. Change the plurals, simple present, past and past participle and converts y to i for example agreed will be change to agree, sleepy will be changed to sleepi
2. Change double suffixes to single suffixes for example specialization will be changed to specialize
3. Change remaining words as in *step 2* by changing special in to special
4. Change remaining single suffixes by changing special to speci
5. It removes e or remove double letter at end for example attribute will be changed to attrib or will changed to wil

Although Apache OpenNLP 1.5.3 does not contain the `PorterStemmer` class, its source code can be downloaded from `https://svn.apache.org/repos/asf/opennlp/trunk/opennlp-tools/src/main/java/opennlp/tools/stemmer/PorterStemmer.java`. It can then be added to your project.

In the following example, we demonstrate the `PorterStemmer` class against an array of words. The input could easily have originated from some other text source. An instance of the `PorterStemmer` class is created and then its `stem` method is applied to each word of the array:

```
String words[] = {"bank", "banking", "banks", "banker", "banked",
    "bankart"};
```

```
PorterStemmer ps = new PorterStemmer();
for(String word : words) {
    String stem = ps.stem(word);
    System.out.println("Word: " + word + "  Stem: " + stem);
}
```

When executed, you will get the following output:

```
Word: bank  Stem: bank
Word: banking  Stem: bank
Word: banks  Stem: bank
Word: banker  Stem: banker
Word: banked  Stem: bank
Word: bankart  Stem: bankart
```

The last word is used in combination with the word *lesion* as in *Bankart lesion*. This is an injury of the shoulder and doesn't have much to do with the previous words. It does show that only common affixes are used when finding the stem.

Other potentially useful `PorterStemmer` class methods can be found in the following table:

Method	Meaning
add	This will add a `char` to the end of the current stem word
stem	The method used without an argument will return `true` if a different stem occurs
reset	Reset the stemmer so a different word can be used

Stemming with LingPipe

The `PorterStemmerTokenizerFactory` class is used to find stems using LingPipe. In this example, we will use the same words array as in the *Using the Porter Stemmer* section. The `IndoEuropeanTokenizerFactory` class is used to perform the initial tokenization, followed by the use of the Porter Stemmer. These classes are defined here:

```
TokenizerFactory tokenizerFactory =
  IndoEuropeanTokenizerFactory.INSTANCE;
TokenizerFactory porterFactory =
    new PorterStemmerTokenizerFactory(tokenizerFactory);
```

An array to hold the stems is declared next. We reuse the `words` array declared in the previous section. Each word is processed individually. The word is tokenized and its stem is stored in `stems`, as shown in the following code block. The words and their stems are then displayed:

```
String[] stems = new String[words.length];
for (int i = 0; i < words.length; i++) {
```

```
    Tokenization tokenizer = new Tokenization(words[i],porterFactory);
    stems = tokenizer.tokens();
    System.out.print("Word: " + words[i]);
    for (String stem : stems) {
        System.out.println("  Stem: " + stem);
    }
}
```

When executed, we get the following output:

```
Word: bank   Stem: bank
Word: banking   Stem: bank
Word: banks   Stem: bank
Word: banker   Stem: banker
Word: banked   Stem: bank
Word: bankart   Stem: bankart
```

We have demonstrated the Porter Stemmer using OpenNLP and LingPipe examples. It is worth noting that there are other types of stemmers available, including Ngrams and various mixed probabilistic/algorithmic approaches.

Using lemmatization

Lemmatization is supported by a number of NLP APIs. In this section, we will illustrate how lemmatization can be performed using the StanfordCoreNLP and OpenNLPLemmatizer classes. The lemmatization process determines the lemma of a word. A lemma can be thought of as the dictionary form of a word. For example, the lemma of *was* is *be*.

Using the StanfordLemmatizer class

We will use the StanfordCoreNLP class with a pipeline to demonstrate lemmatization. We start by setting up the pipeline with four annotators, including lemma, as shown here:

```
StanfordCoreNLP pipeline;
Properties props = new Properties();
props.put("annotators", "tokenize, ssplit, pos, lemma");
pipeline = new StanfordCoreNLP(props);
```

These annotators are needed and are explained as follows:

Annotator	Operation to be performed
tokenize	Tokenization
ssplit	Sentence-splitting
pos	POS-tagging
lemma	Lemmatization
ner	NER
parse	Syntactic-parsing
dcoref	Coreference-resolution

A `paragraph` variable is used with the `Annotation` constructor and the `annotate` method is then executed, as shown here:

```
String paragraph = "Similar to stemming is Lemmatization. "
    +"This is the process of finding its lemma, its form " +
    +"as found in a dictionary.";
Annotation document = new Annotation(paragraph);
pipeline.annotate(document);
```

We now need to iterate over the sentences and tokens of the sentences. The `Annotation` and `CoreMap` class' `get` methods will return values of the type specified. If there are no values of the specified type, it will return `null`. We will use these classes to obtain a list of lemmas.

First, a list of sentences is returned and then each word of each sentence is processed to find lemmas. The list of `sentences` and `lemmas` is declared here:

```
List<CoreMap> sentences =
    document.get(SentencesAnnotation.class);
List<String> lemmas = new LinkedList<>();
```

Two for-each statements iterate over the sentences to populate the `lemmas` list. Once this is completed, the list is displayed:

```
for (CoreMap sentence : sentences) {
    for (CoreLabelword : sentence.get(TokensAnnotation.class)) {
        lemmas.add(word.get(LemmaAnnotation.class));
    }
}

System.out.print("[");
```

```
for (String element : lemmas) {
    System.out.print(element + " ");
}
System.out.println("]");
```

The output of this sequence is as follows:

```
[similar to stem be lemmatization . this be the process of find its
lemma , its form as find in a dictionary . ]
```

Comparing this to the original test, we can see that it does a pretty good job:

```
Similar to stemming is Lemmatization. This is the process of finding
its lemma, its form as found in a dictionary.
```

Using lemmatization in OpenNLP

OpenNLP also supports lemmatization using the `JWNLDictionary` class. This class'
constructor uses a string that contains the path of the dictionary files used to identify roots.
We will use a WordNet dictionary that has been developed at Princeton University
(`wordnet.princeton.edu`). The actual dictionary is a series of files stored in a directory.
These files contain a list of words and their *root*. For the examples used in this section, we
will use the dictionary found at
`https://code.google.com/p/xssm/downloads/detail?name=SimilarityUtils.zip&can=2&q=`.

The `JWNLDictionary` class' `getLemmas` method is passed the word we want to process
and a second parameter that specifies the POS for the word. It is important that the POS
matches the actual word type if we want accurate results.

In the following code sequence, we create an instance of the `JWNLDictionary` class using a
path ending with `\dict\`. This is the location of the dictionary. We also define our sample
text. The constructor can throw `IOException` and `JWNLException`, which we deal with in
a `try...catch` block sequence:

```
try {
    dictionary = new JWNLDictionary("...\dict\");
    paragraph = "Eat, drink, and be merry, for life is but a dream";
    ...
} catch (IOException | JWNLException ex)
    //
}
```

Following the text initialization, add the following statements. First, we tokenize the string using the WhitespaceTokenizer class, as explained in the *Using the WhitespaceTokenizer class* section. Then, each token is passed to the getLemmas method with an empty string as the POS type. The original token and its lemmas are then displayed:

```
String tokens[] =
    WhitespaceTokenizer.INSTANCE.tokenize(paragraph);
for (String token : tokens) {
    String[] lemmas = dictionary.getLemmas(token, "");
    for (String lemma : lemmas) {
        System.out.println("Token: " + token + "   Lemma: "
            + lemma);
    }
}
```

The output is as follows:

```
Token: Eat,   Lemma: at
Token: drink,   Lemma: drink
Token: be   Lemma: be
Token: life   Lemma: life
Token: is   Lemma: is
Token: is   Lemma: i
Token: a   Lemma: a
Token: dream   Lemma: dream
```

The lemmatization process works well, except for the is token, which returns two lemmas. The second one is not valid. This illustrates the importance of using the proper POS for a token. We could have used one or more of the POS tags as the argument to the getLemmas method. However, this begs the question: how do we determine the correct POS? This topic is discussed in detail in Chapter 5, *Detecting Parts of Speech*.

A short list of POS tags is found in the following table. This list is adapted from https://www.ling.upenn.edu/courses/Fall_2003/ling001/penn_treebank_pos.html. The complete list of The University of Pennsylvania (Penn) Treebank tagset can be found at http://www.comp.leeds.ac.uk/ccalas/tagsets/upenn.html:

Tag	Description
JJ	Adjective
NN	Noun, singular, or mass
NNS	Noun, plural
NNP	Proper noun, singular
NNPS	Proper noun, plural

Tag	Description
POS	Possessive ending
PRP	Personal pronoun
RB	Adverb
RP	Particle
VB	Verb, base form
VBD	Verb, past tense
VBG	Verb, gerund, or present participle

Normalizing using a pipeline

In this section, we will combine many of the normalization techniques using a pipeline. To demonstrate this process, we will expand upon the example used in the *Using LingPipe* section to remove stopwords. We will add two additional factories to normalize text: `LowerCaseTokenizerFactory` and `PorterStemmerTokenizerFactory`.

The `LowerCaseTokenizerFactory` factory is added before the creation of `EnglishStopTokenizerFactory`, and `PorterStemmerTokenizerFactory` is added after the creation of `EnglishStopTokenizerFactory`, as shown here:

```
paragraph = "A simple approach is to create a class "
    + "to hold and remove stopwords.";
TokenizerFactory factory =
    IndoEuropeanTokenizerFactory.INSTANCE;
factory = new LowerCaseTokenizerFactory(factory);
factory = new EnglishStopTokenizerFactory(factory);
factory = new PorterStemmerTokenizerFactory(factory);
Tokenizer tokenizer =
    factory.tokenizer(paragraph.toCharArray(), 0,
    paragraph.length());
for (String token : tokenizer) {
    System.out.println(token);
}
```

The output is as follows:

```
simpl
approach
creat
class
```

```
hold
remov
stopword
.
```

What we have left are the stems of the words in lowercase with the stopwords removed.

Summary

In this chapter, we illustrated various approaches to tokenizing text and performing normalization on text. We started with simple tokenization techniques based on core Java classes, such as the `String` class' `split` method and the `StringTokenizer` class. These approaches can be useful when we decide to forgo the use of the NLP API classes.

We demonstrated how tokenization can be performed using the OpenNLP, Stanford, and LingPipe APIs. We found variations in how tokenization can be performed and options that can be applied in these APIs. A brief comparison of their output was provided.

Normalization was discussed, which can involve converting characters to lowercase, expanding abbreviations, removing stopwords, stemming, and lemmatization. We illustrated how these techniques can be applied using both core Java classes and the NLP APIs.

In the next chapter, `Chapter 3`, *Finding Sentences*, we will investigate the issues involved in determining the end of a sentence using various NLP APIs.

3
Finding Sentences

Partitioning text into sentences is also called **sentence boundary disambiguation (SBD)**. This process is useful for many downstream NLP tasks that require analysis within sentences; for example, POS and phrase analysis typically work within a sentence.

In this chapter, we will explain why SBD is difficult. Then, we will examine some core Java approaches that may work in some situations, and move on to the use of models by various NLP APIs. We will also examine training and validating approaches for sentence-detection models. We can add additional rules to refine the process further, but this will work only up to a certain point. After that, models must be trained to handle both common and specialized situations. The latter part of this chapter focuses on these models and their use.

We will cover the following topics in this chapter:

- The SBD process
- What makes SBD difficult?
- Using NLP APIs
- Training a sentence-detector model

The SBD process

The SBD process is language-dependent and is often not straightforward. Common approaches to detect sentences include using a set of rules or training a model to detect them. A set of simple rules for detecting a sentence follows. The end of a sentence is detected if the following is true:

- The text is terminated by a period, question mark, or exclamation mark
- The period is not preceded by an abbreviation or followed by a digit

Although this works well for most sentences, it will not work for all of them. For example, it is not always easy to determine what an abbreviation is, and sequences such as ellipses may be confused with periods.

Most search engines are not concerned with SBD. They are only interested in a query's tokens and their positions. POS-taggers and other NLP tasks that perform the extraction of data will frequently process individual sentences. The detection of sentence boundaries will help separate phrases that might appear to span sentences. For example, consider the following sentences:

"The construction process was over. The hill where the house was built was short."

If we were searching for the phrase *over the hill,* we would inadvertently pick up it here.

Many of the examples in this chapter will use the following text to demonstrate SBD. This text consists of three simple sentences followed by a more complicated sentence:

```
private static String paragraph = "When determining the end of sentences "
    + "we need to consider several factors. Sentences may end with "
    + "exclamation marks! Or possibly questions marks? Within "
    + "sentences we may find numbers like 3.14159, abbreviations "
    + "such as found in Mr. Smith, and possibly ellipses either "
    + "within a sentence ..., or at the end of a sentence...";
```

What makes SBD difficult?

Breaking text into sentences is difficult for a number of reasons:

- Punctuation is frequently ambiguous
- Abbreviations often contain periods
- Sentences may be embedded within each other by the use of quotes
- With more specialized text, such as tweets and chat sessions, we may need to consider the use of new lines or the completion of clauses

Punctuation ambiguity is best illustrated by the period. It is frequently used to demark the end of a sentence. However, it can be used in a number of other contexts as well, including abbreviations, numbers, email addresses, and ellipses. Other punctuation characters, such as question and exclamation marks, are also used in embedded quotes and specialized text, such as code that may be in a document.

Periods are used in a number of situations:

- To terminate a sentence
- To end an abbreviation
- To end an abbreviation and terminate a sentence
- For ellipses

- For ellipses at the end of a sentence
- Embedded in quotes or brackets

Most sentences we encounter end with a period. This makes them easy to identify. However, when they end with an abbreviation, it is a bit more difficult to identify them. The following sentence contains abbreviations with periods:

"Mr. and Mrs. Smith went to the ball."

In the following two sentences, we have an abbreviation that occurs at the end of the sentence:

"He was an agent of the CIA."

"He was an agent of the C.I.A."

In the last sentence, each letter of the abbreviation is followed by a period. Although not common, this may occur and we cannot simply ignore it.

Another issue that makes SBD difficult is trying to determine whether or not a word is an abbreviation. We cannot simply treat all uppercase sequences as abbreviations. Perhaps the user typed in a word in all caps by accident or the text was preprocessed to convert all characters to lowercase. Also, some abbreviations consist of a sequence of uppercase and lowercase letters. To handle abbreviations, a list of valid abbreviations is sometimes used. However, the abbreviations are often domain-specific.

Ellipses can further complicate the problem. They may be found as a single character (Extended ASCII 0 x 85 or Unicode (U+2026)) or as a sequence of three periods. In addition, there is the Unicode horizontal ellipsis (U+2026), the vertical ellipsis (U+22EE), and the presentation form for the vertical and horizontal ellipsis (U+FE19). Besides these, there are HTML encodings. For Java, `\uFE19` is used. These variations on encoding illustrate the need for good preprocessing of text before it is analyzed.

The following two sentences illustrate possible uses of the ellipses:

"And then there was ... one."

"And the list goes on and on and ..."

The second sentence was terminated by an ellipsis. In some situations, as suggested by the MLA handbook (`http://www.mlahandbook.org/fragment/public_index`), we can use brackets to distinguish ellipses that have been added from ellipses that were part of the original text, as shown here:

"The people [...] used various forms of transportation [...]" (*Young 73*).

We will also find sentences embedded in another sentence, such as:

The man said, "That's not right."

Exclamation marks and questions marks present other problems, even though the occurrence of these characters is more limited than that of the period. There are places other than at the end of a sentence where exclamation marks can occur. In the case of some words, such as Yahoo!, the exclamation mark is a part of the word. In addition, multiple exclamation marks are used for emphasis, such as "Best wishes!!" This can lead to the identification of multiple sentences where they do not actually exist.

Understanding the SBD rules of LingPipe's HeuristicSentenceModel class

There are other rules that can be used to perform SBD. LingPipe's `HeuristicSentenceModel` class uses a series of token rules to perform SBD. We will present them here, as they provide insight into what rules can be useful.

This class uses three sets of tokens and two flags to assist in the process:

- **Possible stops**: This is a set of tokens that can be the last token of a sentence
- **Impossible penultimates**: These tokens cannot be the second to last token in a sentence
- **Impossible starts**: This is a set of tokens that cannot be used to start a sentence
- **Balance parentheses**: This flag indicates that a sentence should not be terminated until all matching parentheses are matched in that sentence
- **Force final boundary**: This specifies that the final token in an input stream should be treated as a sentence terminator, even if it is not a possible stop

Balance parentheses include () and []. However, this rule will fail if the text is malformed. The default token sets are listed in the following table:

Possible stops	Impossible penultimates	Impossible starts
.	Any single letter	closed parentheses
..	Personal and professional titles, ranks, and so on	,
!	Commas, colons, and quotes	;
?	Common abbreviations	:
"	Directions	-

"	Corporate designators	--
).	Time, months, and so on	---
	US political parties	%
	US states (not ME or IN)	"
	Shipping terms	
	Address abbreviations	

Although LingPipe's `HeuristicSentenceModel` class uses these rules, there is no reason that they cannot be used in other implementations of SBD tools.

Heuristic approaches for SBD might not always be as accurate as other techniques. However, they may work in a particular domain and often have the advantages of being faster and using less memory.

Simple Java SBDs

Sometimes, text may be simple enough that Java core support will suffice. There are two approaches that will perform SBD: using regular expressions and using the `BreakIterator` class. We will examine both approaches here.

Using regular expressions

Regular expressions can be difficult to understand. While simple expressions are not usually a problem, as they become more complex, their readability worsens. This is one of the limitations of regular expressions when trying to use them for SBD.

We will present two different regular expressions. The first expression is simple, but does not do a very good job. It illustrates a solution that may be too simple for some problem domains. The second is more sophisticated and does a better job.

In this example, we create a regular expression class that matches periods, question marks, and exclamation marks. The `String` class' `split` method is used to split the text into sentences:

```
String simple = "[.?!]";
String[] splitString = (paragraph.split(simple));
for (String string : splitString) {
    System.out.println(string);
}
```

The output is as follows:

```
    When determining the end of sentences we need to consider several
factors
    Sentences may end with exclamation marks
    Or possibly questions marks
    Within sentences we may find numbers like 3
    14159, abbreviations such as found in Mr
    Smith, and possibly ellipses either within a sentence ..., or at the
end of a sentence...
```

As expected, the method splits the paragraph into characters, regardless of whether they are part of a number or abbreviation.

A second approach follows, which produces better results. This example has been adapted from an example found at `http://stackoverflow.com/questions/5553410/regular-expression-match-a-sentence`. The `Pattern` class, which compiles the following regular expression, is used:

```
[^.!?\s][^.!?]*(?:[.!?](?!['"]?\s|$)[^.!?]*)*[.!?]?['"]?(?=\s|$)
```

The comment in the following code sequence provides an explanation of what each part represents:

```
Pattern sentencePattern = Pattern.compile(
    "# Match a sentence ending in punctuation or EOS.\n"
    + "[^.!?\\s]     # First char is non-punct, non-ws\n"
    + "[^.!?]*       # Greedily consume up to punctuation.\n"
    + "(?:           # Group for unrolling the loop.\n"
    + "  [.!?]       # (special) inner punctuation ok if\n"
    + "  (?!['\"]?\\s|$)  # not followed by ws or EOS.\n"
    + "  [^.!?]*     # Greedily consume up to punctuation.\n"
    + ")*            # Zero or more (special normal*)\n"
    + "[.!?]?        # Optional ending punctuation.\n"
    + "['\"]?        # Optional closing quote.\n"
    + "(?=\\s|$)",
    Pattern.MULTILINE | Pattern.COMMENTS);
```

Another representation of this expression can be generated using the display tool found at `http://regexper.com/`. As shown in the following diagram, it graphically depicts the expression and can clarify how it works:

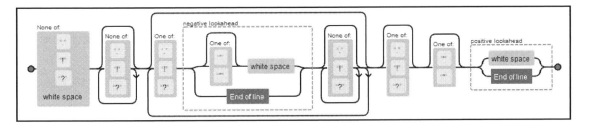

The `matcher` method is executed against the sample paragraph and then the results are displayed:

```
Matcher matcher = sentencePattern.matcher(paragraph);
while (matcher.find()) {
    System.out.println(matcher.group());
}
```

The output follows. The sentence terminators are retained, but there are still problems with abbreviations:

```
        When determining the end of sentences we need to consider several
factors.
        Sentences may end with exclamation marks!
        Or possibly questions marks?
        Within sentences we may find numbers like 3.14159, abbreviations such
as found in Mr.
        Smith, and possibly ellipses either within a sentence ..., or at the
end of a sentence...
```

Using the BreakIterator class

The `BreakIterator` class can be used to detect various text boundaries, such as those between characters, words, sentences, and lines. Different methods are used to create different instances of the `BreakIterator` class as follows:

- For characters, the `getCharacterInstance` method is used
- For words, the `getWordInstance` method is used
- For sentences, the `getSentenceInstance` method is used
- For lines, the `getLineInstance` method is used

Detecting breaks between characters is important at times, for example, when we need to process characters that are composed of multiple Unicode characters, such as ü. This character is sometimes formed by combining the `\u0075` (u) and `\u00a8` (¨) Unicode characters. The class will identify these types of characters. This capability is further detailed at `https://docs.oracle.com/javase/tutorial/i18n/text/char.html`.

The `BreakIterator` class can be used to detect the end of a sentence. It uses a cursor that references the current boundary. It supports a `next` and a `previous` method that moves the cursor forward and backwards in the text, respectively. `BreakIterator` has a single, protected default constructor. To obtain an instance of the `BreakIterator` class to detect the end of a sentence, use the static `getSentenceInstance` method, as shown here:

```
BreakIterator sentenceIterator =
  BreakIterator.getSentenceInstance();
```

There is also an overloaded version of the method. It takes a `Locale` instance as an argument:

```
Locale currentLocale = new Locale("en", "US");
BreakIterator sentenceIterator =
    BreakIterator.getSentenceInstance(currentLocale);
```

Once an instance has been created, the `setText` method will associate the text to be processed with the iterator:

```
sentenceIterator.setText(paragraph);
```

`BreakIterator` identifies the boundaries found in text using a series of methods and fields. All of these return integer values, and they are detailed in the following table:

Method	Usage
first	Returns the first boundary of the text
next	Returns the boundary following the current boundary
previous	Returns the boundary preceding the current boundary
DONE	The final integer, which is assigned a value of -1 (indicating that there are no more boundaries to be found)

To use the iterator in a sequential fashion, the first boundary is identified using the `first` method, and then the `next` method is called repeatedly to find the subsequent boundaries. The process is terminated when `DONE` is returned. This technique is illustrated in the following code sequence, which uses the previously declared `sentenceIterator` instance:

```
int boundary = sentenceIterator.first();
while (boundary != BreakIterator.DONE) {
    int begin = boundary;
    System.out.print(boundary + "-");
    boundary = sentenceIterator.next();
    int end = boundary;
    if (end == BreakIterator.DONE) {
        break;
    }
    System.out.println(boundary + " ["
        + paragraph.substring(begin, end) + "]");
}
```

On execution, we get the following output:

```
    0-75 [When determining the end of sentences we need to consider several
factors. ]
    75-117 [Sentences may end with exclamation marks! ]
    117-146 [Or possibly questions marks? ]
    146-233 [Within sentences we may find numbers like 3.14159 ,
abbreviations such as found in Mr. ]
    233-319 [Smith, and possibly ellipses either within a sentence ... , or
at the end of a sentence...]
    319-
```

This output works for simple sentences but is not successful with more complex sentences.

The uses of both regular expressions and the `BreakIterator` class have limitations. They are useful for text consisting of relatively simple sentences. However, when the text becomes more complex, it is better to use the NLP APIs instead, as discussed in the next section.

Using NLP APIs

There are a number of NLP API classes that support SBD. Some are rule-based, whereas others use models that have been trained using common and uncommon text. We will illustrate the use of sentence-detection classes using the OpenNLP, Stanford, and LingPipe APIs.

The models can also be trained. The discussion of this approach is illustrated in the *Training a sentence detector model* section. Specialized models are needed when working with specialized text, such as medical or legal text.

Using OpenNLP

OpenNLP uses models to perform SBD. An instance of the SentenceDetectorME class is created, based on a model file. Sentences are returned by the sentDetect method, and position information is returned by the sentPosDetect method.

Using the SentenceDetectorME class

A model is loaded from a file using the SentenceModel class. An instance of the SentenceDetectorME class is then created using the model, and the sentDetect method is invoked to perform SBD. The method returns an array of strings, with each element holding a sentence.

This process is demonstrated in the following example. A try-with-resources block is used to open the en-sent.bin file, which contains a model. Then, the paragraph string is processed. Next, various IO type-exceptions are caught (if necessary). Finally, a for-each statement is used to display the sentences:

```
try (InputStream is = new FileInputStream(
        new File(getModelDir(), "en-sent.bin"))) {
    SentenceModel model = new SentenceModel(is);
    SentenceDetectorME detector = new SentenceDetectorME(model);
    String sentences[] = detector.sentDetect(paragraph);
    for (String sentence : sentences) {
        System.out.println(sentence);
    }
} catch (FileNotFoundException ex) {
    // Handle exception
} catch (IOException ex) {
    // Handle exception
}
```

On execution, we get the following output:

```
    When determining the end of sentences we need to consider several
factors.
    Sentences may end with exclamation marks!
    Or possibly questions marks?
    Within sentences we may find numbers like 3.14159, abbreviations such
as found in Mr. Smith, and possibly ellipses either within a sentence ...,
or at the end of a sentence...
```

The output worked well for this paragraph. It caught both simple sentences and the more complex sentences. Of course, text that is processed is not always perfect. The following paragraph has extra spaces in some spots and is missing spaces where it needs them. This problem is likely to occur in the analysis of chat sessions:

```
paragraph = " This sentence starts with spaces and ends with "
    + "spaces . This sentence has no spaces between the next "
    + "one.This is the next one.";
```

When we use this paragraph with the previous example, we get the following output:

```
    This sentence starts with spaces and ends with spaces   .
    This sentence has no spaces between the next one.This is the next one.
```

The leading spaces of the first sentence were removed, but the ending spaces were not. The third sentence was not detected and was merged with the second sentence.

The getSentenceProbabilities method returns an array of doubles representing the confidence of the sentences detected from the last use of the sentDetect method. Add the following code after the for-each statement that displayed the sentences:

```
double probablities[] = detector.getSentenceProbabilities();
for (double probablity : probablities) {
    System.out.println(probablity);
}
```

By executing with the original paragraph, we get the following output:

```
0.9841708738988814
0.908052385070974
0.9130082376342675
1.0
```

The numbers shown are the probability representing the confidence.

Using the sentPosDetect method

The `SentenceDetectorME` class possesses a `sentPosDetect` method that returns `Span` objects for each sentence. Use the same code as found in the previous section, except for two changes: replace the `sentDetect` method with the `sentPosDetect` method, and the for-each statement with the method used here:

```
Span spans[] = detector.sentPosDetect(paragraph);
for (Span span : spans) {
    System.out.println(span);
}
```

The output that follows uses the original paragraph. The `Span` objects contain positional information returned from the default execution of the `toString` method:

```
[0..74)
[75..116)
[117..145)
[146..317)
```

The `Span` class possesses a number of methods. The following code sequence demonstrates the use of the `getStart` and `getEnd` methods to clearly show the text represented by those spans:

```
for (Span span : spans) {
    System.out.println(span + "[" + paragraph.substring(
        span.getStart(), span.getEnd()) +"]");
}
```

The output shows the sentences identified:

```
      [0..74)[When determining the end of sentences we need to consider
several factors.]
      [75..116)[Sentences may end with exclamation marks!]
      [117..145)[Or possibly questions marks?]
      [146..317)[Within sentences we may find numbers like 3.14159,
abbreviations such as found in Mr. Smith, and possibly ellipses either
within a sentence ..., or at the end of a sentence...]
```

There are a number of other `Span` methods that can be valuable. These are listed in the following table:

Method	Meaning
contains	An overloaded method that determines whether another Span object or index is contained with the target
crosses	Determines whether two spans overlap

`length`	The length of the span
`startsWith`	Determines whether the span starts the target span

Using the Stanford API

The Stanford NLP library supports several techniques used to perform sentence-detection. In this section, we will demonstrate this process using the following classes:

- `PTBTokenizer`
- `DocumentPreprocessor`
- `StanfordCoreNLP`

Although all of them perform SBD, each uses a different approach for performing the process.

Using the PTBTokenizer class

The `PTBTokenizer` class uses rules to perform SBD and has a variety of tokenization options. The constructor for this class possesses three parameters:

- A `Reader` class that encapsulates the text to be processed
- An object that implements the `LexedTokenFactory` interface
- A string holding the tokenization options

These options allow us to specify the text, the tokenizer to be used, and any options that we may need to use for a specific text stream.

In the following code sequence, an instance of the `StringReader` class is created to encapsulate the text. The `CoreLabelTokenFactory` class is used with the options left as `null` for this example:

```
PTBTokenizer ptb = new PTBTokenizer(new StringReader(paragraph),
    new CoreLabelTokenFactory(), null);
```

We will use the `WordToSentenceProcessor` class to create a `List` instance of the `List` class to hold the sentences and their tokens. Its `process` method takes the tokens produced by the `PTBTokenizer` instance to create the list of the `List` class, as shown here:

```
WordToSentenceProcessor wtsp = new WordToSentenceProcessor();
List<List<CoreLabel>> sents = wtsp.process(ptb.tokenize());
```

This `List` instance of the `List` class can be displayed in several ways. In the following sequence, the `toString` method of the `List` class displays the list enclosed in brackets, with its elements separated by commas:

```
for (List<CoreLabel> sent : sents) {
    System.out.println(sent);
}
```

The output of this sequence produces the following:

```
[When, determining, the, end, of, sentences, we, need, to, consider,
several, factors, .]
[Sentences, may, end, with, exclamation, marks, !]
[Or, possibly, questions, marks, ?]
[Within, sentences, we, may, find, numbers, like, 3.14159, ,,
abbreviations, such, as, found, in, Mr., Smith, ,, and, possibly, ellipses,
either, within, a, sentence, ..., ,, or, at, the, end, of, a, sentence,
...]
```

An alternate approach, shown here, displays each sentence on a separate line:

```
for (List<CoreLabel> sent : sents) {
    for (CoreLabel element : sent) {
        System.out.print(element + " ");
    }
    System.out.println();
}
```

The output is as follows:

```
When determining the end of sentences we need to consider several
factors .
Sentences may end with exclamation marks !
Or possibly questions marks ?
Within sentences we may find numbers like 3.14159 , abbreviations such
as found in Mr. Smith , and possibly ellipses either within a sentence ...
, or at the end of a sentence ...
```

If we are only interested in the positions of the words and sentences, we can use the `endPosition` method, as illustrated here:

```
for (List<CoreLabel> sent : sents) {
    for (CoreLabel element : sent) {
        System.out.print(element.endPosition() + " ");
    }
    System.out.println();
}
```

When this is executed, we get the following output. The last number on each line is the index of the sentence boundary:

```
4 16 20 24 27 37 40 45 48 57 65 73 74
84 88 92 97 109 115 116
119 128 138 144 145
152 162 165 169 174 182 187 195 196 210 215 218 224 227 231 237 238 242
251 260 267 274 276 285 287 288 291 294 298 302 305 307 316 317
```

The first elements of each sentence are displayed in the following sequence along with its index:

```
for (List<CoreLabel> sent : sents) {
    System.out.println(sent.get(0) + " "
        + sent.get(0).beginPosition());
}
```

The output is as follows:

```
When 0
Sentences 75
Or 117
Within 146
```

If we are interested in the last elements of a sentence, we can use the following sequence. The number of elements of a list is used to display the terminating character and its ending position:

```
for (List<CoreLabel> sent : sents) {
    int size = sent.size();
    System.out.println(sent.get(size-1) + " "
        + sent.get(size-1).endPosition());
}
```

This will produce the following output:

```
. 74
! 116
? 145
... 317
```

There are a number of options available when the constructor of the PTBTokenizer class is invoked. These options are enclosed as the constructor's third parameter. The option string consists of the options separated by commas, as shown here:

```
"americanize=true,normalizeFractions=true,asciiQuotes=true".
```

Several of these options are listed in this table:

Option	Meaning
`invertible`	Used to indicate that the tokens and whitespace must be preserved so that the original string can be reconstructed
`tokenizeNLs`	Indicates that the ends of lines must be treated as tokens
`americanize`	If true, this will rewrite British spellings as American spellings
`normalizeAmpersandEntity`	Will convert the XML &amp character to an ampersand
`normalizeFractions`	Converts common fraction characters, such as ½, to the long form (1/2)
`asciiQuotes`	Will convert quote characters to the simpler ' and " characters
`unicodeQuotes`	Will convert quote characters to characters that range from U+2018 to U+201D

The following sequence illustrates the use of this option string:

```
paragraph = "The colour of money is green. Common fraction "
    + "characters such as ½  are converted to the long form 1/2. "
    + "Quotes such as "cat" are converted to their simpler form.";
ptb = new PTBTokenizer(
    new StringReader(paragraph), new CoreLabelTokenFactory(),
    "americanize=true,normalizeFractions=true,asciiQuotes=true");
wtsp = new WordToSentenceProcessor();
sents = wtsp.process(ptb.tokenize());
for (List<CoreLabel> sent : sents) {
    for (CoreLabel element : sent) {
        System.out.print(element + " ");
    }
    System.out.println();
}
```

The output is as follows:

```
The color of money is green .
Common fraction characters such as 1/2 are converted to the long form
1/2 .
Quotes such as " cat " are converted to their simpler form .
```

The British spelling of the word "colour" was converted to its American equivalent. The fraction ½ was expanded to three characters: 1/2. In the last sentence, the smart quotes were converted to their simpler form.

Using the DocumentPreprocessor class

When an instance of the `DocumentPreprocessor` class is created, it uses its `Reader` parameter to produce a list of sentences. It also implements the `Iterable` interface, which makes it easy to traverse the list.

In the following example, the paragraph is used to create a `StringReader` object, and this object is used to instantiate the `DocumentPreprocessor` instance:

```
Reader reader = new StringReader(paragraph);
DocumentPreprocessor dp = new DocumentPreprocessor(reader);
for (List sentence : dp) {
    System.out.println(sentence);
}
```

On execution, we get the following output:

```
[When, determining, the, end, of, sentences, we, need, to, consider,
several, factors, .]
[Sentences, may, end, with, exclamation, marks, !]
[Or, possibly, questions, marks, ?]
[Within, sentences, we, may, find, numbers, like, 3.14159, ,,
abbreviations, such, as, found, in, Mr., Smith, ,, and, possibly, ellipses,
either, within, a, sentence, ..., ,, or, at, the, end, of, a, sentence,
...]
```

By default, `PTBTokenizer` is used to tokenize the input. The `setTokenizerFactory` method can be used to specify a different tokenizer. There are several other methods that can be useful, as detailed in the following table:

Method	Purpose
`setElementDelimiter`	Its argument specifies an XML element. Only the text inside of those elements will be processed.
`setSentenceDelimiter`	The processor will assume that the string argument is a sentence delimiter.
`setSentenceFinalPuncWords`	Its string array argument specifies the end of sentences delimiters.
`setKeepEmptySentences`	When used with whitespace models, if its argument is `true`, empty sentences will be retained.

The class can process either plain text or XML documents.

To demonstrate how an XML file can be processed, we will create a simple XML file called XMLText.xml, containing the following data:

```
<?xml version="1.0" encoding="UTF-8"?>
<?xml-stylesheet type="text/xsl"?>
<document>
    <sentences>
        <sentence id="1">
            <word>When</word>
            <word>the</word>
            <word>day</word>
            <word>is</word>
            <word>done</word>
            <word>we</word>
            <word>can</word>
            <word>sleep</word>
            <word>.</word>
        </sentence>
        <sentence id="2">
            <word>When</word>
            <word>the</word>
            <word>morning</word>
            <word>comes</word>
            <word>we</word>
            <word>can</word>
            <word>wake</word>
            <word>.</word>
        </sentence>
        <sentence id="3">
            <word>After</word>
            <word>that</word>
            <word>who</word>
            <word>knows</word>
            <word>.</word>
        </sentence>
    </sentences>
</document>
```

We will reuse the code from the previous example. However, we will open the XMLText.xml file instead, and use DocumentPreprocessor.DocType.XML as the second argument of the constructor of the DocumentPreprocessor class, as shown in the following code. This will specify that the processor should treat the text as XML text. In addition, we will specify that only those XML elements that are within the <sentence> tag should be processed:

```
try {
    Reader reader = new FileReader("XMLText.xml");
    DocumentPreprocessor dp = new DocumentPreprocessor(
        reader, DocumentPreprocessor.DocType.XML);
    dp.setElementDelimiter("sentence");
    for (List sentence : dp) {
        System.out.println(sentence);
    }
} catch (FileNotFoundException ex) {
    // Handle exception
}
```

The output of this example is as follows:

```
[When, the, day, is, done, we, can, sleep, .]
[When, the, morning, comes, we, can, wake, .]
[After, that, who, knows, .]
```

A cleaner output is possible using `ListIterator`, as shown here:

```
for (List sentence : dp) {
    ListIterator list = sentence.listIterator();
     while (list.hasNext()) {
        System.out.print(list.next() + " ");
    }
    System.out.println();
}
```

Its output is the following:

```
When the day is done we can sleep .
When the morning comes we can wake .
After that who knows .
```

If we had not specified an element delimiter, each word would have been displayed like this:

```
[When]
[the]
[day]
[is]
[done]
...
[who]
[knows]
[.]
```

Using the StanfordCoreNLP class

The `StanfordCoreNLP` class supports sentence-detection using the `ssplit` annotator. In the following example, the `tokenize` and `ssplit` annotators are used. A pipeline object is created and the `annotate` method is applied against the pipeline, using the paragraph as its argument:

```
Properties properties = new Properties();
properties.put("annotators", "tokenize, ssplit");
StanfordCoreNLP pipeline = new StanfordCoreNLP(properties);
Annotation annotation = new Annotation(paragraph);
pipeline.annotate(annotation);
```

The output contains a lot of information. Only the output for the first line is shown here:

```
Sentence #1 (13 tokens):
When determining the end of sentences we need to consider several
factors.
[Text=When CharacterOffsetBegin=0 CharacterOffsetEnd=4]
[Text=determining CharacterOffsetBegin=5 CharacterOffsetEnd=16] [Text=the
CharacterOffsetBegin=17 CharacterOffsetEnd=20] [Text=end
CharacterOffsetBegin=21 CharacterOffsetEnd=24] [Text=of
CharacterOffsetBegin=25 CharacterOffsetEnd=27] [Text=sentences
CharacterOffsetBegin=28 CharacterOffsetEnd=37] [Text=we
CharacterOffsetBegin=38 CharacterOffsetEnd=40] [Text=need
CharacterOffsetBegin=41 CharacterOffsetEnd=45] [Text=to
CharacterOffsetBegin=46 CharacterOffsetEnd=48] [Text=consider
CharacterOffsetBegin=49 CharacterOffsetEnd=57] [Text=several
CharacterOffsetBegin=58 CharacterOffsetEnd=65] [Text=factors
CharacterOffsetBegin=66 CharacterOffsetEnd=73] [Text=.
CharacterOffsetBegin=73 CharacterOffsetEnd=74]
```

Alternatively, we can use the `xmlPrint` method. This will produce the output in XML format, which can often be easier for extracting the information of interest. This method is shown here, and it requires that the `IOException` be handled:

```
try {
    pipeline.xmlPrint(annotation, System.out);
} catch (IOException ex) {
    // Handle exception
}
```

A partial listing of the output is as follows:

```
<?xml version="1.0" encoding="UTF-8"?>
<?xml-stylesheet href="CoreNLP-to-HTML.xsl" type="text/xsl"?>
<root>
  <document>
    <sentences>
      <sentence id="1">
        <tokens>
          <token id="1">
            <word>When</word>
            <CharacterOffsetBegin>0</CharacterOffsetBegin>
            <CharacterOffsetEnd>4</CharacterOffsetEnd>
          </token>
...
          <token id="34">
            <word>...</word>
            <CharacterOffsetBegin>316</CharacterOffsetBegin>
            <CharacterOffsetEnd>317</CharacterOffsetEnd>
          </token>
        </tokens>
      </sentence>
    </sentences>
  </document>
</root>
```

Using LingPipe

LingPipe uses a hierarchy of classes to support SBD, as shown in the following diagram:

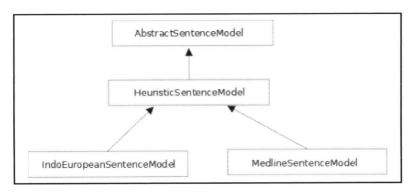

At the base of this hierarchy is the **AbstractSentenceModel** class, whose primary method is an overloaded `boundaryIndices` method. This method returns an integer array of a boundary index where each element of the array represents a sentence boundary.

Derived from this class is the **HeuristicSentenceModel** class. This class uses a series of possible stops, impossible penultimates, and impossible starts token sets. These were discussed earlier in the *Understanding the SBD rules of LingPipe's HeuristicSentenceModel class* section.

The **IndoEuropeanSentenceModel** and **MedlineSentenceModel** classes are derived from the **HeuristicSentenceModel** class. They have been trained for English and specialized for medical text, respectively. We will illustrate both of these classes in the following sections.

Using the IndoEuropeanSentenceModel class

The `IndoEuropeanSentenceModel` model is used for English text. Its two-argument constructor will specify:

- Whether the final token must be a stop
- Whether parentheses should be balanced

The default constructor does not force the final token to be a stop or expect that parentheses should be balanced. The sentence model needs to be used with a tokenizer. We will use the default constructor of the `IndoEuropeanTokenizerFactory` class for this purpose, as shown here:

```
TokenizerFactory TOKENIZER_FACTORY=
 IndoEuropeanTokenizerFactory.INSTANCE;
com.aliasi.sentences.SentenceModel sentenceModel = new
IndoEuropeanSentenceModel();
```

A tokenizer is created and its `tokenize` method is invoked to populate two lists:

```
List<String> tokenList = new ArrayList<>();
List<String> whiteList = new ArrayList<>();
Tokenizer tokenizer= TOKENIZER_FACTORY.tokenizer(
    paragraph.toCharArray(),0, paragraph.length());
tokenizer.tokenize(tokenList, whiteList);
```

The `boundaryIndices` method returns an array of integer boundary indexes. The method requires two `String` array arguments containing tokens and whitespaces. The `tokenize` method used two lists for these elements. This means we need to convert the list into equivalent arrays, as shown here:

```
String[] tokens = new String[tokenList.size()];
String[] whites = new String[whiteList.size()];
tokenList.toArray(tokens);
whiteList.toArray(whites);
```

We can then use the `boundaryIndices` method and display the indexes:

```
int[] sentenceBoundaries=
 sentenceModel.boundaryIndices(tokens, whites);
for(int boundary : sentenceBoundaries) {
    System.out.println(boundary);
}
```

The output is shown here:

```
12
19
24
```

To display the actual sentences, we will use the following sequence. The whitespace indexes are one off from the token:

```
int start = 0;
for(int boundary : sentenceBoundaries) {
    while(start<=boundary) {
        System.out.print(tokenList.get(start)
     + whiteList.get(start+1));
        start++;
    }
    System.out.println();
}
```

The following output is the result:

```
When determining the end of sentences we need to consider several
factors.
Sentences may end with exclamation marks!
Or possibly questions marks?
```

Unfortunately, it missed the last sentence. This is due to the last sentence ending in an ellipsis. If we add a period to the end of the sentence, we get the following output:

```
    When determining the end of sentences we need to consider several
factors.
    Sentences may end with exclamation marks!
    Or possibly questions marks?
    Within sentences we may find numbers like 3.14159, abbreviations such
as found in Mr. Smith, and possibly ellipses either within a sentence ...,
or at the end of a sentence....
```

Using the SentenceChunker class

An alternative approach is to use the `SentenceChunker` class to perform SBD. The constructor of this class requires a `TokenizerFactory` object and a `SentenceModel` object, as shown here:

```
TokenizerFactory tokenizerfactory =
  IndoEuropeanTokenizerFactory.INSTANCE;
SentenceModel sentenceModel = new IndoEuropeanSentenceModel();
```

The `SentenceChunker` instance is created using the `tokenizerfactory` and sentence instances:

```
SentenceChunker sentenceChunker =
    new SentenceChunker(tokenizerfactory, sentenceModel);
```

The `SentenceChunker` class implements the `Chunker` interface, which uses a `chunk` method. This method returns an object that implements the `Chunking` interface. This object specifies "chunks" of text with a character sequence (`CharSequence`).

The `chunk` method uses a character array and indexes within the array to specify which portions of the text need to be processed. A `Chunking` object is returned like this:

```
Chunking chunking = sentenceChunker.chunk(
    paragraph.toCharArray(),0, paragraph.length());
```

We will use the `Chunking` object for two purposes. First, we will use its `chunkSet` method to return a set of `Chunk` objects. Then, we will obtain a string holding all the sentences:

```
Set<Chunk> sentences = chunking.chunkSet();
String slice = chunking.charSequence().toString();
```

A `Chunk` object stores character offsets of the sentence boundaries. We will use its `start` and `end` methods in conjunction with the slice to display the sentences, as shown in the following code. Each element and sentence holds the sentence's boundary. We use this information to display each sentence in the slice:

```
for (Chunk sentence : sentences) {
    System.out.println("[" + slice.substring(sentence.start(),
        sentence.end()) + "]");
}
```

The following is the output. However, it still has problems with sentences ending with an ellipsis, so a period has been added to the end of the last sentence before the text is processed.

```
    [When determining the end of sentences we need to consider several
factors.]
    [Sentences may end with exclamation marks!]
    [Or possibly questions marks?]
    [Within sentences we may find numbers like 3.14159, abbreviations such
as found in Mr. Smith, and possibly ellipses either within a sentence ...,
or at the end of a sentence....]
```

Although the `IndoEuropeanSentenceModel` class works reasonably well for English text, it may not always work well for specialized text. In the next section, we will examine the use of the `MedlineSentenceModel` class, which has been trained to work with medical text.

Using the MedlineSentenceModel class

The LingPipe sentence model uses **MEDLINE**, which is a large collection of biomedical literature. This collection is stored in XML format and is maintained by the United States National Library of Medicine (`http://www.nlm.nih.gov/`).

LingPipe uses its `MedlineSentenceModel` class to perform SBD. This model has been trained against the MEDLINE data. It uses simple text and tokenizes it into tokens and whitespace. The MEDLINE model is then used to find the text's sentences.

In the following example, we will use a paragraph from `http://www.ncbi.nlm.nih.gov/pmc/articles/PMC3139422/` to demonstrate the use of the model, as declared here:

```
paragraph = "HepG2 cells were obtained from the American Type
  Culture "
    + "Collection (Rockville, MD, USA) and were used only until "
```

```
+ "passage 30. They were routinely grown at 37°C in Dulbecco's "
+ "modified Eagle's medium (DMEM) containing 10 % fetal bovine "
+ "serum (FBS), 2 mM glutamine, 1 mM sodium pyruvate, and 25 "
+ "mM glucose (Invitrogen, Carlsbad, CA, USA) in a humidified "
+ "atmosphere containing 5% CO2. For precursor and 13C-sugar "
+ "experiments, tissue culture treated polystyrene 35 mm "
+ "dishes (Corning Inc, Lowell, MA, USA) were seeded with 2 "
+ "× 106 cells and grown to confluency in DMEM.";
```

The code that follows is based on the `SentenceChunker` class, as demonstrated in the previous section. The difference is in the use of the `MedlineSentenceModel` class:

```
TokenizerFactory tokenizerfactory =
    IndoEuropeanTokenizerFactory.INSTANCE;
MedlineSentenceModel sentenceModel = new
    MedlineSentenceModel();
SentenceChunker sentenceChunker =
    new SentenceChunker(tokenizerfactory,
 sentenceModel);
    = sentenceChunker.chunk(
    paragraph.toCharArray(), 0, paragraph.length());
Set<Chunk> sentences = chunking.chunkSet();
String slice = chunking.charSequence().toString();
for (Chunk sentence : sentences) {
    System.out.println("["
        + slice.substring(sentence.start(),
 sentence.end())
        + "]");
}
```

The output is as follows:

```
    [HepG2 cells were obtained from the American Type Culture Collection
(Rockville, MD, USA) and were used only until passage 30.]
    [They were routinely grown at 37°C in Dulbecco's modified Eagle's medium
(DMEM) containing 10 % fetal bovine serum (FBS), 2 mM glutamine, 1 mM
sodium pyruvate, and 25 mM glucose (Invitrogen, Carlsbad, CA, USA) in a
humidified atmosphere containing 5% CO2.]
    [For precursor and 13C-sugar experiments, tissue culture treated
polystyrene 35 mm dishes (Corning Inc, Lowell, MA, USA) were seeded with 2
× 106 cells and grown to confluency in DMEM.]
```

When executed against medical text, this model will perform better than other models.

Training a sentence-detector model

We will use OpenNLP's `SentenceDetectorME` class to illustrate the training process. This class has a static `train` method that uses sample sentences found in a file. The method returns a model that is usually serialized to a file for later use.

Models use special annotated data to clearly specify where a sentence ends. Frequently, a large file is used to provide a good sample for training purposes. Part of the file is used for training purposes, and the rest is used to verify the model after it has been trained.

The training file used by OpenNLP consists of one sentence per line. Usually, at least 10 to 20 sample sentences are needed to avoid processing errors. To demonstrate this process, we will use a file called `sentence.train`. It consists of Chapter 5, *Twenty Thousand Leagues Under the Sea*, by Jules Verne. The text of the book can be found at `http://www.gutenberg.org/files/164/164-h/164-h.htm#chap05`. The file can be downloaded from `https://github.com/PacktPublishing/Natural-Language-Processing-with-Java-Second-Edition` or from this book's GitHub repository.

A `FileReader` object is used to open the file. This object is used as the argument of the `PlainTextByLineStream` constructor. The stream that results consists of a string for each line of the file. This is used as the argument of the `SentenceSampleStream` constructor, which converts the sentence strings to `SentenceSample` objects. These objects hold the beginning index of each sentence. This process is shown as follows, where the statements are enclosed in a `try` block to handle exceptions that may be thrown by these statements:

```
try {
    ObjectStream<String> lineStream = new PlainTextByLineStream(
        new FileReader("sentence.train"));
    ObjectStream<SentenceSample> sampleStream
        = new SentenceSampleStream(lineStream);
    ...
} catch (FileNotFoundException ex) {
    ex.printStackTrace();
    // Handle exception
} catch (IOException ex) {
    ex.printStackTrace();
    // Handle exception
}
```

Now, the `train` method can be used like this:

```
SentenceModel model = SentenceDetectorME.train("en",
        sampleStream, true,
    null, TrainingParameters.defaultParams());
```

The output of the method is a trained model. The parameters of this method are detailed in the following table:

Parameter	Meaning
`"en"`	Specifies that the language of the text is English
`sampleStream`	The training text stream
`true`	Specifies whether end tokens shown should be used
`null`	A dictionary for abbreviations
`TrainingParameters.defaultParams()`	Specifies that the default training parameters should be used

In the following sequence, `OutputStream` is created and used to save the model in the `modelFile` file. This allows the model to be reused for other applications:

```
OutputStream modelStream = new BufferedOutputStream(
    new FileOutputStream("modelFile"));
model.serialize(modelStream);
```

The output of this process is as follows. All the iterations have not been shown here to save space. The default cuts off indexing events to 5 and iterations to 100:

```
Indexing events using cutoff of 5
    Computing event counts...  done. 93 events
    Indexing...  done.
Sorting and merging events... done. Reduced 93 events to 63.
Done indexing.
Incorporating indexed data for training...
done.
    Number of Event Tokens: 63
        Number of Outcomes: 2
       Number of Predicates: 21
...done.
Computing model parameters ...
Performing 100 iterations.
    1:  ... loglikelihood=-64.4626877920749      0.9032258064516129
    2:  ... loglikelihood=-31.11084296202819     0.9032258064516129
    3:  ... loglikelihood=-26.418795734248626    0.9032258064516129
    4:  ... loglikelihood=-24.327956749903198    0.9032258064516129
    5:  ... loglikelihood=-22.766489585258565    0.9032258064516129
    6:  ... loglikelihood=-21.46379347841989     0.9139784946236559
    7:  ... loglikelihood=-20.356036369911394    0.9139784946236559
    8:  ... loglikelihood=-19.406935608514992    0.9139784946236559
    9:  ... loglikelihood=-18.58725539754483     0.9139784946236559
```

```
10:   ... loglikelihood=-17.873030559849326      0.9139784946236559
...
99:   ... loglikelihood=-7.214933901940582       0.978494623655914
100:  ... loglikelihood=-7.183774954664058       0.978494623655914
```

Using the Trained model

We can then use the model, as illustrated in the following code sequence. This is based on the techniques illustrated in the *Using the SentenceDetectorME class* section:

```
try (InputStream is = new FileInputStream(
        new File(getModelDir(), "modelFile"))) {
    SentenceModel model = new SentenceModel(is);
    SentenceDetectorME detector = new
     SentenceDetectorME(model);
    String sentences[] = detector.sentDetect(paragraph);
    for (String sentence : sentences) {
        System.out.println(sentence);
    }
} catch (FileNotFoundException ex) {
    // Handle exception
} catch (IOException ex) {
    // Handle exception
}
```

The output is as follows:

```
    When determining the end of sentences we need to consider several
factors.
    Sentences may end with exclamation marks! Or possibly questions marks?
    Within sentences we may find numbers like 3.14159,
    abbreviations such as found in Mr.
    Smith, and possibly ellipses either within a sentence ..., or at the
end of a sentence...
```

This model did not process the last sentence very well, which reflects a mismatch between the sample text and the text the model is used against. Using relevant training data is important. Otherwise, downstream tasks based on this output will suffer.

ing the model using the
eDetectorEvaluator class

We reserved a part of the sample file for evaluation purposes so that we can use the SentenceDetectorEvaluator class to evaluate the model. We modified the sentence.train file by extracting the last 10 sentences and placing them in a file called evalSample. Then, we used this file to evaluate the model. In the following example, we've reused the lineStream and sampleStream variables to create a stream of SentenceSample objects based on the file's contents:

```
lineStream = new PlainTextByLineStream(
    new FileReader("evalSample"));
sampleStream = new SentenceSampleStream(lineStream);
```

An instance of the SentenceDetectorEvaluator class is created using the previously created SentenceDetectorME class variable, detector. The second argument of the constructor is a SentenceDetectorEvaluationMonitor object, which we will not use here. Then, the evaluate method is called:

```
SentenceDetectorEvaluator sentenceDetectorEvaluator
    = new SentenceDetectorEvaluator(detector, null);
sentenceDetectorEvaluator.evaluate(sampleStream);
```

The getFMeasure method will return an instance of the FMeasure class, which provides measurements of the quality of the model:

```
System.out.println(sentenceDetectorEvaluator.getFMeasure());
```

The output follows. Precision is the fraction of correct instances that are included, and recall reflects the sensitivity of the model. F-measure is a score that combines recall and precision. In essence, it reflects how well the model works. It is best to keep the precision above 90% for tokenization and SBD tasks:

```
Precision: 0.8181818181818182
Recall: 0.9
F-Measure: 0.8571428571428572
```

Summary

In this chapter, we discussed many of the issues that make sentence-detection a difficult task, such as problems that result from periods being used for numbers and abbreviations. The use of ellipses and embedded quotes can also be problematic.

Java provides a couple of techniques to detect the end of a sentence. We saw how regular expressions and the `BreakIterator` class can be used. These techniques are useful for simple sentences, but they do not work that well for more complicated sentences.

The use of various NLP APIs was also illustrated. Some of these process the text based on rules, while others use models. We also demonstrated how models can be trained and evaluated.

In the next chapter, `Chapter 4`, *Finding People and Things*, you will learn how to find people and things using text.

4
Finding People and Things

The process of finding people and things is referred to as **Named Entity Recognition (NER)**. Entities such as people and places are associated with categories that have names, which identify what they are. A named category can be as simple as *people*. Common entity types include the following:

- People
- Locations
- Organizations
- Money
- Time
- URLs

Finding names, locations, and various things in a document are important and useful NLP tasks. They are used in many places, such as conducting simple searches, processing queries, resolving references, the disambiguation of text, and finding the meaning of text. For example, NER is sometimes interested in only finding those entities that belong to a single category. Using categories, the search can be isolated to those item types. Other NLP tasks use NER, such as in **Part-Of-Speech (POS)** taggers and in performing cross-referencing tasks.

The NER process involves two tasks:

- Detection of entities
- Classification of entities

Detection is concerned with finding the position of an entity within text. Once it is located, it is important to determine what type of entity was discovered. After these two tasks have been performed, the results can be used to solve other tasks, such as searching and determining the meaning of the text. For example, tasks may include identifying names from a movie or book review, and helping to find other movies or books that might be of interest. Extracting location information can assist in providing references to nearby services.

We will cover the following topics in this chapter:

- Why is NER difficult?
- Techniques for name recognition
- Using regular expressions for NER
- Using NLP APIs
- Building a new dataset with the NER annotation tool
- Training a model

Why is NER difficult?

Like many NLP tasks, NER is not always simple. Although the tokenization of a text will reveal its components, understanding what they are can be difficult. Using proper nouns will not always work because of the ambiguity of language. For example, Penny and Faith, while valid names, may also be used for a measurement of currency and a belief, respectively. We can also find words such as Georgia that are used as the name of a country, a state, and a person. We can also not make a list of all people or places or entities as they are not predefined. Consider the following two simple sentences:

- Jobs are harder to find nowadays
- Jobs said dots will always connect

In these two sentences, jobs seems to be the entity but they are not related, and in second sentence it's not even an entity. We need to use some complex techniques to check for the occurrence of entities in the context. Sentences may use the same entity's name in different ways. Say, for example, IBM and International Business Machines; both terms are used in text to refer to the same entity, but for NER, this is challenging. Take another example: Suzuki and Nissan may be interpreted as names of people, instead of names of companies, by NER.

Some phrases can be challenging. Consider the phrase *"Metropolitan Convention and Exhibit Hall"* may contain words that in themselves are valid entities. So when the domain is well-known, a list of entities can be identified very easily and it is also easy to implement.

NER is typically applied at the sentence level, otherwise a phrase can easily bridge sentences, leading to the incorrect identification of an entity. For example, take the following two sentences:

"Bob went south. Dakota went west."

If we ignored the sentence boundaries, then we could inadvertently find the location entity South Dakota.

Specialized text such as URLs, email addresses, and specialized numbers can be difficult to isolate. This identification is made even more difficult if we have to take into account variations of the entity's form. For example, are parentheses used with phone numbers? Are dashes, or periods, or some other character used to separate its parts? Do we need to consider international phone numbers?

These factors contribute to the need for good NER techniques.

Techniques for name recognition

There are a number of NER techniques available. Some use regular expressions and others are based on a predefined dictionary. Regular expressions have a lot of expressive power and can isolate entities. A dictionary of entity names can be compared to tokens of text to find matches.

Another common NER approach uses trained models to detect their presence. These models are dependent on the type of entity we are looking for and the target language. A model that works well for one domain, such as web pages, may not work well for a different domain, such as medical journals.

When a model is trained, it uses an annotated block of text, which identifies the entities of interest. To measure how well a model has been trained, several measures are used:

- **Precision**: It is the percentage of entities found that match exactly the spans found in the evaluation data
- **Recall**: It is the percentage of entities defined in the corpus that were found in the same location
- **Performance measure**: It is the harmonic mean of precision and recall given by
  $F1 = 2 * Precision * Recall / (Recall + Precision)$

We will use these measures when we cover the evaluation of models.

NER is also known as entity identification and entity chunking. **Chunking** is the analysis of text to identify its parts, such as nouns, verbs, or other components. As humans, we tend to chunk a sentence into distinct parts. These parts form a structure that we use to determine its meaning. The NER process will create spans of text such as *Queen of England*. However, there may be other entities within these spans, such as *England*.

An NER system is built using different techniques and can be categorized as the following:

- A rule-based approach uses rules crafted by a domain expert to recognize entities. A rule-based system parses the text and generates a parse tree or some other abstraction format. It can be a list-based lookup where a bag of words is used, or a linguistic approach, which requires deep knowledge of entity identification.
- The machine learning approach uses pattern-based learning with statistical models where the nouns are identified and classified. Machine learning again can be categorized into three different types:
    - Supervised learning uses labeled data to make a model
    - Semi-supervised learning uses labeled data, as well as other information, to make a model
    - Unsupervised learning uses unlabeled data and learns from the input
- NE extraction is normally used for extracting data from web pages. It not only learns, but also forms or builds a list for NER.

Lists and regular expressions

One technique is to use lists of standard entities along with regular expressions to identify named entities. Named entities are sometimes referred to as proper nouns. The standard entities list could be a list of states, common names, months, or frequently referenced locations. Gazetteers, which are lists that contain geographical information used with maps, provide a source of location-related entities. However, maintaining such lists can be time-consuming. They can also be specific to language and locale. Making changes to the list can be tedious. We will demonstrate this approach in the *Using the ExactDictionaryChunker class* section later in this chapter.

Regular expressions can be useful in identifying entities. Their powerful syntax provides enough flexibility in many situations to accurately isolate the entity of interest. However, this flexibility can also make them difficult to understand and maintain. We will demonstrate several regular expression approaches in this chapter.

Statistical classifiers

Statistical classifiers determine whether a word is the start of an entity, the continuation of an entity, or not an entity at all. Sample text is tagged to isolate entities. Once a classifier has been developed, it can be trained on different sets of data for different problem domains. The disadvantage of this approach is that it requires someone to annotate the sample text, which is a time-consuming process. In addition, it is domain dependent.

We will examine several approaches to performing NER. First, we will start by explaining how regular expressions are used to identify entities.

Using regular expressions for NER

Regular expressions can be used to identify entities in a document. We will investigate two general approaches:

- The first one uses regular expressions as supported by Java. These can be useful in situations where the entities are relatively simple and consistent in their form.
- The second approach uses classes designed to specifically use regular expressions. To demonstrate this, we will use LingPipe's `RegExChunker` class.

When working with regular expressions, it is advantageous to avoid reinventing the wheel. There are many sources for predefined and tested expressions. One such library can be found at `http://regexlib.com/Default.aspx`. We will use several of the regular expressions in this library for our examples.

To test how well these approaches work, we will use the following text for most of our examples:

```
private static String regularExpressionText
    = "He left his email address (rgb@colorworks.com) and his "
    + "phone number,800-555-1234. We believe his current address "
    + "is 100 Washington Place, Seattle, CO 12345-1234. I "
    + "understand you can also call at 123-555-1234 between "
    + "8:00 AM and 4:30 most days. His URL is http://example.com "
    + "and he was born on February 25, 1954 or 2/25/1954.";
```

Using Java's regular expressions to find entities

To demonstrate how these expressions can be used, we will start with several simple examples. The initial example starts with the following declaration. It is a simple expression designed to identify certain types of phone number:

```
String phoneNumberRE = "\\d{3}-\\d{3}-\\d{4}";
```

We will use the following code to test our simple expressions. The `compile` method of the `Pattern` class takes a regular expression and compiles it into a `Pattern` object. Its `matcher` method can then be executed against the target text, which returns a `Matcher` object. This object allows us to repeatedly identify regular expression matches:

```
Pattern pattern = Pattern.compile(phoneNumberRE);
Matcher matcher = pattern.matcher(regularExpressionText);
while (matcher.find()) {
    System.out.println(matcher.group() + " [" + matcher.start()
        + ":" + matcher.end() + "]");
}
```

The `find` method will return `true` when a match occurs. Its `group` method returns the text that matches the expression. Its `start` and `end` methods give us the position of the matched text in the target text.

When executed, we will get the following output:

```
800-555-1234 [68:80]
123-555-1234 [196:208]
```

A number of other regular expressions can be used in a similar manner. These are listed in the following table. The third column is the output produced when the corresponding regular expression is used in the previous code sequence:

Entity type	Regular expression	Output
URL	`\\b(https?|ftp|file|ldap)://[-A-Za-z0-9+&@#/%?=~_|!:,.;]*[-A-Za-z0-9+&@#/%=~_|]`	`http://example.com [256:274]`
ZIP code	`[0-9]{5}(\\-?[0-9]{4})?`	`12345-1234 [150:160]`
Email	`[a-zA-Z0-9'._%+-]+@(?:[a-zA-Z0-9-]+\\.)+[a-zA-Z]{2,4}`	`rgb@colorworks.com [27:45]`
Time	`(([0-1]?[0-9])|([2][0-3])):([0-5]?[0-9])(:([0-5]?[0-9]))?`	`8:00 [217:221]` `4:30 [229:233]`

Entity type	Regular expression	Output

Date	`((0?[13578]|10|12)(-|\\/)`
	 `(([1-9])|(0[1-9])|([12])([0-9]?)|(3[01]?))(-|\\/)`
	 `((19)([2-9])(\\d{1})|(20)([01])(\\d{1})|([8901])`
	 `(\\d{1}))|(0?[2469]|11)(-|\\/)(([1-9])`
	 `|(0[1-9])|([12])([0-9]?)|(3[0]?))`
	 `(-|\\/)((19)([2-9])(\\d{1})|(20)([01])`
	 `(\\d{1})|([8901])(\\d{1})))`
		2/25/1954
		 [315:324]

There are many other regular expressions that we could have used. However, these examples illustrate the basic techniques. As demonstrated with the date regular expression, some of these can be quite complex.

It is common for regular expressions to miss some entities and to falsely report other non-entities as entities. For example, we could replace the text with the following expression:

```
regularExpressionText =
    "(888)555-1111 888-SEL-HIGH 888-555-2222-J88-W3S";
```

Executing the code will return this:

```
888-555-2222 [27:39]
```

It missed the first two phone numbers and falsely reported the part number as a phone number.

We can also search for more than one regular expression at a time using the | operator. In the following statement, three regular expressions are combined using this operator. They are declared using the corresponding entries in the previous table:

```
Pattern pattern = Pattern.compile(phoneNumberRE + "|"
    + timeRE + "|" + emailRegEx);
```

When executed using the original `regularExpressionText` text defined at the beginning of the previous section, we get the following output:

```
rgb@colorworks.com [27:45]
800-555-1234 [68:80]
123-555-1234 [196:208]
8:00 [217:221]
4:30 [229:233]
```

Using the RegExChunker class of LingPipe

The RegExChunker class uses chunks to find entities in text. The class uses a regular expression to represent an entity. Its chunk method returns a Chunking object that can be used just as we used it in our earlier examples.

The RegExChunker class's constructor takes three arguments:

- String: This is a regular expression
- String: This is a type of entity or category
- double: A value for the score

We will demonstrate this class using a regular expression representing time in the following example. The regular expression is the same as that used in the *Using Java's regular expressions to find entities* section earlier in this chapter. The Chunker instance is then created:

```
String timeRE =
    "(([0-1]?[0-9])|([2][0-3])):([0-5]?[0-9])(:([0-5]?[0-9]))?";
        Chunker chunker = new RegExChunker(timeRE,"time",1.0);
```

The Chunk method is used, along with the displayChunkSet method, as shown here:

```
Chunking chunking = chunker.chunk(regularExpressionText);
Set<Chunk> chunkSet = chunking.chunkSet();
displayChunkSet(chunker, regularExpressionText);
```

The displayChunkSet method is shown in the following code segment. The chunkSet method returns a set collection of Chunk instances. We can use various methods to display specific parts of the chunk:

```
public void displayChunkSet(Chunker chunker, String text) {
    Chunking chunking = chunker.chunk(text);
    Set<Chunk> set = chunking.chunkSet();
    for (Chunk chunk : set) {
        System.out.println("Type: " + chunk.type() + " Entity: ["
            + text.substring(chunk.start(), chunk.end())
            + "] Score: " + chunk.score());
    }
}
```

The output is as follows:

```
Type: time Entity: [8:00] Score: 1.0
Type: time Entity: [4:30] Score: 1.0+95
```

Alternatively, we can declare a simple class to encapsulate the regular expression, which lends itself to reuse in other situations. Next, the `TimeRegexChunker` class is declared and it supports the identification of time entities:

```
public class TimeRegexChunker extends RegExChunker {
    private final static String TIME_RE =
      "(([0-1]?[0-9])|([2][0-3])):([0-5]?[0-9])(:([0-5]?[0-9]))?";
    private final static String CHUNK_TYPE = "time";
    private final static double CHUNK_SCORE = 1.0;
    public TimeRegexChunker() {
        super(TIME_RE,CHUNK_TYPE,CHUNK_SCORE);
    }
}
```

To use this class, replace this section's initial declaration of `chunker` with the following declaration:

```
Chunker chunker = new TimeRegexChunker();
```

The output will be the same as before.

Using NLP APIs

We will demonstrate the NER process using OpenNLP, Stanford API, and LingPipe. Each of these provide alternative techniques that can often do a good job of identifying entities in the text. The following declaration will serve as the sample text to demonstrate the APIs:

```
String sentences[] = {"Joe was the last person to see Fred. ",
  "He saw him in Boston at McKenzie's pub at 3:00 where he "
  + " paid $2.45 for an ale. ",
  "Joe wanted to go to Vermont for the day to visit a cousin who "
  + "works at IBM, but Sally and he had to look for Fred"};
```

Using OpenNLP for NER

We will demonstrate the use of the `TokenNameFinderModel` class to perform NLP using the OpenNLP API. Additionally, we will demonstrate how to determine the probability that the entity identified is correct.

The general approach is to convert the text into a series of tokenized sentences, create an instance of the `TokenNameFinderModel` class using an appropriate model, and then use the `find` method to identify the entities in the text.

The following example demonstrates the use of the `TokenNameFinderModel` class. We will use a simple sentence initially, and then use multiple sentences. The sentence is defined here:

```
String sentence = "He was the last person to see Fred.";
```

We will use the models found in the `en-token.bin` and `en-ner-person.bin` files for the tokenizer and name finder models, respectively. The `InputStream` object for these files is opened using a try-with-resources block, as shown here:

```
try (InputStream tokenStream = new FileInputStream(
        new File(getModelDir(), "en-token.bin"));
        InputStream modelStream = new FileInputStream(
            new File(getModelDir(), "en-ner-person.bin"));) {
    ...

} catch (Exception ex) {
    // Handle exceptions
}
```

Within the `try` block, the `TokenizerModel` and `Tokenizer` objects are created:

```
TokenizerModel tokenModel = new TokenizerModel(tokenStream);
Tokenizer tokenizer = new TokenizerME(tokenModel);
```

Next, an instance of the `NameFinderME` class is created using the `person` model:

```
TokenNameFinderModel entityModel =
    new TokenNameFinderModel(modelStream);
NameFinderME nameFinder = new NameFinderME(entityModel);
```

We can now use the `tokenize` method to tokenize the text and the `find` method to identify the person in the text. The `find` method will use the tokenized `String` array as input and return an array of `Span` objects, as shown here:

```
String tokens[] = tokenizer.tokenize(sentence);
Span nameSpans[] = nameFinder.find(tokens);
```

We discussed the `Span` class in `Chapter 3`, *Finding Sentences*. As you may remember, this class holds positional information about the entities found. The actual string entities are still in the `tokens` array:

The following `for` statement displays the person found in the sentence. Its positional information and the person are displayed on separate lines:

```
for (int i = 0; i < nameSpans.length; i++) {
    System.out.println("Span: " + nameSpans[i].toString());
    System.out.println("Entity: "
        + tokens[nameSpans[i].getStart()]);
}
```

The output is as follows:

```
Span: [7..9) person
Entity: Fred
```

We will often work with multiple sentences. To demonstrate this, we will use the previously defined `sentences` string array. The previous `for` statement is replaced with the following sequence. The `tokenize` method is invoked against each sentence and then the entity information is displayed, like it was earlier:

```
for (String sentence : sentences) {
    String tokens[] = tokenizer.tokenize(sentence);
    Span nameSpans[] = nameFinder.find(tokens);
    for (int i = 0; i < nameSpans.length; i++) {
        System.out.println("Span: " + nameSpans[i].toString());
        System.out.println("Entity: "
            + tokens[nameSpans[i].getStart()]);
    }
    System.out.println();
}
```

The output is as follows. There is an extra blank line between the two people detected because the second sentence did not contain a `person`:

```
Span: [0..1) person
Entity: Joe
Span: [7..9) person
Entity: Fred
Span: [0..1) person
Entity: Joe
Span: [19..20) person
Entity: Sally
Span: [26..27) person
Entity: Fred
```

Determining the accuracy of the entity

When `TokenNameFinderModel` identifies entities in text, it computes a probability for that entity. We can access this information using the `probs` method, as shown in the following line of code. This method returns an array of doubles, which corresponds to the elements of the `nameSpans` array:

```
double[] spanProbs = nameFinder.probs(nameSpans);
```

Add this statement to the previous example immediately after the use of the `find` method. Then, add the following statement at the end of the nested `for` statement:

```
System.out.println("Probability: " + spanProbs[i]);
```

When this example is executed, you will get the following output. The probability fields reflect the confidence level of the entity assignment. For the first entity, the model is 80.529 percent confident that `Joe` is a `person`:

```
Span: [0..1) person
Entity: Joe
Probability: 0.8052914774025202
Span: [7..9) person
Entity: Fred
Probability: 0.9042160889302772
Span: [0..1) person
Entity: Joe
Probability: 0.9620970782763985
Span: [19..20) person
Entity: Sally
Probability: 0.964568603518126
Span: [26..27) person
Entity: Fred
Probability: 0.990383039618594
```

Using other entity types

OpenNLP supports different libraries, as listed in the following table. These models can be downloaded from `http://opennlp.sourceforge.net/models-1.5/`.
The `en` prefix specifies English as the language and `ner` indicates that the model is for NER:

English finder models	Filename
Location name finder model	en-ner-location.bin
Money name finder model	en-ner-money.bin

Organization name finder model	`en-ner-organization.bin`
Percentage name finder model	`en-ner-percentage.bin`
Person name finder model	`en-ner-person.bin`
Time name finder model	`en-ner-time.bin`

If we modify the statement to use a different model file, we can see how they work against the sample sentences:

```
InputStream modelStream = new FileInputStream(
    new File(getModelDir(), "en-ner-time.bin"));) {
```

The various outputs are shown in the following table:

Model	Output
`en-ner-location.bin`	Span: [4..5) location Entity: Boston Probability: 0.8656908776583051 Span: [5..6) location Entity: Vermont Probability: 0.9732488014011262
`en-ner-money.bin`	Span: [14..16) money Entity: 2.45 Probability: 0.7200919701507937
`en-ner-organization.bin`	Span: [16..17) organization Entity: IBM Probability: 0.9256970736336729
`en-ner-time.bin`	The model was not able to detect time in this text sequence

When the `en-ner-money.bin` model is used, the index in the tokens array in the earlier code sequence has to be increased by 1. Otherwise, all that is returned is the dollar sign.

The model failed to find the time entities in the sample text. This illustrates that the model did not have enough confidence to find any time entities in the text.

Processing multiple entity types

We can also handle multiple entity types at the same time. This involves creating instances of the `NameFinderME` class based on each model within a loop and applying the model against each sentence, keeping track of the entities as they are found.

We will illustrate this process with the following example. It requires rewriting the previous `try` block to create the `InputStream` instance within the block, as shown here:

```
try {
    InputStream tokenStream = new FileInputStream(
        new File(getModelDir(), "en-token.bin"));
    TokenizerModel tokenModel = new TokenizerModel(tokenStream);
    Tokenizer tokenizer = new TokenizerME(tokenModel);
    ...
} catch (Exception ex) {
    // Handle exceptions
}
```

Within the `try` block, we will define a `String` array to hold the names of the model files. As shown here, we will use models for people, locations, and organizations:

```
String modelNames[] = {"en-ner-person.bin",
    "en-ner-location.bin", "en-ner-organization.bin"};
```

An `ArrayList` instance is created to hold the entities as they are discovered:

```
ArrayList<String> list = new ArrayList();
```

A `foreach` statement is used to load one model at a time and then to create an instance of the `NameFinderME` class:

```
for(String name : modelNames) {
    TokenNameFinderModel entityModel = new TokenNameFinderModel(
        new FileInputStream(new File(getModelDir(), name)));
    NameFinderME nameFinder = new NameFinderME(entityModel);
    ...
}
```

Previously, we did not try to identify which sentences the entities were found in. This is not hard to do, but we need to use a simple `for` statement instead of a `foreach` statement to keep track of the sentence indexes. This is shown in the following example, where the previous example has been modified to use the `index` integer variable to hold the sentences. Otherwise, the code works the same way as earlier:

```
for (int index = 0; index < sentences.length; index++) {
    String tokens[] = tokenizer.tokenize(sentences[index]);
```

```
    Span nameSpans[] = nameFinder.find(tokens);
    for(Span span : nameSpans) {
        list.add("Sentence: " + index
            + " Span: " + span.toString() + " Entity: "
            + tokens[span.getStart()]);
    }
}
```

The entities discovered are then displayed:

```
for(String element : list) {
    System.out.println(element);
}
```

The output is as follows:

```
Sentence: 0 Span: [0..1) person Entity: Joe
Sentence: 0 Span: [7..9) person Entity: Fred
Sentence: 2 Span: [0..1) person Entity: Joe
Sentence: 2 Span: [19..20) person Entity: Sally
Sentence: 2 Span: [26..27) person Entity: Fred
Sentence: 1 Span: [4..5) location Entity: Boston
Sentence: 2 Span: [5..6) location Entity: Vermont
Sentence: 2 Span: [16..17) organization Entity: IBM
```

Using the Stanford API for NER

We will demonstrate the CRFClassifier class as it's going to be used to perform NER. This class implements what is known as a linear chain **conditional random field (CRF)** sequence model.

To demonstrate the use of the CRFClassifier class, we will start with a declaration of the classifier file string, as shown here:

```
String model = getModelDir() +
    "\\english.conll.4class.distsim.crf.ser.gz";
```

The classifier is then created using the model:

```
CRFClassifier<CoreLabel> classifier =
    CRFClassifier.getClassifierNoExceptions(model);
```

The `classify` method takes a single string representing the text to be processed. To use the `sentences` text, we need to convert it to a simple string:

```
String sentence = "";
for (String element : sentences) {
    sentence += element;
}
```

The `classify` method is then applied to the text:

```
List<List<CoreLabel>> entityList = classifier.classify(sentence);
```

A `List` instance of `List` instances of `CoreLabel` objects is returned. The object returned is a list that contains another list. The contained list is a `List` instance of `CoreLabel` objects. The `CoreLabel` class represents a word with additional information attached to it. The `internal` list contains a list of these words. In the outer for-each statement in the following code sequence, the reference variable, `internalList`, represents one sentence of the text. In the inner for-each statement, each word in that inner list is displayed. The `word` method returns the word and the `get` method returns the type of the word.

The words and their types are then displayed:

```
for (List<CoreLabel> internalList: entityList) {
    for (CoreLabel coreLabel : internalList) {
        String word = coreLabel.word();
        String category = coreLabel.get(
            CoreAnnotations.AnswerAnnotation.class);
        System.out.println(word + ":" + category);
    }
}
```

Part of the output follows. It has been truncated because every word is displayed. The O represents the other category:

```
Joe:PERSON
was:O
the:O
last:O
person:O
to:O
see:O
Fred:PERSON
.:O
```

```
He:O ... look:O for:O Fred:PERSON
```

To filter out the words that are not relevant, replace the `println` statement with the following statements. This will eliminate the other categories:

```
if (!"O".equals(category)) {
    System.out.println(word + ":" + category);
}
```

The output is simpler now:

```
Joe:PERSON
Fred:PERSON
Boston:LOCATION
McKenzie:PERSON
Joe:PERSON
Vermont:LOCATION
IBM:ORGANIZATION
Sally:PERSON
Fred:PERSON
```

Using LingPipe for NER

We previously demonstrated the use of LingPipe using regular expressions in the *Using regular expressions for NER* section earlier in this chapter. Here, we will demonstrate how named entity models and the `ExactDictionaryChunker` class are used to perform NER analysis.

Using LingPipe's named entity models

LingPipe has a few named entity models that we can use with chunking. These files consist of a serialized object that can be read from a file and then applied to text. These objects implement the `Chunker` interface. The chunking process results in a series of `Chunking` objects that identify the entities of interest.

A list of NER models is found in the following table. These models can be downloaded from `http://alias-i.com/lingpipe/web/models.html`:

Genre	Corpus	File
English news	MUC-6	ne-en-news-muc6.AbstractCharLmRescoringChunker
English genes	GeneTag	ne-en-bio-genetag.HmmChunker
English genomics	GENIA	ne-en-bio-genia.TokenShapeChunker

We will use the model found in the `ne-en-news-muc6.AbstractCharLmRescoringChunker` file to demonstrate how this class is used. We will start with a `try...catch` block to deal with exceptions, as shown in the following example. The file is opened and used with the `AbstractExternalizable` class's static `readObject` method to create an instance of a `Chunker` class. This method will read in the serialized model:

```
try {
    File modelFile = new File(getModelDir(),
        "ne-en-news-muc6.AbstractCharLmRescoringChunker");
     Chunker chunker = (Chunker)
        AbstractExternalizable.readObject(modelFile);
    ...
} catch (IOException | ClassNotFoundException ex) {
    // Handle exception
}
```

The `Chunker` and `Chunking` interfaces provide methods that work with a set of chunks of text. Its `chunk` method returns an object that implements the `Chunking` instance. The following sequence displays the chunks found in each sentence of the text, as shown here:

```
for (int i = 0; i < sentences.length; ++i) {
    Chunking chunking = chunker.chunk(sentences[i]);
    System.out.println("Chunking=" + chunking);
}
```

The output of this sequence is as follows:

```
    Chunking=Joe was the last person to see Fred.  : [0-3:PERSON@-Infinity,
31-35:ORGANIZATION@-Infinity]
    Chunking=He saw him in Boston at McKenzie's pub at 3:00 where he paid
$2.45 for an ale.  : [14-20:LOCATION@-Infinity, 24-32:PERSON@-Infinity]
    Chunking=Joe wanted to go to Vermont for the day to visit a cousin who
works at IBM, but Sally and he had to look for Fred : [0-3:PERSON@-
Infinity, 20-27:ORGANIZATION@-Infinity, 71-74:ORGANIZATION@-Infinity,
109-113:ORGANIZATION@-Infinity]
```

Instead, we can use methods of the `Chunk` class to extract specific pieces of information, as illustrated in the following code. We will replace the previous `for` statement with the following `foreach` statement. This calls the `displayChunkSet` method that was developed in the *Using the RegExChunker class of LingPipe* section earlier in this chapter:

```
for (String sentence : sentences) {
    displayChunkSet(chunker, sentence);
}
```

The output that follows shows the result. However, it does not always match the entity type correctly:

```
Type: PERSON Entity: [Joe] Score: -Infinity
Type: ORGANIZATION Entity: [Fred] Score: -Infinity
Type: LOCATION Entity: [Boston] Score: -Infinity
Type: PERSON Entity: [McKenzie] Score: -Infinity
Type: PERSON Entity: [Joe] Score: -Infinity
Type: ORGANIZATION Entity: [Vermont] Score: -Infinity
Type: ORGANIZATION Entity: [IBM] Score: -Infinity
Type: ORGANIZATION Entity: [Fred] Score: -Infinity
```

Using the ExactDictionaryChunker class

The `ExactDictionaryChunker` class provides an easy way to create a dictionary of entities and their types, which can be used to find them later in text. It uses a `MapDictionary` object to store entries, and then the `ExactDictionaryChunker` class is used to extract chunks based on the dictionary.

The `AbstractDictionary` interface supports basic operations for entities, categories, and scores. The score is used in the matching process. The `MapDictionary` and `TrieDictionary` classes implement the `AbstractDictionary` interface. The `TrieDictionary` class stores information using a character trie structure. This approach uses less memory so when the memory is limited this approach works well. We will use the `MapDictionary` class for our example.

To illustrate this approach, we will start with a declaration of the `MapDictionary` class:

```
private MapDictionary<String> dictionary;
```

The dictionary will contain the entities that we are interested in finding. We need to initialize the model, as performed in the following `initializeDictionary` method. The `DictionaryEntry` constructor used here accepts three arguments:

- `String`: The name of the entity
- `String`: The category of the entity
- `Double`: Represents a score for the entity

The score is used when determining matches. A few entities are declared and added to the dictionary:

```
private static void initializeDictionary() {
    dictionary = new MapDictionary<String>();
    dictionary.addEntry(
        new DictionaryEntry<String>("Joe","PERSON",1.0));
    dictionary.addEntry(
        new DictionaryEntry<String>("Fred","PERSON",1.0));
    dictionary.addEntry(
        new DictionaryEntry<String>("Boston","PLACE",1.0));
    dictionary.addEntry(
        new DictionaryEntry<String>("pub","PLACE",1.0));
    dictionary.addEntry(
        new DictionaryEntry<String>("Vermont","PLACE",1.0));
    dictionary.addEntry(
        new DictionaryEntry<String>("IBM","ORGANIZATION",1.0));
    dictionary.addEntry(
        new DictionaryEntry<String>("Sally","PERSON",1.0));
}
```

An `ExactDictionaryChunker` instance will use this dictionary. The arguments of the `ExactDictionaryChunker` class are detailed here:

- `Dictionary<String>`: It is a dictionary containing the entities
- `TokenizerFactory`: It is a tokenizer used by the chunker
- `boolean`: If it is `true`, the chunker should return all matches
- `boolean`: If it is `true`, matches are case sensitive

Matches can be overlapping. For example, in the phrase *The First National Bank*, the entity *Bank* could be used by itself or in conjunction with the rest of the phrase. The third parameter that is, `boolean` determines whether all of the matches are returned.

In the following sequence, the dictionary is initialized. We then create an instance of the `ExactDictionaryChunker` class using the Indo-European tokenizer, where we return all matches and ignore the case of the tokens:

```
initializeDictionary();
ExactDictionaryChunker dictionaryChunker
    = new ExactDictionaryChunker(dictionary,
        IndoEuropeanTokenizerFactory.INSTANCE, true, false);
```

The `dictionaryChunker` object is used with each sentence, as shown in the following code sequence. We will use the `displayChunkSet` method, as developed in the *Using the RegExChunker class of LingPipe* section earlier in this chapter:

```
for (String sentence : sentences) {
    System.out.println("\nTEXT=" + sentence);
    displayChunkSet(dictionaryChunker, sentence);
}
```

On execution, we get the following output:

```
TEXT=Joe was the last person to see Fred.
Type: PERSON Entity: [Joe] Score: 1.0
Type: PERSON Entity: [Fred] Score: 1.0
TEXT=He saw him in Boston at McKenzie's pub at 3:00 where he paid $2.45 for
an ale.
Type: PLACE Entity: [Boston] Score: 1.0
Type: PLACE Entity: [pub] Score: 1.0
TEXT=Joe wanted to go to Vermont for the day to visit a cousin who works at
IBM, but Sally and he had to look for Fred
Type: PERSON Entity: [Joe] Score: 1.0
Type: PLACE Entity: [Vermont] Score: 1.0
Type: ORGANIZATION Entity: [IBM] Score: 1.0
Type: PERSON Entity: [Sally] Score: 1.0
Type: PERSON Entity: [Fred] Score: 1.0
```

This does a pretty good job, but it requires a lot of effort to create the dictionary for a large vocabulary.

Building a new dataset with the NER annotation tool

There are many annotation tools available in different forms. Some are standalone and can be configured or installed on a local machine, some are cloud-based, some are free, and some are paid. In this section, we will focus on free annotation tools, get an idea of how to use them, and see what we can achieve with annotation.

To see how we can use annotations to create a dataset, we will look at these tools:

- brat
- Stanford Annotator

brat stands for *brat rapid annotation tool* and can be found at `http://brat.nlplab.org/index.html`. It can be used online or offline. Installing it on your local machine is simple: follow the steps listed at `http://brat.nlplab.org/installation.html`. Once installed and running, open the browser. You need to create a `text1.txt` file in the `data/test` directory with the following content:

```
Joe was the last person to see Fred. He saw him in Boston at McKenzie's pub
at 3:00 where he paid $2.45 for an ale. Joe wanted to go to Vermont for the
day to visit a cousin who works at IBM, but Sally and he had to look for
Fred.
```

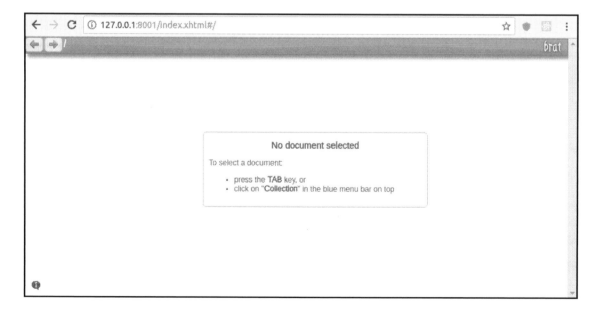

As it shows **No document selected**, using the *Tab* key, the document can be selected. We will create a text file name `text1.txt` as discussed about with the same content we used for processing in earlier examples:

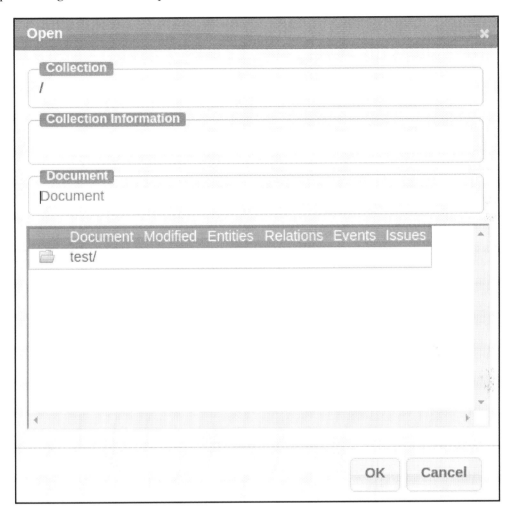

It will display the contents of the `text1.txt` file:

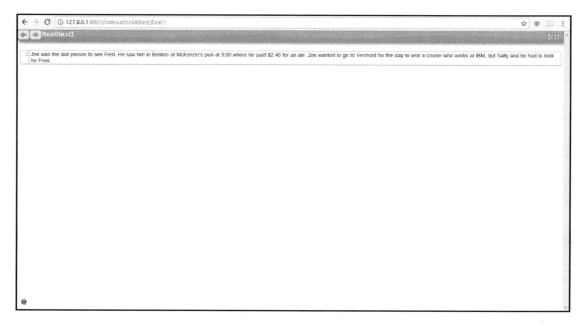

To annotate the document, first we have to log in:

Once logged in, select any word you wish to annotate, and this will open the **New Annotation** window with the listed/configured **Entity type** and **Event type**. All this information is stored and preconfigured in the `annotation.conf` file in the `data/test` directory. You can modify the file as per your requirements:

Annotations will be displayed on the text as we go on selecting the text:

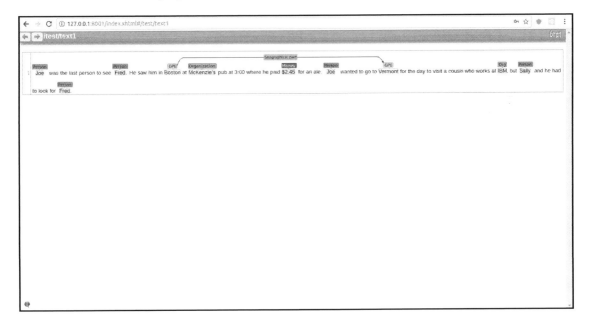

Once saved, the annotation file can be found as `text1.ann` [`Filename.ann`].

The other tool is the Stanford Annotation tool, which can be downloaded from `https://` `nlp.stanford.edu/software/stanford-manual-annotation-tool-2004-05-16.tar.gz`. Once downloaded, extract and double-click on `annotator.jar`, or execute the following command:

```
> java -jar annotator.jar
```

It will show the following:

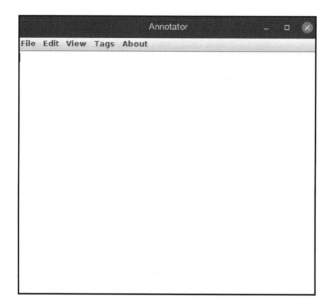

Either you can open any text file, or you can write your content and save the file. The text we used in the previous example on annotation will be used again, just to show how to use the Stanford Annotation tool.

Once the content is available, the next step is to create the tags. From the **Tags** menu, select the **Add Tag** option, which will open the **Tag creation** window, as shown in the following screenshot:

Enter the tag name and click on **OK**. You will then be asked to select the color for the tag. It will display the tag in the right-hand pane of the main window, as shown in the following screenshot:

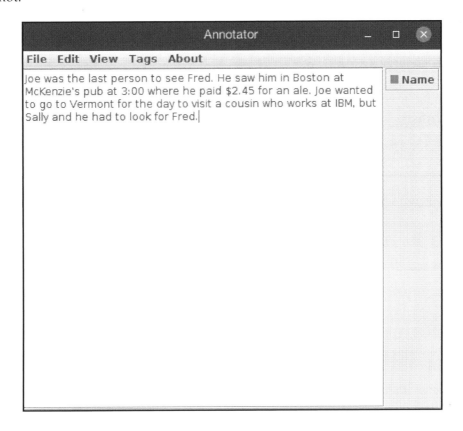

Similarly, we can create as many tags as we want to use. Once a tag is created, the next step is to annotate the text. To annotate text, let's say, `Joe`, select the text using the mouse and click on the **Name** tag on the right. It will add markup to the text, as shown here:

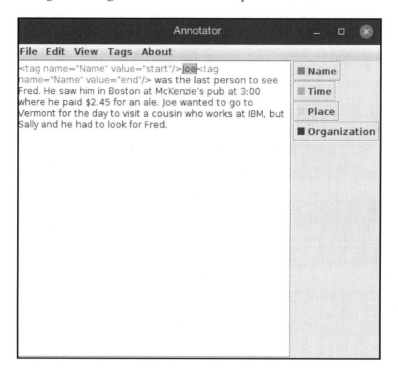

In the same way, as we did for Joe we can mark any other text as required, and save the file. The tag can also be saved so that it can be reused on other text. The saved files are normal text files and can be viewed in any text editor.

Training a model

We will use OpenNLP to demonstrate how a model is trained. The training file used must:

- Contain marks to demarcate the entities
- Have one sentence per line

We will use the following model file, named `en-ner-person.train`:

```
<START:person> Joe <END> was the last person to see <START:person> Fred
<END>.
He saw him in Boston at McKenzie's pub at 3:00 where he paid $2.45 for an
ale.
<START:person> Joe <END> wanted to go to Vermont for the day to visit a
cousin who works at IBM, but <START:person> Sally <END> and he had to look
for <START:person> Fred <END>.
```

Several methods in this example are capable of throwing exceptions. These statements will be placed in a try-with-resource block, as shown here, where the model's output stream is created:

```
try (OutputStream modelOutputStream = new BufferedOutputStream(
        new FileOutputStream(new File("modelFile")));) {
    ...
} catch (IOException ex) {
    // Handle exception
}
```

Within the block, we create an `OutputStream<String>` object using the `PlainTextByLineStream` class. This class's constructor takes a `FileInputStream` instance and returns each line as a `String` object. The `en-ner-person.train` file is used as the input file, as shown here. The `UTF-8` string refers to the encoding sequence used:

```
ObjectStream<String> lineStream = new PlainTextByLineStream(
    new FileInputStream("en-ner-person.train"), "UTF-8");
```

The `lineStream` object contains streams that are annotated with tags delineating the entities in the text. These need to be converted to `NameSample` objects so that the model can be trained. This conversion is performed by the `NameSampleDataStream` class, as shown here. A `NameSample` object holds the names of the entities found in the text:

```
ObjectStream<NameSample> sampleStream =
    new NameSampleDataStream(lineStream);
```

The `train` method can now be executed as follows:

```
TokenNameFinderModel model = NameFinderME.train(
    "en", "person",  sampleStream,
    Collections.<String, Object>emptyMap(), 100, 5);
```

The arguments of the method are as detailed in the following table:

Parameter	Meaning
"en"	Language code
"person"	Entity type
sampleStream	Sample data
null	Resources
100	Number of iterations
5	Cutoff

The model is then serialized to an output file:

```
model.serialize(modelOutputStream);
```

The output of this sequence is as follows. It has been shortened to conserve space. Basic information about the creation of the model is provided:

```
Indexing events using cutoff of 5
   Computing event counts...  done. 53 events
   Indexing...  done.
Sorting and merging events... done. Reduced 53 events to 46.
Done indexing.
Incorporating indexed data for training...
done.
   Number of Event Tokens: 46
       Number of Outcomes: 2
     Number of Predicates: 34
...done.
Computing model parameters ...
Performing 100 iterations.
   1:  ... loglikelihood=-36.73680056967707   0.05660377358490566
   2:  ... loglikelihood=-17.499660626361216  0.9433962264150944
   3:  ... loglikelihood=-13.216835449617108  0.9433962264150944
   4:  ... loglikelihood=-11.461783667999262  0.9433962264150944
   5:  ... loglikelihood=-10.380239416084963  0.9433962264150944
   6:  ... loglikelihood=-9.570622475692486   0.9433962264150944
   7:  ... loglikelihood=-8.919945779143012   0.9433962264150944
 ...
  99:  ... loglikelihood=-3.513810438211968   0.9622641509433962
 100:  ... loglikelihood=-3.507213816708068   0.9622641509433962
```

Evaluating a model

A model can be evaluated using the `TokenNameFinderEvaluator` class. The evaluation process uses marked up sample text to perform the evaluation.

For this simple example, a file called `en-ner-person.eval` was created that contained the following text:

```
<START:person> Bill <END> went to the farm to see <START:person> Sally
<END>.
Unable to find <START:person> Sally <END> he went to town.
There he saw <START:person> Fred <END> who had seen <START:person> Sally
<END> at the book store with <START:person> Mary <END>.
```

The following code is used to perform the evaluation. The previous model is used as the argument of the `TokenNameFinderEvaluator` constructor. A `NameSampleDataStream` instance is created, based on the evaluation file. The `TokenNameFinderEvaluator` class's `evaluate` method performs the evaluation:

```
TokenNameFinderEvaluator evaluator =
    new TokenNameFinderEvaluator(new NameFinderME(model));
lineStream = new PlainTextByLineStream(
    new FileInputStream("en-ner-person.eval"), "UTF-8");
sampleStream = new NameSampleDataStream(lineStream);
evaluator.evaluate(sampleStream);
```

To determine how well the model worked with the evaluation data, the `getFMeasure` method is executed. The results are then displayed:

```
FMeasure result = evaluator.getFMeasure();
System.out.println(result.toString());
```

The following output displays the `Precision`, `Recall`, and `F-Measure`. It indicates that 50 percent of the entities found exactly match the evaluation data. `Recall` is the percentage of entities defined in the corpus that were found in the same location. The performance measure is the harmonic mean and is defined as *F1 = 2 * Precision * Recall / (Recall + Precision)*:

```
Precision: 0.5 Recall: 0.25 F-Measure: 0.3333333333333333
```

The data and evaluation sets should be much larger in order to create a better model. The intent here was to demonstrate the basic approach used to train and evaluate a POS model.

Summary

NER involves detecting entities and then classifying them. Common categories include names, locations, and things. This is an important task that many applications use to support searching, resolving references, and finding meanings in text. The process is frequently used in downstream tasks.

We investigated several techniques for performing NER. Regular expressions are one approach that is supported by both core Java classes and NLP APIs. This technique is useful for many applications, and there are a large number of regular expression libraries available.

Dictionary-based approaches are also possible and work well for some applications. However, they require considerable effort to populate at times. We used LingPipe's `MapDictionary` class to illustrate this approach.

Trained models can also be used to perform NER. We examined several of these and demonstrated how to train a model using the OpenNLP `NameFinderME` class. This process was very similar to the earlier training processes.

In the next chapter, `Chapter 5`, *Detecting Parts of Speech* we will learn how to detect parts of speech such as nouns, adjectives, and prepositions.

5
Detecting Part of Speech

Previously, we identified parts of text, such as people, places, and things. In this chapter, we will investigate the process of finding **Part-Of-Speech** (**POS**). These are the parts that we recognize in English as grammatical elements, such as nouns and verbs. We will find that the context of the word is an important aspect of determining what type of word it is.

We will examine the tagging process, which essentially assigns a POS to a tag. This process is at the heart of detecting POS. We will briefly discuss why tagging is important, and then examine the various factors that make detecting POS difficult. Various **Natural Language Processing** (**NLP**) APIs are then used to illustrate the tagging process. We will also demonstrate how to train a model to address specialized text.

We will cover the following topics in this chapter:

- The tagging process
- Using the NLP APIs

The tagging process

Tagging is the process of assigning a description to a token or a portion of text. This description is called a tag. POS tagging is the process of assigning a POS tag to a token. These tags are normally grammatical tags such as noun, verb, and adjective. For example, consider the following sentence:

"The cow jumped over the moon."

For many of these initial examples, we will illustrate the result of a POS tagger using the OpenNLP tagger that will be discussed in the *Using OpenNLP POS taggers* section later in this chapter. If we use that tagger with the previous example, we will get the following results. Notice that the words are followed by a forward slash and then their POS tag. These tags will be explained shortly:

```
The/DT cow/NN jumped/VBD over/IN the/DT moon./NN
```

Words can potentially have more than one tag associated with them, depending on their context. For example, the word *saw* could be a noun or a verb. When a word can be classified into different categories, information such as its position, words in its vicinity, or similar information is used to probabilistically determine the appropriate category. For example, if a word is preceded by a determiner and followed by a noun, then tag the word as an adjective.

The general tagging process consists of tokenizing the text, determining possible tags, and resolving ambiguous tags. Algorithms are used to perform POS identification (tagging). There are two general approaches:

- **Rule-based**: Rule-based taggers use a set of rules, and a dictionary of words and possible tags. The rules are used when a word has multiple tags. Rules often use the previous and/or following words to select a tag.

- **Stochastic**: Stochastic taggers are either based on the Markov model or are cue-based, which uses either decision trees or maximum entropy. Markov models are finite state machines, where each state has two probability distributions. Its objective is to find the optimal sequence of tags for a sentence. **Hidden Markov Models (HMM)** are also used. In these models, the state transitions are not visible.

A maximum entropy tagger uses statistics to determine the POS for a word and often uses a corpus to train a model. A corpus is a collection of words marked up with POS tags. Corpora exist for a number of languages. These take a lot of effort to develop. Frequently used corpora include the Penn Treebank (https://www.seas.upenn.edu/~pdtb//) or Brown Corpus (http://www.essex.ac.uk/linguistics/external/clmt/w3c/corpus_ling/content/corpora/list/private/brown/brown.html).

A sample from the Penn Treebank corpus, which illustrates POS markup, is as follows:

```
Well/UH what/WP do/VBP you/PRP think/VB about/IN
the/DT idea/NN of/IN ,/, uh/UH ,/, kids/NNS having/VBG
to/TO do/VB public/JJ service/NN work/NN for/IN a/DT
year/NN ?/.
```

There are traditionally nine parts of speech in English: nouns, verbs, articles, adjectives, prepositions, pronouns, adverbs, conjunctions, and interjections. However, a more complete analysis often requires additional categories and subcategories. There have been as many as 150 different parts of speech identified. In some situations, it may be necessary to create new tags. A short list is shown in the following table. These are the tags we will be using frequently in this chapter:

Part	Meaning
NN	Noun, singular, or mass
DT	Determiner
VB	Verb, base form
VBD	Verb, past tense
VBZ	Verb, third person singular present
IN	Preposition or subordinating conjunction
NNP	Proper noun, singular
TO	To
JJ	Adjective

A more comprehensive list is shown in the following table. This list is adapted from `https://www.ling.upenn.edu/courses/Fall_2003/ling001/penn_treebank_pos.html`. The complete list of *The University of Pennsylvania (Penn) Treebank Tag Set* can be found at `http://www.comp.leeds.ac.uk/ccalas/tagsets/upenn.html`. A set of tags is referred to as a *tag set*:

Tag	Description	Tag	Description
CC	Coordinating conjunction	PRP$	Possessive pronoun
CD	Cardinal number	RB	Adverb
DT	Determiner	RBR	Adverb, comparative
EX	Existential there	RBS	Adverb, superlative
FW	Foreign word	RP	Particle
IN	Preposition or subordinating conjunction	SYM	Symbol
JJ	Adjective	TO	To
JJR	Adjective, comparative	UH	Interjection
JJS	Adjective, superlative	VB	Verb, base form
LS	List item marker	VBD	Verb, past tense
MD	Modal	VBG	Verb, gerunds or present participle
NN	Noun, singular, or mass	VBN	Verb, past participle
NNS	Noun, plural	VBP	Verb, non-third person singular present
NNP	Proper noun, singular	VBZ	Verb, third person singular present
NNPS	Proper noun, plural	WDT	Wh-determiner
PDT	Predeterminer	WP	Wh-pronoun

Tag	Description	Tag	Description
POS	Possessive ending	WP$	Possessive wh-pronoun
PRP	Personal pronoun	WRB	Wh-adverb

The development of a manual corpus is labor intensive. However, some statistical techniques have been developed to create corpora. A number of corpora are available. One of the first ones was the Brown Corpus (`http://clu.uni.no/icame/manuals/BROWN/INDEX.HTM`). Newer ones include the British National Corpus (`http://www.natcorp.ox.ac.uk/corpus/index.xml`), with over 100 million words, and the American National Corpus (`http://www.anc.org/`).

The importance of POS taggers

Proper tagging of a sentence can enhance the quality of downstream processing tasks. If we know that *sue* is a verb and not a noun, then this can assist in establishing the correct relationship between tokens. Determining the POS, phrases, clauses, and any relationship between them is called *parsing*. This is in contrast to tokenization, where we are only interested in identifying *word* elements and we are not concerned about their meaning.

POS tagging is used for many downstream processes, such as question analysis and analyzing the sentiment of text. Some social media sites are frequently interested in assessing the sentiment of their client's communication. Text indexing will frequently use POS data. Speech processing can use tags to help decide how to pronounce words.

What makes POS difficult?

There are many aspects of a language that can make POS tagging difficult. Most English words will have two or more tags associated with them. A dictionary is not always sufficient to determine a word's POS. For example, the meaning of words such as *bill* and *force* are dependent on their context. The following sentence demonstrates how they can both be used in the same sentence as nouns and verbs.

"Bill used the force to force the manger to tear the bill in two."

Using the OpenNLP tagger with this sentence produces the following output:

```
Bill/NNP used/VBD the/DT force/NN to/TO force/VB the/DT manger/NN to/TO
tear/VB the/DT bill/NN in/IN two./PRP$
```

The use of textese, a combination of different forms of text including abbreviations, hashtags, emoticons, and slang, in communications mediums such as tweets and text makes it more difficult to tag sentences. For example, the following message is difficult to tag:

"AFAIK she H8 cth! BTW had a GR8 tym at the party BBIAM."

Its equivalent is:

"As far as I know, she hates cleaning the house! By the way, had a great time at the party. Be back in a minute."

Using the OpenNLP tagger, we will get the following output:

```
AFAIK/NNS she/PRP H8/CD cth!/.
BTW/NNP had/VBD a/DT GR8/CD tym/NN at/IN the/DT party/NN BBIAM./.
```

In the *Using the MaxentTagger class to tag textese* section later in this chapter, we will provide a demonstration of how LingPipe can handle textese. A short list of common textese terms is given in the following table:

Phrase	Textese	Phrase	Textese
As far as I know	AFAIK	By the way	BTW
Away from keyboard	AFK	You're on your own	YOYO
Thanks	THNX or THX	As soon as possible	ASAP
Today	2day	What do you mean by that	WDYMBT
Before	B4	Be back in a minute	BBIAM
See you	C U	Can't	CNT
Haha	hh	Later	l8R
Laughing out loud	LOL	On the other hand	OTOH
Rolling on the floor laughing	ROFL or ROTFL	I don't know	IDK
Great	GR8	Cleaning the house	CTH
At the moment	ATM	In my humble opinion	IMHO

There are several lists of textese; a large list can be found at http://www.ukrainecalling.com/textspeak.aspx.

Tokenization is an important step in the POS tagging process. If the tokens are not split properly, we can get erroneous results. There are several other potential problems, including the following:

- If we use lowercase, then words such as *sam* can be confused with the person or the System for Award Management (`www.sam.gov`)
- We have to take into account contractions such as *can't* and recognize that different characters may be used for the apostrophe
- Although phrases such as *vice versa* can be treated as a unit, it has been used for a band in England, the title of a novel, and the title of a magazine
- We can't ignore hyphenated words such as *first-cut* and *prime-cut* that have meanings different from their individual use
- Some words have embedded numbers, such as iPhone 5S
- Special character sequences such as a URL or email address also need to be handled

Some words are found embedded in quotes or parentheses, which can make their meaning confusing. Consider the following example:

"Whether "Blue" was correct or not (it's not) is debatable."

"Blue" could refer to the color blue or conceivably the nickname of a person. The output of the tagger for this sentence is as follows:

```
Whether/IN "Blue"/NNP was/VBD correct/JJ or/CC not/RB (it's/JJ not)/NN
is/VBZ debatable/VBG
```

Using the NLP APIs

We will demonstrate POS tagging using OpenNLP, Stanford API, and LingPipe. Each of the examples will use the following sentence. It is the first sentence of Chapter 5 from *At A Venture*, of *Twenty Thousands Leagues Under the Sea*, by Jules Verne:

```
private String[] sentence = {"The", "voyage", "of", "the",
    "Abraham", "Lincoln", "was", "for", "a", "long", "time", "marked",
    "by", "no", "special", "incident."};
```

The text to be processed may not always be defined in this fashion. Sometimes, the sentence will be available as a single string:

```
String theSentence = "The voyage of the Abraham Lincoln was for a "
    + "long time marked by no special incident.";
```

We might need to convert a string to an array of strings. There are numerous techniques for converting this string to an array of words. The following `tokenizeSentence` method performs this operation:

```
public String[] tokenizeSentence(String sentence) {
    String words[] = sentence.split("S+");
    return words;
}
```

The following code demonstrates the use of this method:

```
String words[] = tokenizeSentence(theSentence);
for(String word : words) {
    System.out.print(word + " ");
}
System.out.println();
```

The output is as follows:

```
The voyage of the Abraham Lincoln was for a long time marked by no special
incident.
```

Alternatively, we could use a tokenizer such as OpenNLP's `WhitespaceTokenizer` class, as shown here:

```
String words[] =
        WhitespaceTokenizer.INSTANCE.tokenize(sentence);
```

Using OpenNLP POS taggers

OpenNLP provides several classes in support of POS tagging. We will demonstrate how to use the `POSTaggerME` class to perform basic tagging and the `ChunkerME` class to perform chunking. Chunking involves grouping related words according to their types. This can provide additional insight into the structure of a sentence. We will also examine the creation and use of a `POSDictionary` instance.

Using the OpenNLP POSTaggerME class for POS taggers

The OpenNLP `POSTaggerME` class uses maximum entropy to process the tags. The tagger determines the type of tag based on the word itself and the word's context. Any given word may have multiple tags associated with it. The tagger uses a probability model to determine the specific tag to be assigned.

POS models are loaded from a file. The `en-pos-maxent.bin` model is used frequently and is based on the Penn TreeBank tag set. Various pretrained POS models for OpenNLP can be found at `http://opennlp.sourceforge.net/models-1.5/`.

We start with a try-catch block to handle any `IOException` that might be generated when loading a model, as shown here.

We use the `en-pos-maxent.bin` file for the model:

```
try (InputStream modelIn = new FileInputStream(
    new File(getModelDir(), "en-pos-maxent.bin"));) {
    ...
}
catch (IOException e) {
    // Handle exceptions
}
```

Next, create the `POSModel` and `POSTaggerME` instances, as shown here:

```
POSModel model = new POSModel(modelIn);
POSTaggerME tagger = new POSTaggerME(model);
```

The `tag` method can now be applied to the tagger using the text to be processed as its argument:

```
String tags[] = tagger.tag(sentence);
```

The words and their tags are then displayed, as shown here:

```
for (int i = 0; i<sentence.length; i++) {
    System.out.print(sentence[i] + "/" + tags[i] + " ");
}
```

The output is as follows. Each word is followed by its type:

```
The/DT voyage/NN of/IN the/DT Abraham/NNP Lincoln/NNP was/VBD for/IN a/DT
long/JJ time/NN marked/VBN by/IN no/DT special/JJ incident./NN
```

With any sentence, there may be more than one possible assignment of tags to words. The `topKSequences` method will return a set of sequences based on their probability of being correct. In the following code sequence, the `topKSequences` method is executed using the `sentence` variable and then displayed:

```
Sequence topSequences[] = tagger.topKSequences(sentence);
for (inti = 0; i<topSequences.length; i++) {
    System.out.println(topSequences[i]);
}
```

Its output follows, in which the first number represents a weighted score and the tags within the brackets are the sequence of tags scored:

```
   -0.5563571615737618 [DT, NN, IN, DT, NNP, NNP, VBD, IN, DT, JJ, NN,
VBN, IN, DT, JJ, NN]
   -2.9886144610050907 [DT, NN, IN, DT, NNP, NNP, VBD, IN, DT, JJ, NN,
VBN, IN, DT, JJ, .]
   -3.771930515521527 [DT, NN, IN, DT, NNP, NNP, VBD, IN, DT, JJ, NN, VBN,
IN, DT, NN, NN]
```

 Ensure that you include the correct Sequence class. For this example, use import opennlp.tools.util.Sequence;.

The Sequence class has several methods, as detailed in the following table:

Method	Meaning
getOutcomes	Returns a list of strings representing the tags for the sentence
getProbs	Returns an array of double variables representing the probability for each tag in the sequence
getScore	Returns a weighted value for the sequence

In the following sequence, we use several of these methods to demonstrate what they do. For each sequence, the tags and their probabilities are displayed, separated by a forward slash:

```
for (int i = 0; i<topSequences.length; i++) {
    List<String> outcomes = topSequences[i].getOutcomes();
    double probabilities[] = topSequences[i].getProbs();
    for (int j = 0; j <outcomes.size(); j++) {
        System.out.printf("%s/%5.3f ",outcomes.get(j),
        probabilities[j]);
    }
    System.out.println();
}
System.out.println();
```

The output is as follows. Each pair of lines represents one sequence where the output has been wrapped:

```
    DT/0.992 NN/0.990 IN/0.989 DT/0.990 NNP/0.996 NNP/0.991 VBD/0.994
IN/0.996 DT/0.996 JJ/0.991 NN/0.994 VBN/0.860 IN/0.985 DT/0.960 JJ/0.919
NN/0.832
    DT/0.992 NN/0.990 IN/0.989 DT/0.990 NNP/0.996 NNP/0.991 VBD/0.994
IN/0.996 DT/0.996 JJ/0.991 NN/0.994 VBN/0.860 IN/0.985 DT/0.960 JJ/0.919
./0.073
    DT/0.992 NN/0.990 IN/0.989 DT/0.990 NNP/0.996 NNP/0.991 VBD/0.994
IN/0.996 DT/0.996 JJ/0.991 NN/0.994 VBN/0.860 IN/0.985 DT/0.960 NN/0.073
NN/0.419
```

Using OpenNLP chunking

The process of chunking involves breaking a sentence into parts or chunks. These chunks can then be annotated with tags. We will use the ChunkerME class to illustrate how this is accomplished. This class uses a model loaded into a ChunkerModel instance. The ChunkerME class's chunk method performs the actual chunking process. We will also examine the use of the chunkAsSpans method to return information about the span of these chunks. This allows us to see how long a chunk is and what elements make up the chunk.

We will use the en-pos-maxent.bin file to create a model for the POSTaggerME instance. We need to use this instance to tag the text as we did in the *Using OpenNLP POSTaggerME class for POS taggers* section earlier in this chapter. We will also use the en-chunker.bin file to create a ChunkerModel instance to be used with the ChunkerME instance.

These models are created using input streams, as shown in the following example. We use a try-with-resources block to open and close files and to deal with any exceptions that may be thrown:

```
try (
        InputStream posModelStream = new FileInputStream(
            getModelDir() + "\\en-pos-maxent.bin");
        InputStream chunkerStream = new FileInputStream(
            getModelDir() + "\\en-chunker.bin");) {
    ...
} catch (IOException ex) {
    // Handle exceptions
}
```

The following code sequence creates and uses a tagger to find the POS of the sentence. The sentence and its tags are then displayed:

```
POSModel model = new POSModel(posModelStream);
POSTaggerME tagger = new POSTaggerME(model);

String tags[] = tagger.tag(sentence);
for(int i=0; i<tags.length; i++) {
    System.out.print(sentence[i] + "/" + tags[i] + " ");
}
System.out.println();
```

The output is as follows. We have shown this output so that it will be clear how the chunker works:

```
The/DT voyage/NN of/IN the/DT Abraham/NNP Lincoln/NNP was/VBD for/IN a/DT
long/JJ time/NN marked/VBN by/IN no/DT special/JJ incident./NN
```

A `ChunkerModel` instance is created using the input stream. From this, the `ChunkerME` instance is created, followed by the use of the `chunk` method, as shown here. The `chunk` method will use the sentence's token and its tags to create an array of strings. Each string will hold information about the token and its chunk:

```
ChunkerModel chunkerModel = new
    ChunkerModel(chunkerStream);
ChunkerME chunkerME = new ChunkerME(chunkerModel);
String result[] = chunkerME.chunk(sentence, tags);
```

Each token in the `results` array and its chunk tag are displayed, as shown here:

```
for (int i = 0; i < result.length; i++) {
    System.out.println("[" + sentence[i] + "] " + result[i]);
}
```

The output is as follows. The token is enclosed in brackets, followed by the chunk tag. These tags are explained in the following table:

First part	
B	Beginning of tag
I	Continuation of tag
E	End of tag (will not appear if tag is one word long)
Second part	
NP	Noun chunk
VB	Verb chunk

Multiple words are grouped together, such as "The voyage" and "the Abraham Lincoln":

```
[The] B-NP
[voyage] I-NP
[of] B-PP
[the] B-NP
[Abraham] I-NP
[Lincoln] I-NP
[was] B-VP
[for] B-PP
[a] B-NP
[long] I-NP
[time] I-NP
[marked] B-VP
[by] B-PP
[no] B-NP
[special] I-NP
[incident.] I-NP
```

If we are interested in getting more detailed information about the chunks, we can use the ChunkerME class's chunkAsSpans method. This method returns an array of Span objects. Each object represents one span found in the text.

There are several other ChunkerME class methods available. Here, we will illustrate the use of the getType, getStart, and getEnd methods. The getType method returns the second part of the chunk tag, and the getStart and getEnd methods return the beginning and ending index of the tokens in the original sentence array, respectively. The length method returns the length of the span in a number of tokens.

In the following sequence, the chunkAsSpans method is executed using the sentence and tags arrays. The spans array is then displayed. The outer for loop processes one Span object at a time, displaying the basic span information.
The inner for loop displays the spanned text enclosed within brackets:

```
Span[] spans = chunkerME.chunkAsSpans(sentence, tags);
for (Span span : spans) {
    System.out.print("Type: " + span.getType() + " - "
        + " Begin: " + span.getStart()
        + " End:" + span.getEnd()
        + " Length: " + span.length() + "  [");
    for (int j = span.getStart(); j < span.getEnd(); j++) {
        System.out.print(sentence[j] + " ");
    }
    System.out.println("]");
}
```

The following output clearly shows the span type, its position in the `sentence` array, its `Length`, and then the actual spanned text:

```
Type: NP -  Begin: 0 End:2 Length: 2   [The voyage ]
Type: PP -  Begin: 2 End:3 Length: 1   [of ]
Type: NP -  Begin: 3 End:6 Length: 3   [the Abraham Lincoln ]
Type: VP -  Begin: 6 End:7 Length: 1   [was ]
Type: PP -  Begin: 7 End:8 Length: 1   [for ]
Type: NP -  Begin: 8 End:11 Length: 3   [a long time ]
Type: VP -  Begin: 11 End:12 Length: 1   [marked ]
Type: PP -  Begin: 12 End:13 Length: 1   [by ]
Type: NP -  Begin: 13 End:16 Length: 3   [no special incident. ]
```

Using the POSDictionary class

A tag dictionary specifies what the valid tags for a word are. This can prevent a tag from being applied inappropriately to a word. In addition, some search algorithms execute faster, since they do not have to consider other less probable tags.

In this section, we will demonstrate how to:

- Obtain the tag dictionary for a tagger
- Determine what tags a word has
- Show how to change the tags for a word
- Add a new tag dictionary to a new tagger factory

As with the previous example, we will use a try-with-resources block to open our input streams for the POS model and then create our model and tagger factory, as shown here:

```java
try (InputStream modelIn = new FileInputStream(
        new File(getModelDir(), "en-pos-maxent.bin"));) {
    POSModel model = new POSModel(modelIn);
    POSTaggerFactory posTaggerFactory = model.getFactory();
    ...
} catch (IOException e) {
    //Handle exceptions
}
```

Obtaining the tag dictionary for a tagger

We used the POSModel class's getFactory method to get a POSTaggerFactory instance. We will use its getTagDictionary method to obtain its TagDictionary instance. This is illustrated here:

```
MutableTagDictionary tagDictionary =
    (MutableTagDictionary)posTaggerFactory.getTagDictionary();
```

The MutableTagDictionary interface extends the TagDictionary interface. The TagDictionary interface possesses a getTags method, and the MutableTagDictionary interface adds a put method that allows tags to be added to the dictionary. These interfaces are implemented by the POSDictionary class.

Determining a word's tags

To obtain the tags for a given word, use the getTags method. This returns an array of tags represented by strings. The tags are then displayed, as shown here:

```
String tags[] = tagDictionary.getTags("force");
for (String tag : tags) {
    System.out.print("/" + tag);
}
System.out.println();
```

The output is as follows:

```
/NN/VBP/VB
```

This means that the word "force" can be interpreted in three different ways.

Changing a word's tags

The MutableTagDictionary interface's put method allows us to add tags to a word. The method has two arguments: the word and its new tags. The method returns an array containing the previous tags.

In the following example, we replace the old tags with a new tag. The old tags are then displayed:

```
String oldTags[] = tagDictionary.put("force", "newTag");
for (String tag : oldTags) {
    System.out.print("/" + tag);
}
System.out.println();
```

The following output lists the old tags for the word:

```
/NN/VBP/VB
```

These tags have been replaced by the new tag, as demonstrated here, where the current tags are displayed:

```
tags = tagDictionary.getTags("force");
for (String tag : tags) {
    System.out.print("/" + tag);
}
System.out.println();
```

All we get is the following:

```
/newTag
```

To retain the old tags, we will need to create an array of strings to hold the old and the new tags, and then use the array as the second argument of the put method, as shown here:

```
String newTags[] = new String[tags.length+1];
for (int i=0; i<tags.length; i++) {
    newTags[i] = tags[i];
}
newTags[tags.length] = "newTag";
oldTags = tagDictionary.put("force", newTags);
```

If we redisplay the current tags, as shown here, we can see that the old tags have been retained and the new one has been added:

```
/NN/VBP/VB/newTag
```

> When adding tags, be careful to assign the tags in the proper order, as it will influence which tag is assigned.

Adding a new tag dictionary

A new tag dictionary can be added to a POSTaggerFactory instance. We will illustrate this process by creating a new POSTaggerFactory and then adding the tagDictionary we developed earlier. First, we create a new factory using the default constructor, as shown in the following code.

This is followed by calling the `setTagDictionary` method against the new factory:

```
POSTaggerFactory newFactory = new POSTaggerFactory();
newFactory.setTagDictionary(tagDictionary);
```

To confirm that the `tag` dictionary has been added, we display the tags for the word `"force"`, as shown here:

```
tags = newFactory.getTagDictionary().getTags("force");
for (String tag : tags) {
    System.out.print("/" + tag);
}
System.out.println();
```

The tags are the same, as shown here:

```
/NN/VBP/VB/newTag
```

Creating a dictionary from a file

If we need to create a new dictionary, then one approach is to create an XML file containing all of the words and their tags, and then create the dictionary from the file. OpenNLP supports this approach with the `POSDictionary` class's `create` method.

The XML file consists of the `dictionary` root element, followed by a series of `entry` elements. The `entry` element uses the `tags` attribute to specify the tags for the word. The word is contained within the `entry` element as a `token` element. A simple example using two words stored in the `dictionary.txt` file is as follows:

```
<dictionary case_sensitive="false">
    <entry tags="JJ VB">
        <token>strong</token>
    </entry>
    <entry tags="NN VBP VB">
        <token>force</token>
    </entry>
</dictionary>
```

To create the dictionary, we use the `create` method based on an input stream, as shown here:

```
try (InputStream dictionaryIn =
    new FileInputStream(new File("dictionary.txt"));) {
    POSDictionary dictionary =
     POSDictionary.create(dictionaryIn);
    ...
```

```
    } catch (IOException e) {
        // Handle exceptions
    }
```

The `POSDictionary` class has an `iterator` method that returns an iterator object. Its `next` method returns a string for each word in the dictionary. We can use these methods to display the contents of the dictionary, as shown here:

```
Iterator<String> iterator = dictionary.iterator();
while (iterator.hasNext()) {
    String entry = iterator.next();
    String tags[] = dictionary.getTags(entry);
    System.out.print(entry + " ");
    for (String tag : tags) {
        System.out.print("/" + tag);
    }
    System.out.println();
}
```

The output that follows displays what we can expect:

```
strong /JJ/VB
force /NN/VBP/VB
```

Using Stanford POS taggers

In this section, we will examine two different approaches supported by the Stanford API to perform tagging. The first technique uses the `MaxentTagger` class. As its name implies, it uses maximum entropy to find the POS. We will also use this class to demonstrate a model designed to handle textese-type text. The second approach will use the pipeline approach with annotators. The English taggers use the Penn Treebank English POS tag set.

Using Stanford MaxentTagger

The `MaxentTagger` class uses a model to perform the tagging task. There are a number of models that come bundled with the API, all with the file extension `.tagger`. They include English, Chinese, Arabic, French, and German models.

The English models are listed here. The prefix, `wsj`, refers to models based on the Wall Street Journal. The other terms refer to techniques used to train the model. These concepts are not covered here:

- `wsj-0-18-bidirectional-distsim.tagger`
- `wsj-0-18-bidirectional-nodistsim.tagger`

- wsj-0-18-caseless-left3words-distsim.tagger
- wsj-0-18-left3words-distsim.tagger
- wsj-0-18-left3words-nodistsim.tagger
- english-bidirectional-distsim.tagger
- english-caseless-left3words-distsim.tagger
- english-left3words-distsim.tagger

The example reads in a series of sentences from a file. Each sentence is then processed and various ways of accessing and displaying the words and tags are shown.

We start with a try-with-resources block to deal with IO exceptions, as shown here. The wsj-0-18-bidirectional-distsim.tagger file is used to create an instance of the MaxentTagger class.

A List instance of List instances of HasWord objects is created using the MaxentTagger class's tokenizeText method. The sentences are read in from the sentences.txt file. The HasWord interface represents words and contains two methods: a setWord and a word method. The latter method returns a word as a string. Each sentence is represented by a List instance of HasWord objects:

```
try {
    MaxentTagger tagger = new MaxentTagger(getModelDir() +
        "//wsj-0-18-bidirectional-distsim.tagger");
    List<List<HasWord>> sentences = MaxentTagger.tokenizeText(
        new BufferedReader(new FileReader("sentences.txt")));
    ...
} catch (FileNotFoundException ex) {
    // Handle exceptions
}
```

The sentences.txt file contains the first four sentences of Chapter 5, *At A Venture,* of the book *Twenty Thousand Leagues Under the Sea*:

```
The voyage of the Abraham Lincoln was for a long time marked by no special
incident.
But one circumstance happened which showed the wonderful dexterity of Ned
Land, and proved what confidence we might place in him.
The 30th of June, the frigate spoke some American whalers, from whom we
learned that they knew nothing about the narwhal.
But one of them, the captain of the Monroe, knowing that Ned Land had
shipped on board the Abraham Lincoln, begged for his help in chasing a
whale they had in sight.
```

A loop is added to process each sentence of the `sentences` list. The `tagSentence` method returns a `List` instance of `TaggedWord` objects, as shown in the following code. The `TaggedWord` class implements the `HasWord` interface and adds a `tag` method that returns the tag associated with the word. As shown here, the `toString` method is used to display each sentence:

```
List<TaggedWord> taggedSentence =
    tagger.tagSentence(sentence);
for (List<HasWord> sentence : sentences) {
    List<TaggedWord> taggedSentence=
        tagger.tagSentence(sentence);
    System.out.println(taggedSentence);
}
```

The output is as follows:

```
    [The/DT, voyage/NN, of/IN, the/DT, Abraham/NNP, Lincoln/NNP, was/VBD,
for/IN, a/DT, long/JJ, --- time/NN, marked/VBN, by/IN, no/DT, special/JJ,
incident/NN, ./.]
    [But/CC, one/CD, circumstance/NN, happened/VBD, which/WDT, showed/VBD,
the/DT, wonderful/JJ, dexterity/NN, of/IN, Ned/NNP, Land/NNP, ,/,, and/CC,
proved/VBD, what/WP, confidence/NN, we/PRP, might/MD, place/VB, in/IN,
him/PRP, ./.]
    [The/DT, 30th/JJ, of/IN, June/NNP, ,/,, the/DT, frigate/NN, spoke/VBD,
some/DT, American/JJ, whalers/NNS, ,/,, from/IN, whom/WP, we/PRP,
learned/VBD, that/IN, they/PRP, knew/VBD, nothing/NN, about/IN, the/DT,
narwhal/NN, ./.]
    [But/CC, one/CD, of/IN, them/PRP, ,/,, the/DT, captain/NN, of/IN,
the/DT, Monroe/NNP, ,/,, knowing/VBG, that/IN, Ned/NNP, Land/NNP, had/VBD,
shipped/VBN, on/IN, board/NN, the/DT, Abraham/NNP, Lincoln/NNP, ,/,,
begged/VBN, for/IN, his/PRP$, help/NN, in/IN, chasing/VBG, a/DT, whale/NN,
they/PRP, had/VBD, in/IN, sight/NN, ./.]
```

Alternatively, we can use the `Sentence` class's `listToString` method to convert the tagged sentence to a simple `String` object.

A value of `false` for its second parameter is used by the `toString` method of `HasWord` to create the resulting string, as shown here:

```
List<TaggedWord> taggedSentence =
    tagger.tagSentence(sentence);
for (List<HasWord> sentence : sentences) {
    List<TaggedWord> taggedSentence=
        tagger.tagSentence(sentence);
    System.out.println(Sentence.listToString(taggedSentence, false));
}
```

This produces a more aesthetically pleasing output:

```
    The/DT voyage/NN of/IN the/DT Abraham/NNP Lincoln/NNP was/VBD for/IN
a/DT long/JJ time/NN marked/VBN by/IN no/DT special/JJ incident/NN ./.
    But/CC one/CD circumstance/NN happened/VBD which/WDT showed/VBD the/DT
wonderful/JJ dexterity/NN of/IN Ned/NNP Land/NNP ,/, and/CC proved/VBD
what/WP confidence/NN we/PRP might/MD place/VB in/IN him/PRP ./.
    The/DT 30th/JJ of/IN June/NNP ,/, the/DT frigate/NN spoke/VBD some/DT
American/JJ whalers/NNS ,/, from/IN whom/WP we/PRP learned/VBD that/IN
they/PRP knew/VBD nothing/NN about/IN the/DT narwhal/NN ./.
    But/CC one/CD of/IN them/PRP ,/, the/DT captain/NN of/IN the/DT
Monroe/NNP ,/, knowing/VBG that/IN Ned/NNP Land/NNP had/VBD shipped/VBN
on/IN board/NN the/DT Abraham/NNP Lincoln/NNP ,/, begged/VBN for/IN
his/PRP$ help/NN in/IN chasing/VBG a/DT whale/NN they/PRP had/VBD in/IN
sight/NN ./.
```

We can use the following code sequence to produce the same results. The `word` and `tag` methods extract the words and their tags:

```
List<TaggedWord> taggedSentence =
    tagger.tagSentence(sentence);
for (TaggedWord taggedWord : taggedSentence) {
    System.out.print(taggedWord.word() + "/" +
        taggedWord.tag() + " ");
}
System.out.println();
```

If we are only interested in finding specific occurrences of a given tag, we can use a sequence such as the following, which will list only the singular nouns (NN):

```
List<TaggedWord> taggedSentence =
    tagger.tagSentence(sentence);
for (TaggedWord taggedWord : taggedSentence) {
    if (taggedWord.tag().startsWith("NN")) {
        System.out.print(taggedWord.word() + " ");
    }
}
System.out.println();
```

The singular nouns are displayed for each sentence, as shown here:

```
    NN Tagged: voyage Abraham Lincoln time incident
    NN Tagged: circumstance dexterity Ned Land confidence
    NN Tagged: June frigate whalers nothing narwhal
    NN Tagged: captain Monroe Ned Land board Abraham Lincoln help whale
sight
```

Using the MaxentTagger class to tag textese

We can use a different model to handle Twitter text that may include textese. The **General Architecture for Text Engineering** (**GATE**) (`https://gate.ac.uk/wiki/twitter-postagger.html`) has developed a model for Twitter text. The model is used here to process textese:

```
MaxentTagger tagger = new MaxentTagger(getModelDir()
    + "//gate-EN-twitter.model");
```

Here, we use the `MaxentTagger` class's `tagString` method from the *What makes POS difficult?* section earlier in this chapter to process the textese:

```
System.out.println(tagger.tagString("AFAIK she H8 cth!"));
System.out.println(tagger.tagString( "BTW had a GR8 tym at the party
BBIAM."));
```

The output will be as follows:

```
AFAIK_NNP she_PRP H8_VBP cth!_NN
BTW_UH had_VBD a_DT GR8_NNP tym_NNP at_IN the_DT party_NN BBIAM._NNP
```

Using the Stanford pipeline to perform tagging

We have used the Stanford pipeline in several previous examples. In this example, we will use the Stanford pipeline to extract POS tags. As with our previous Stanford examples, we create a pipeline based on a set of annotators: `tokenize`, `ssplit`, and `pos`.

These will tokenize, split the text into sentences, and then find the POS tags:

```
Properties props = new Properties();
props.put("annotators", "tokenize, ssplit, pos");
StanfordCoreNLP pipeline = new StanfordCoreNLP(props);
```

To process the text, we will use the `theSentence` variable as input to `Annotator`. The pipeline's `annotate` method is then invoked, as shown here:

```
Annotation document = new Annotation(theSentence);
pipeline.annotate(document);
```

Since the pipeline can perform different types of processing, a list of CoreMap objects is used to access the words and tags. The Annotation class's get method returns the list of sentences, as shown here:

```
List<CoreMap> sentences =
    document.get(SentencesAnnotation.class);
```

The contents of the CoreMap objects can be accessed using its get method. The method's argument is the class for the information needed. As shown in the following code example, tokens are accessed using the TextAnnotation class, and the POS tags can be retrieved using the PartOfSpeechAnnotation class. Each word of each sentence and its tags are displayed:

```
for (CoreMap sentence : sentences) {
    for (CoreLabel token : sentence.get(TokensAnnotation.class)) {
        String word = token.get(TextAnnotation.class);
        String pos = token.get(PartOfSpeechAnnotation.class);
        System.out.print(word + "/" + pos + " ");
    }
    System.out.println();
}
```

The output will be as follows:

```
The/DT voyage/NN of/IN the/DT Abraham/NNP Lincoln/NNP was/VBD for/IN a/DT
long/JJ time/NN marked/VBN by/IN no/DT special/JJ incident/NN ./.
```

The pipeline can use additional options to control how the tagger works. For example, by default, the english-left3words-distsim.tagger tagger model is used. We can specify a different model using the pos.model property, as shown here. There is also a pos.maxlen property to control the maximum sentence size:

```
props.put("pos.model",
"C:/.../Models/english-caseless-left3words-distsim.tagger");
```

Sometimes, it is useful to have a tagged document that is XML formatted. The StanfordCoreNLP class's xmlPrint method will write out such a document. The method's first argument is the annotator to be displayed. Its second argument is the OutputStream object to write to. In the following code sequence, the previous tagging results are written to standard output. It is enclosed in a try...catch block to handle IO exceptions:

```
try {
    pipeline.xmlPrint(document, System.out);
} catch (IOException ex) {
    // Handle exceptions
}
```

A partial listing of the results is as follows. Only the first two words and the last word are displayed. Each token tag contains the word, its position, and its POS tag:

```
<?xml version="1.0" encoding="UTF-8"?>
<?xml-stylesheet href="CoreNLP-to-HTML.xsl" type="text/xsl"?>
<root>
<document>
<sentences>
<sentence id="1">
<tokens>
<token id="1">
<word>The</word>
<CharacterOffsetBegin>0</CharacterOffsetBegin>
<CharacterOffsetEnd>3</CharacterOffsetEnd>
<POS>DT</POS>
</token>
<token id="2">
<word>voyage</word>
<CharacterOffsetBegin>4</CharacterOffsetBegin>
<CharacterOffsetEnd>10</CharacterOffsetEnd>
<POS>NN</POS>
</token>
          . . .
<token id="17">
<word>.</word>
<CharacterOffsetBegin>83</CharacterOffsetBegin>
<CharacterOffsetEnd>84</CharacterOffsetEnd>
<POS>.</POS>
</token>
</tokens>
</sentence>
</sentences>
</document>
</root>
```

The `prettyPrint` method works in a similar manner:

```
pipeline.prettyPrint(document, System.out);
```

However, the output is not really that pretty, as shown here. The original sentence is displayed, followed by each word, its position, and its tag. The output has been formatted to make it more readable:

```
The voyage of the Abraham Lincoln was for a long time marked by no
special incident.
  [Text=The CharacterOffsetBegin=0 CharacterOffsetEnd=3 PartOfSpeech=DT]
  [Text=voyage CharacterOffsetBegin=4 CharacterOffsetEnd=10
PartOfSpeech=NN]
```

```
    [Text=of CharacterOffsetBegin=11 CharacterOffsetEnd=13 PartOfSpeech=IN]
    [Text=the CharacterOffsetBegin=14 CharacterOffsetEnd=17
PartOfSpeech=DT]
    [Text=Abraham CharacterOffsetBegin=18 CharacterOffsetEnd=25
PartOfSpeech=NNP]
    [Text=Lincoln CharacterOffsetBegin=26 CharacterOffsetEnd=33
PartOfSpeech=NNP]
    [Text=was CharacterOffsetBegin=34 CharacterOffsetEnd=37
PartOfSpeech=VBD]
    [Text=for CharacterOffsetBegin=38 CharacterOffsetEnd=41
PartOfSpeech=IN]
    [Text=a CharacterOffsetBegin=42 CharacterOffsetEnd=43 PartOfSpeech=DT]
    [Text=long CharacterOffsetBegin=44 CharacterOffsetEnd=48
PartOfSpeech=JJ]
    [Text=time CharacterOffsetBegin=49 CharacterOffsetEnd=53
PartOfSpeech=NN]
    [Text=marked CharacterOffsetBegin=54 CharacterOffsetEnd=60
PartOfSpeech=VBN]
    [Text=by CharacterOffsetBegin=61 CharacterOffsetEnd=63
PartOfSpeech=IN]
    [Text=no CharacterOffsetBegin=64 CharacterOffsetEnd=66 PartOfSpeech=DT]
    [Text=special CharacterOffsetBegin=67 CharacterOffsetEnd=74
PartOfSpeech=JJ]
    [Text=incident CharacterOffsetBegin=75 CharacterOffsetEnd=83
PartOfSpeech=NN]
    [Text=. CharacterOffsetBegin=83 CharacterOffsetEnd=84 PartOfSpeech=.]
```

Using LingPipe POS taggers

LingPipe uses the `Tagger` interface to support POS tagging. This interface has a single method: `tag`. It returns a `List` instance of the `Tagging` objects. These objects are the words and their tags. The interface is implemented by the `ChainCrf` and `HmmDecoder` classes.

The `ChainCrf` class uses linear-chain conditional random field decoding and estimation for determining tags. The `HmmDecoder` class uses an HMM to perform tagging. We will illustrate this class next.

The `HmmDecoder` class uses the `tag` method to determine the most likely (best) tags. It also has a `tagNBest` method, which scores the possible tagging and returns an iterator of this scored tagging. There are three POS models that come with the LingPipe, which can be downloaded from `http://alias-i.com/lingpipe/web/models.html`. These are listed in the following table. For our demonstration, we will use the Brown Corpus model:

Model	File
English general text: Brown Corpus	`pos-en-general-brown.HiddenMarkovModel`
English biomedical text: MedPost Corpus	`pos-en-bio-medpost.HiddenMarkovModel`
English biomedical text: GENIA Corpus	`pos-en-bio-genia.HiddenMarkovModel`

Using the HmmDecoder class with Best_First tags

We start with a try-with-resources block to handle exceptions and the code to create the `HmmDecoder` instance, as shown in the following code.

The model is read from the file and then used as the argument of the `HmmDecoder` constructor:

```
try (
        FileInputStream inputStream =
            new FileInputStream(getModelDir()
            + "//pos-en-general-brown.HiddenMarkovModel");
        ObjectInputStream objectStream =
            new ObjectInputStream(inputStream);) {
    HiddenMarkovModel hmm = (HiddenMarkovModel)
        objectStream.readObject();
    HmmDecoder decoder = new HmmDecoder(hmm);
    ...
} catch (IOException ex) {
 // Handle exceptions
} catch (ClassNotFoundException ex) {
 // Handle exceptions
};
```

We will perform tagging on the `theSentence` variable. First, it needs to be tokenized. We will use an `IndoEuropean` tokenizer, as shown here. The `tokenizer` method requires that the text string be converted to an array of characters. The `tokenize` method then returns an array of tokens as strings:

```
TokenizerFactory TOKENIZER_FACTORY =
    IndoEuropeanTokenizerFactory.INSTANCE;
char[] charArray = theSentence.toCharArray();
Tokenizer tokenizer =
```

```
    TOKENIZER_FACTORY.tokenizer(
        charArray, 0, charArray.length);
String[] tokens = tokenizer.tokenize();
```

The actual tagging is performed by the `HmmDecoder` class's `tag` method. However, this method requires a `List` instance of `String` tokens. This list is created using the `Arrays` class's `asList` method. The `Tagging` class holds a sequence of tokens and tags:

```
List<String> tokenList = Arrays.asList(tokens);
Tagging<String> tagString = decoder.tag(tokenList);
```

We are now ready to display the tokens and their tags. The following loop uses the `token` and `tag` methods to access the tokens and tags, respectively, in the `Tagging` object. They are then displayed:

```
for (int i = 0; i < tagString.size(); ++i) {
    System.out.print(tagString.token(i) + "/"
    + tagString.tag(i) + " ");
}
```

The output is as follows:

```
The/at voyage/nn of/in the/at Abraham/np Lincoln/np was/bedz for/in a/at
long/jj time/nn marked/vbn by/in no/at special/jj incident/nn ./.
```

Using the HmmDecoder class with NBest tags

The tagging process considers multiple combinations of tags. The `HmmDecoder` class's `tagNBest` method returns an iterator of the `ScoredTagging` objects that reflect the confidence of different orders. This method takes a token list and a number specifying the maximum number of results desired.

The previous sentence is not ambiguous enough to demonstrate the combination of tags. Instead, we will use the following sentence:

```
String[] sentence = {"Bill", "used", "the", "force",
    "to", "force", "the", "manager", "to",
    "tear", "the", "bill","in", "to."};
List<String> tokenList = Arrays.asList(sentence);
```

An example of using this method is shown here, starting with declarations for the number of results:

```
int maxResults = 5;
```

Using the `decoder` object created in the previous section, we apply the `tagNBest` method to it as follows:

```
Iterator<ScoredTagging<String>> iterator =
    decoder.tagNBest(tokenList, maxResults);
```

The iterator will allows us to access each of the five different scores. The `ScoredTagging` class possesses a `score` method that returns a value reflecting how well it believes it performs. In the following code sequence, a `printf` statement displays this score. This is followed by a loop where the token and its tag are displayed.

The result is a score, followed by the word sequence with the tag attached:

```
while (iterator.hasNext()) {
    ScoredTagging<String> scoredTagging = iterator.next();
    System.out.printf("Score: %7.3f    Sequence: ",
        scoredTagging.score());
    for (int i = 0; i < tokenList.size(); ++i) {
        System.out.print(scoredTagging.token(i) + "/"
            + scoredTagging.tag(i) + " ");
    }
    System.out.println();
}
```

The output is as follows. Notice that the word `"force"` can have a tag of `nn`, `jj`, or `vb`:

```
    Score: -148.796    Sequence: Bill/np used/vbd the/at force/nn to/to
force/vb the/at manager/nn to/to tear/vb the/at bill/nn in/in two./nn
    Score: -154.434    Sequence: Bill/np used/vbn the/at force/nn to/to
force/vb the/at manager/nn to/to tear/vb the/at bill/nn in/in two./nn
    Score: -154.781    Sequence: Bill/np used/vbd the/at force/nn to/in
force/nn the/at manager/nn to/to tear/vb the/at bill/nn in/in two./nn
    Score: -157.126    Sequence: Bill/np used/vbd the/at force/nn to/to
force/vb the/at manager/jj to/to tear/vb the/at bill/nn in/in two./nn
    Score: -157.340    Sequence: Bill/np used/vbd the/at force/jj to/to
force/vb the/at manager/nn to/to tear/vb the/at bill/nn in/in two./nn
```

Determining tag confidence with the HmmDecoder class

Statistical analysis can be performed using a lattice structure, which is useful for analyzing alternative word orderings. This structure represents forward/backward scores. The `HmmDecoder` class's `tagMarginal` method returns an instance of the `TagLattice` class, which represents a lattice.

We can examine each token of the lattice using an instance of the
ConditionalClassification class. In the following example, the tagMarginal method
returns a TagLattice instance. A loop is used to obtain the
ConditionalClassification instance for each token in the lattice.

We are using the same tokenList instance that we developed in the previous section:

```
TagLattice<String> lattice = decoder.tagMarginal(tokenList);
for (int index = 0; index < tokenList.size(); index++) {
    ConditionalClassification classification =
        lattice.tokenClassification(index);
    ...
}
```

The ConditionalClassification class has a score and a category method. The score
method returns a relative score for a given category. The category method returns this
category, which is the tag. The token, its score, and its category are displayed as shown
here:

```
System.out.printf("%-8s",tokenList.get(index));
for (int i = 0; i < 4; ++i) {
    double score = classification.score(i);
    String tag = classification.category(i);
    System.out.printf("%7.3f/%-3s ",score,tag);
}
System.out.println();
```

The output is shown as follows:

```
Bill     0.974/np    0.018/nn    0.006/rb    0.001/nps
used     0.935/vbd   0.065/vbn   0.000/jj    0.000/rb
the      1.000/at    0.000/jj    0.000/pps   0.000/pp$$
force    0.977/nn    0.016/jj    0.006/vb    0.001/rb
to       0.944/to    0.055/in    0.000/rb    0.000/nn
force    0.945/vb    0.053/nn    0.002/rb    0.001/jj
the      1.000/at    0.000/jj    0.000/vb    0.000/nn
manager  0.982/nn    0.018/jj    0.000/nn$   0.000/vb
to       0.988/to    0.012/in    0.000/rb    0.000/nn
tear     0.991/vb    0.007/nn    0.001/rb    0.001/jj
the      1.000/at    0.000/jj    0.000/vb    0.000/nn
bill     0.994/nn    0.003/jj    0.002/rb    0.001/nns
in       0.990/in    0.004/rp    0.002/nn    0.001/jj
two.     0.960/nn    0.013/np    0.011/nns   0.008/rb
```

Training the OpenNLP POSModel

Training an OpenNLP `POSModel` is similar to the previous training examples. A training file is needed and should be large enough to provide a good sample set. Each sentence of the training file must be on a line by itself. Each line consists of a token, followed by the underscore character and then the tag.

The following training data was created using the first five sentences of Chapter 5, *At A Venture*, of *Twenty Thousands Leagues Under the Sea*. Although this is not a large sample set, it is easy to create and adequate for illustration purposes. It is saved in a file named `sample.train`:

```
    The_DT voyage_NN of_IN the_DT Abraham_NNP Lincoln_NNP was_VBD for_IN
a_DT long_JJ time_NN marked_VBN by_IN no_DT special_JJ incident._NN
    But_CC one_CD circumstance_NN happened_VBD which_WDT showed_VBD the_DT
wonderful_JJ dexterity_NN of_IN Ned_NNP Land,_NNP and_CC proved_VBD what_WP
confidence_NN we_PRP might_MD place_VB in_IN him._PRP$
    The_DT 30th_JJ of_IN June,_NNP the_DT frigate_NN spoke_VBD some_DT
American_NNP whalers,_, from_IN whom_WP we_PRP learned_VBD that_IN they_PRP
knew_VBD nothing_NN about_IN the_DT narwhal._NN
    But_CC one_CD of_IN them,_PRP$ the_DT captain_NN of_IN the_DT
Monroe,_NNP knowing_VBG that_IN Ned_NNP Land_NNP had_VBD shipped_VBN on_IN
board_NN the_DT Abraham_NNP Lincoln,_NNP begged_VBD for_IN his_PRP$ help_NN
in_IN chasing_VBG a_DT whale_NN they_PRP had_VBD in_IN sight._NN
```

We will demonstrate the creation of the model using the `POSModel` class's `train` method and how the model can be saved to a file. We start with the declaration of the `POSModel` instance variable:

```
POSModel model = null;
```

A try-with-resources block opens the sample file:

```
try (InputStream dataIn = new FileInputStream("sample.train");) {
    ...
} catch (IOException e) {
    // Handle exceptions
}
```

An instance of the `PlainTextByLineStream` class is created and used with the `WordTagSampleStream` class to create an `ObjectStream<POSSample>` instance. This puts the sample data into the format required by the `train` method:

```
ObjectStream<String> lineStream =
    new PlainTextByLineStream(dataIn, "UTF-8");
ObjectStream<POSSample> sampleStream =
    new WordTagSampleStream(lineStream);
```

The `train` method uses its parameters to specify the language, the sample stream, the training parameters, and any dictionaries (none, in this case) needed, as shown here:

```
model = POSTaggerME.train("en", sampleStream,
    TrainingParameters.defaultParams(), null, null);
```

The output of this process is lengthy. The following output has been shortened to conserve space:

```
Indexing events using cutoff of 5
   Computing event counts...  done. 90 events
   Indexing...  done.
Sorting and merging events... done. Reduced 90 events to 82.
Done indexing.
Incorporating indexed data for training...
done.
   Number of Event Tokens: 82
       Number of Outcomes: 17
     Number of Predicates: 45
...done.
Computing model parameters ...
Performing 100 iterations.
   1:  ... loglikelihood=-254.98920096505964  0.14444444444444443
   2:  ... loglikelihood=-201.19283975630537  0.6
   3:  ... loglikelihood=-174.8849213436524  0.6111111111111112
   4:  ... loglikelihood=-157.58164262220754  0.6333333333333333
   5:  ... loglikelihood=-144.69272379986646  0.6555555555555556
 ...
  99:  ... loglikelihood=-33.461128002846024  0.9333333333333333
 100:  ... loglikelihood=-33.29073273669207  0.9333333333333333
```

To save the model to a file, we use the following code. The output stream is created and the `POSModel` class's `serialize` method saves the model to the `en_pos_verne.bin` file:

```
try (OutputStream modelOut = new BufferedOutputStream(
        new FileOutputStream(new File("en_pos_verne.bin")));) {
    model.serialize(modelOut);
} catch (IOException e) {
```

```
    // Handle exceptions
}
```

Summary

POS tagging is a powerful technique for identifying the grammatical parts of a sentence. It provides useful processing for downstream tasks, such as question analysis and analyzing the sentiment of text. We will return to this subject when we address parsing in `Chapter 7, Information Retrieval`.

Tagging is not an easy process, due to the ambiguities found in most languages. The increasing use of textese only makes the process more difficult. Fortunately, there are models that can do a good job of identifying this type of text. However, as new terms and slang are introduced, these models need to be kept up to date.

We investigated the use of OpenNLP, the Stanford API, and LingPipe in support of tagging. These libraries used several different approaches to tagging words, including both rule-based and model-based approaches. We saw how dictionaries can be used to enhance the tagging process.

We briefly touched on the model training process. Pretagged sample texts are used as input to the process, and a model emerges as output. Although we did not address validation of the model, this can be accomplished in a similar manner as what we accomplished in earlier chapters.

The various POS tagger approaches can be compared, based on a number of factors such as their accuracy and how fast they run. Although we did not cover these issues here, there are numerous web resources available. One comparison that examines how fast they run can be found at `http://mattwilkens.com/2008/11/08/evaluating-pos-taggers-speed/`.

In the next chapter, `Chapter 6`, *Representing Text with Features*, we will examine techniques to classify documents based on their content.

6
Representing Text with Features

Text contains features that need to be extracted, bearing in mind their context, but processing a whole section of text together to include context is very difficult for machines.

In this chapter, we will see how text is presented using N-grams and what role they play in associating the context. We will see word embedding, in which the words' representations are converted or mapped to numbers (real numbers) so that machines can understand and process them in a better way. This may lead to the issue of high dimensionality due to the amount of text. So, next, we will see how to reduce the dimensions of vectors in such a way that the context is preserved.

In this chapter we will cover the following topics:

- N-grams
- Word embedding
- GloVe
- word2vec
- Dimensionality reduction
- Principle component analysis
- Distributed stochastic neighbor embedding

N-grams

N-grams is a probabilistic model used for predicting the next word, text, or letter. It captures language in a statistical structure as machines are better at dealing with numbers instead of text. Many companies use this approach in spelling correction and suggestions, breaking words, or summarizing text. Let's try to understand it. N-grams are simply a sequence of words or letters, mostly words. Consider the sentence "This is n-gram model" It has four words or tokens, so it's a 4-gram; 3-grams from the same text will be "This is n-gram" and "is n-gram model". Two words are a bigram, and one word is a unigram. Let's try this using Java with OpenNLP:

```
String sampletext = "This is n-gram model";
System.out.println(sampletext);
StringList tokens = new
StringList(WhitespaceTokenizer.INSTANCE.tokenize(sampletext));
System.out.println("Tokens " + tokens);
NGramModel nGramModel = new NGramModel();
nGramModel.add(tokens,3,4);
System.out.println("Total ngrams: " + nGramModel.numberOfGrams());
for (StringList ngram : nGramModel) {
    System.out.println(nGramModel.getCount(ngram) + " - " + ngram);
}
```

We started with a string and, using a tokenizer, we get all the tokens. Using nGramModel, we calculate the *n* in N-grams; in the preceding example, it's 3-gram, and the output is as follows:

```
This is n-gram model
Tokens [This,is,n-gram,model]
Total ngrams: 3
1 - [is,n-gram,model]
1 - [This,is,n-gram]
1 - [This,is,n-gram,model]
```

If we change the n-gram line to 2, the output is as follows:

```
This is n-gram model
Tokens [This,is,n-gram,model]
Total ngrams: 6
1 - [is,n-gram,model]
1 - [n-gram,model]
1 - [This,is,n-gram]
1 - [This,is,n-gram,model]
1 - [is,n-gram]
1 - [This,is]
```

Using `n-gram`, we can find the probability of a word sequence: the probability of which word will come next or before the given word *x*. From the previous bigram, we can conclude the probability of `model` appearing after the word `n-gram` is higher than any other word.

The next step is to prepare a frequency table to find the word that will come next; for example, for bigrams, the table will be something like this:

Word 1	Word 2	Count/frequency
was	the	55,000
are	the	25,000
is	the	45,000

From this table, we can say the word *was* has the best chance of appearing before the word *the* from the given context. This seems simple, but think about text with 20,000 or more words. In such a case, the frequency table may require billions of entries.

The other way is to use probability for estimation, using the sentence *W* with words *w1,w2,.... wn*, we want to find the probability of *wi* from *W* will be:

$$P(wi) = C(wi)/N$$

Here, *N = total number of words* and *c()* denotes the count of the word. Using the chain rule of probability it will be this:

$$P(w1, w2, \ldots wn) = P(w1)P(w2|w1) \ldots P(wn|w1 \ldots wn - 1)$$

Lets try to understand with our sentence that is, "This is n-gram model":

P("This is n-gram model") = P("This") P("is"|"This") P("n-gram"|"This is") P("model" | "This is n-gram")

It seems simpler but for long sentences and computing estimation, it is not simple in this way. But, using the Markov Assumption, the equation can be simplified, as the Markov Assumption says that the probability of a word appearing depends on the previous word:

P("This is n-gram model") = P("This") P("is"|"This") P("n-gram"|"is") P("model" | "n-gram")

So, now, we can say this:

$$P(wi) \approx P(wi|wi - 1)$$

Word embedding

Computers need to be taught to deal with the context. Say, for example, "I like eating apple." The computer need to understand that here, apple is a fruit and not a company. We want text where words have the same meaning to have the same representation, or at least a similar representation, so that machines can understand that the words have the same meaning. The main objective of word embedding is to capture as much context, hierarchical, and morphological information concerning the word as possible.

Word embedding can be categorized in two ways:

- Frequency-based embedding
- Prediction-based embedding

From the name, it is clear that frequency-based embedding uses a counting mechanism, whereas prediction-based embedding uses a probability mechanism.

Frequency-based embedding can be done in different ways, using a count vector, a TD-IDF vector, or a co-occurrence vector/matrix. A count vector tries to learn from all the documents. It will learn an item of vocabulary and count the number of times it appears in the target documents. Let's consider a very simple example, with two documents, *d1* and *d2*:

- *d1* = Count vector, given the total count of words
- *d2* = Count function, returning the total number of values in a set

The next step is to find the tokens, and they are *["Count", "vector", "give", "total", "of", "word", "return", "number", "values", "in", "set"]*.

Given two documents and eleven tokens, the count vector or matrix will look like this:

	Count	vector	give	total	of	word	return	number	values	in	set
d1	2	1	1	1	1	1	0	0	0	0	0
d2	1	0	0	1	1	0	1	1	1	1	1

But, when there are a lot of documents, the amount of text is large, and there is a large corpus of text, the matrix will be difficult to construct and contain many rows and columns. Sometimes, commons words are removed, such as a, an, the, and this.

The second approach is TF-IDF vectors. *TF* stands for *term frequency* and IDF stands for *inverse document frequency*. The idea behind this approach is to remove unnecessary words that will be common in all documents and appear very frequently, but do not add any meaning. This includes words such as a, an, the, this, that, and are. "The" is the most common word in English, so this will appear very frequently in any document.

Lets define *TF* as number of times term appears in a document/number of terms in the document, $IDF = log(N/n)$, where N is the number of documents and n is the number of documents the term appears in. Considering the previous example, term or word count appears twice in *d1* and once in *d2*, so its TF is calculated as:

- *TF(Count / d1) = 2/7*
- *TF(Count/d2) = 1/8*
- *TF(total/d1) = 1/2*
- *TF(total/d2) = 1/2*

Let's calculate IDF for the word or *term total*. The *total* appears in both the documents for one time, so the IDF will be:

$$IDF(total) = log(2/2) = 0$$

So, if the word appears in every document, then there is a possibility that the word is not very relevant and can be ignored. If the term appeared in some document and not in all the documents it may have some relevance for the word count:

$$IDF(count) = log(3/2) = 0.17609$$

To compute the TF-IDF, we will simply multiply the values computed in the previous step:

$$TF\text{-}IDF(total, d1) = 1/2 * 0 = 0$$

$$TF\text{-}IDF(count, d1) = 2/7 * 0.17609 = 0.0503$$

Another approach is to use a co-occurrence vector or matrix. It works on words that occur together, and so will have a similar context, and therefore captures the relationships between words. It works by deciding the length of the context window, which defines the number of words to look for. Consider the sentence "This is word embedding example."

When we say the context window is of size 2, that means we are only interested in the two words before and the two words after the given word. Let's say the word is "word," so when we calculate its co-occurrence, only the two words before "word" and the two words after "word" will be considered. Such a table or matrix is converted into a probability. It has many advantages as it preserves the relationship between words, but the size of such a matrix is huge.

The other method is to use prediction base embedding, which can be done using a **continuous bag of words** (**CBOW**) or skip-gram model. CBOW predicts the probability of a word in a given situation, context, or scenario, which can be of single or multiple words. Consider the sentence "Sample word using continuous bag of words." So, the context will be *["Sample", "word", "using", "continuous", "bag", "of", "words"]*. This will be fed into a neural network. Now, it will help us to predict the words for a given context.

The other approach is to use the skip-gram model, which uses the same approach as CBOW, but the aim is to predict all other words given the one word from the context, is, it should predict the context for the given word.

Both approaches require an understanding of neural networks, where the input is passed through hidden layers using weights. The next layer is the output layer, which is computed using the softmax function, and the values are compared with the original values, which may differ from the first run, and the loss is computed. Loss is the difference between the original and predicted values; this loss is then back-propagated, the weights are adjusted, and the process is repeated until the loss is minimal or close to 0.

In the following few sections, we will see how to use word2vec, which is a combination of the CBOW and skip-gram models.

GloVe

Global Vectors for Word representation (**GloVe**) is a model for word representation. It falls under the category of unsupervised learning. It learns from developing a count matrix for word occurrence. Initially, it starts with the large matrix to store almost all the words and their co-occurrence information, which stores the count of how frequently some words appear in the sequence in given text. Support for GloVe is available in Stanford NLP, but is not implemented in Java. To read more about GloVe, visit `https://nlp.stanford.edu/pubs/glove.pdf`. A brief introduction and some resources for the Stanford GloVe can be found at `https://nlp.stanford.edu/projects/glove/`. To get an idea of what GloVe does, we will be using a Java implementation of GloVe found at `https://github.com/erwtokritos/JGloVe` .

The code also includes the test file and a text file. The text file's contents are as follows:

```
human interface computer
survey user computer system response time
eps user interface system
system human system eps
user response time
trees
graph trees
graph minors trees
graph minors survey
I like graph and stuff
I like trees and stuff
Sometimes I build a graph
Sometimes I build trees
```

GloVe presents similar words from the previous text. The results for finding words similar to graph from the previous text is as follows:

```
INFO: Building vocabulary complete.. There are 19 terms
Iteration #1 , cost = 0.4109707480627031
Iteration #2 , cost = 0.37748817335537205
Iteration #3 , cost = 0.3563396433036622
Iteration #4 , cost = 0.3483667149265019
Iteration #5 , cost = 0.3434632969758875
Iteration #6 , cost = 0.33917154339742045
Iteration #7 , cost = 0.3304641363014488
Iteration #8 , cost = 0.32717383183159243
Iteration #9 , cost = 0.3240225514512226
Iteration #10 , cost = 0.32196412138868596
@trees
@minors
@computer
@a
@like
@survey
@eps
@interface
@and
@human
@user
@time
@response
@system
@Sometimes
```

So, the first matching word is "tree," followed by "minors," and so on. The code it uses to test is as follows:

```
String file = "test.txt";
Options options = new Options();
options.debug = true;
Vocabulary vocab = GloVe.build_vocabulary(file, options);
options.window_size = 3;
List<Cooccurrence> c =  GloVe.build_cooccurrence(vocab, file,
options);
options.iterations = 10;
options.vector_size = 10;
options.debug = true;
DoubleMatrix W = GloVe.train(vocab, c, options);

List<String> similars = Methods.most_similar(W, vocab, "graph",
15);
for(String similar : similars) {
    System.out.println("@" + similar);
}
```

Word2vec

While GloVe is a count-based model where a matrix is created for counting words, word2vec is a predictive model that uses prediction and loss adjustment to find the similarity. It works like a feed-forward neural network and is optimized using various techniques, including **stochastic gradient descent** (**SGD**), which are core concepts of machine learning. It is more useful in predicting the words from the given context words in vector representation. We will be using the implementation of word2vec from `https://github.com/IsaacChanghau/Word2VecfJava`. We will also need the `GoogleNews-vectors-negative300.bin` file from `https://drive.google.com/file/d/0B7XkCwpI5KDYNlNUTTlSS21pQmM/edit?usp=sharing`, as it contains pre-trained vectors for the `GoogleNews` dataset with 300 dimensional vectors for 3 million words and phrases. The example program will find the similar word to kill. The following is the sample output:

```
loading embeddings and creating word2vec...
[main] INFO org.nd4j.linalg.factory.Nd4jBackend - Loaded [CpuBackend]
backend
[main] INFO org.nd4j.nativeblas.NativeOpsHolder - Number of threads used
for NativeOps: 2
[main] INFO org.reflections.Reflections - Reflections took 410 ms to scan 1
urls, producing 29 keys and 189 values
[main] INFO org.nd4j.nativeblas.Nd4jBlas - Number of threads used for BLAS:
2
```

```
[main] INFO org.nd4j.linalg.api.ops.executioner.DefaultOpExecutioner -
Backend used: [CPU]; OS: [Linux]
[main] INFO org.nd4j.linalg.api.ops.executioner.DefaultOpExecutioner -
Cores: [4]; Memory: [5.3GB];
[main] INFO org.nd4j.linalg.api.ops.executioner.DefaultOpExecutioner - Blas
vendor: [OPENBLAS]
[main] INFO org.reflections.Reflections - Reflections took 373 ms to scan 1
urls, producing 373 keys and 1449 values
done...
kill    1.0000001192092896
kills    0.6048964262008667
killing    0.6003166437149048
destroy    0.5964594483375549
exterminate    0.5908634066581726
decapitate    0.5677944421768188
assassinate    0.5450955629348755
behead    0.532557487487793
terrorize    0.5281200408935547
commit_suicide    0.5269641280174255
0.10049013048410416
0.1868356168270111
```

Dimensionality reduction

Word embedding is now a basic building block for natural language processing. GloVe, or word2vec, or any other form of word embedding will generate a two-dimensional matrix, but it is stored in one-dimensional vectors. *Dimensonality* here refers to the size of these vectors, which is not the same as the size of the vocabulary. The following diagram is taken from `https://nlp.stanford.edu/projects/glove/` and shows vocabulary versus vector dimensions:

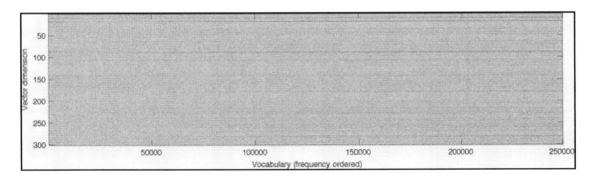

The other issue with large dimensions is the memory required to use word embeddings in the real world; simple 300 dimensional vectors with more than a million tokens will take 6 GB or more of memory to process. Using such a lot of memory is not practical in real-world NLP use cases. The best way is to reduce the number of dimensions to decrease the size. **t-Distributed Stochastic Neighbor Embedding (t-SNE)** and **principal component analysis (PCA)** are two common approaches used to achieve dimensionality reduction. In the next section, we will see how to achieve dimensionality reduction using these two algorithms.

Principle component analysis

Principle component analysis (PCA) is a linear and deterministic algorithm that tries to capture similarities within the data. Once similarities are found, it can be used to remove unnecessary dimensions from high-dimensional data. It works using the concepts of eigenvectors and eigenvalues. A simple example will help you understand eigenvectors and eigenvalues, given that you have a basic understanding of the matrix:

$$\begin{pmatrix} 2 & 3 \\ 2 & 1 \end{pmatrix} * \begin{pmatrix} 3 \\ 2 \end{pmatrix} = \begin{pmatrix} 12 \\ 8 \end{pmatrix}$$

This is equivalent to the following:

$$4 * \begin{pmatrix} 3 \\ 2 \end{pmatrix} = \begin{pmatrix} 12 \\ 8 \end{pmatrix}$$

This is the case of eigenvector, and 4 is the eigenvalue.

The PCA approach is simple. It starts with subtracting the mean from the data; then, it finds the covariance matrix and calculates its eigenvectors and eigenvalues. Once you have the eigenvector and eigenvalue, order them from highest to lowest and thus now we can ignore the component with less significance. If the eigenvalues are small, the loss is negligible. If you have data with n dimensions and you calculate n eigenvectors and eigenvalues, you can select some from n, say, m eigenvectors, where m will always be less than n, so the final dataset will have only m dimensions.

Distributed stochastic neighbor embedding

T-distributed Stochastic Neighbor Embedding (t-SNE), which is widely used in machine learning, is a non-linear, non-deterministic algorithm that creates a two-dimensional map of data with thousands of dimensions.

In other words, it transforms data in a high-dimensional space to fit into a 2D plane. t-SNE tries to hold, or preserve, the local neighbors in the data. It is a very popular approach for dimensionality reduction, as it is very flexible and able to find the structure or relationships in the data where other algorithms fail. It does this by calculating the probability of object *i* picking potential neighbor *j*. It will pick up the similar object from high dimension as it will have a higher probability than a less similar object. It uses the Euclidean distance between the objects as a basis for similarity metrics. t-SNE uses the perplexity feature to fine-tune and decide how to balance local and global data.

t-SNE implementation is available in many languages; we are going to use the one available at `https://github.com/lejon/T-SNE-Java`. Using `git` and `mvn`, you can build and use the examples provided here. Execute the following command:

```
> git clone https://github.com/lejon/T-SNE-Java.git
> cd T-SNE-Java
> mvn install
> cd tsne-demo
> java -jar target/tsne-demos-2.4.0.jar -nohdr -nolbls
src/main/resources/datasets/iris_X.txt
```

The output will be as follows:

```
TSneCsv: Running 2000 iterations of t-SNE on
src/main/resources/datasets/iris_X.txt
NA string is: null
Loaded CSV with: 150 rows and 4 columns.
Dataset types:[class java.lang.Double, class java.lang.Double, class
java.lang.Double, class java.lang.Double]
              V0              V1              V2              V3
    0      5.10000000      3.50000000      1.40000000      0.20000000
    1      4.90000000      3.00000000      1.40000000      0.20000000
    2      4.70000000      3.20000000      1.30000000      0.20000000
    3      4.60000000      3.10000000      1.50000000      0.20000000
    4      5.00000000      3.60000000      1.40000000      0.20000000
    5      5.40000000      3.90000000      1.70000000      0.40000000
    6      4.60000000      3.40000000      1.40000000      0.30000000
    7      5.00000000      3.40000000      1.50000000      0.20000000
    8      4.40000000      2.90000000      1.40000000      0.20000000
    9      4.90000000      3.10000000      1.50000000      0.10000000

Dim:150 x 4
000: [5.1000, 3.5000, 1.4000, 0.2000...]
001: [4.9000, 3.0000, 1.4000, 0.2000...]
002: [4.7000, 3.2000, 1.3000, 0.2000...]
003: [4.6000, 3.1000, 1.5000, 0.2000...]
004: [5.0000, 3.6000, 1.4000, 0.2000...]
.
```

```
         .
         .
145: [6.7000, 3.0000, 5.2000, 2.3000]
146: [6.3000, 2.5000, 5.0000, 1.9000]
147: [6.5000, 3.0000, 5.2000, 2.0000]
148: [6.2000, 3.4000, 5.4000, 2.3000]
149: [5.9000, 3.0000, 5.1000, 1.8000]
X:Shape is = 150 x 4
Using no_dims = 2, perplexity = 20.000000, and theta = 0.500000
Computing input similarities...
Done in 0.06 seconds (sparsity = 0.472756)!
Learning embedding...
Iteration 50: error is 64.67259135061494 (50 iterations in 0.19 seconds)
Iteration 100: error is 61.50118570075227 (50 iterations in 0.20 seconds)
Iteration 150: error is 61.373758889762875 (50 iterations in 0.20 seconds)
Iteration 200: error is 55.78219488135168 (50 iterations in 0.09 seconds)
Iteration 250: error is 2.3581173593529687 (50 iterations in 0.09 seconds)
Iteration 300: error is 2.2349608757095827 (50 iterations in 0.07 seconds)
Iteration 350: error is 1.9906437450336596 (50 iterations in 0.07 seconds)
Iteration 400: error is 1.8958764344779482 (50 iterations in 0.08 seconds)
Iteration 450: error is 1.7360726540960958 (50 iterations in 0.08 seconds)
Iteration 500: error is 1.553250634564741 (50 iterations in 0.09 seconds)
Iteration 550: error is 1.294981722012944 (50 iterations in 0.06 seconds)
Iteration 600: error is 1.0985607573299603 (50 iterations in 0.03 seconds)
Iteration 650: error is 1.0810715645272573 (50 iterations in 0.04 seconds)
Iteration 700: error is 0.8168399675722107 (50 iterations in 0.05 seconds)
Iteration 750: error is 0.7158739920771124 (50 iterations in 0.03 seconds)
Iteration 800: error is 0.6911748222330966 (50 iterations in 0.04 seconds)
Iteration 850: error is 0.6123536061655738 (50 iterations in 0.04 seconds)
Iteration 900: error is 0.5631133416913786 (50 iterations in 0.04 seconds)
Iteration 950: error is 0.5905547118496892 (50 iterations in 0.03 seconds)
Iteration 1000: error is 0.5053631170520657 (50 iterations in 0.04 seconds)
Iteration 1050: error is 0.44752244538411406 (50 iterations in 0.04
seconds)
Iteration 1100: error is 0.40661841893114614 (50 iterations in 0.03
seconds)
Iteration 1150: error is 0.3267394426152807 (50 iterations in 0.05 seconds)
Iteration 1200: error is 0.3393774577158965 (50 iterations in 0.03 seconds)
Iteration 1250: error is 0.37023103950965025 (50 iterations in 0.04
seconds)
Iteration 1300: error is 0.3192975790641602 (50 iterations in 0.04 seconds)
Iteration 1350: error is 0.28140161036965816 (50 iterations in 0.03
seconds)
Iteration 1400: error is 0.30413739839879855 (50 iterations in 0.04
seconds)
Iteration 1450: error is 0.31755361125826165 (50 iterations in 0.04
seconds)
Iteration 1500: error is 0.36301524742916624 (50 iterations in 0.04
```

```
seconds)
Iteration 1550: error is 0.3063801941900375 (50 iterations in 0.03 seconds)
Iteration 1600: error is 0.2928584822753138 (50 iterations in 0.03 seconds)
Iteration 1650: error is 0.2867502934852756 (50 iterations in 0.03 seconds)
Iteration 1700: error is 0.470469997545481 (50 iterations in 0.04 seconds)
Iteration 1750: error is 0.4792376115843584 (50 iterations in 0.04 seconds)
Iteration 1800: error is 0.5100126924750723 (50 iterations in 0.06 seconds)
Iteration 1850: error is 0.37855035406353427 (50 iterations in 0.04
seconds)
Iteration 1900: error is 0.32776847081948496 (50 iterations in 0.04
seconds)
Iteration 1950: error is 0.3875134029990107 (50 iterations in 0.04 seconds)
Iteration 1999: error is 0.32560416632168365 (50 iterations in 0.04
seconds)
Fitting performed in 2.29 seconds.
TSne took: 2.43 seconds
```

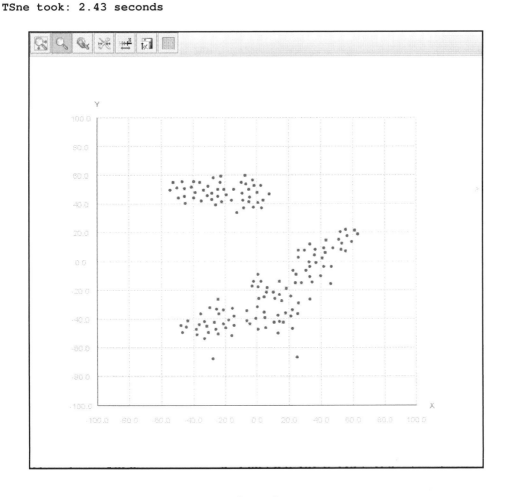

This example uses `iris_X.txt`, which has 150 rows and 4 columns, so the dimensions are 150 x 4. It tries to reduce these dimensions to 2 by setting the perplexity as 20 and the theta as 0.5. It iterates on the data provided in `iris_X.txt` and, using gradient descent, it comes up with a graph on a 2D plane after 2,000 iterations. The graph shows the clusters in the data in a 2D plane, hence effectively reducing the dimensionality. For the mathematical approach to how this was achieved, there are many papers on the topic, and the Wikipedia article (`https://en.wikipedia.org/wiki/T-distributed_stochastic_neighbor_embedding`) explains it too.

Summary

In this chapter, we covered word embedding and why it is important in natural language processing. N-grams were used to show how the words are treated as a vector and how the count of words are stored to find the relevance. GloVe and word2vec are two common approaches to word embedding, where the word counts or probabilities are stored in vectors. Both of these approaches lead to high dimensionality, which is not feasible to process in the real world, especially on mobile devices or devices with less memory. We have seen two different approaches to reduce the dimensionality. In next chapter, `Chapter 7, Information Retrieval` we will see how information retrieval can be done from the unstructured format such as text.

Information Retrieval 7

Information Retrieval (IR) deals with finding information in unstructured data. Any data that has no specific or generalized structure is unstructured data, and processing such data poses a great challenge to machines. Some examples of unstructured data are text files, doc files, XML files, and so on available on local PC or web. So, processing such large amount of unstructured data and finding the relevant information is a challenging task.

We will cover the following topics in this chapter:

- Boolean retrieval
- Dictionaries and tolerant retrieval
- Vector space model
- Scoring and term weighting
- Inverse document frequency
- TF-IDF weighting
- Evaluation of information retrieval systems

Boolean retrieval

Boolean retrieval deals with a retrieval system or algorithm where the IR query can be seen as a Boolean expression of terms using the operations AND, OR, and NOT. A Boolean retrieval model is a model that sees the document as words and can apply query terms using Boolean expressions. A standard example is to consider Shakespeare's collected works. The query is to determine plays that contain the words "Brutus" and "Caesar," but not "Calpurnia." Such a query is feasible using the grep command which is available on Unix-based systems.

It is an effective process when the document size is limited, but to process a large a document quickly, or the amount of data available on the web, and rank it on the basis of an occurrence count, is not possible.

The alternative is to index the document in advance for the terms. The approach is to create an incidence matrix, which records in a form of binary and marks whether the term is present in the given play or not:

	Antony and Cleopatra	Julius Caesar	The Tempest	Hamlet	Othello	Macbeth
Brutus	1	1	0	0	0	1
Caesar	1	1	0	1	0	0
Calpurnia	0	1	0	0	0	0
Mercy	1	0	1	1	1	1
Worser	1	0	1	1	1	0

Now, to answer the previous request for "Brutus" and "Caesar," but not "Calpurnia," this query can be turned into 110100 AND 110111 AND 101111 = 100100, so the answer is that *Antony and Cleopatra* and *Hamlet* are the plays that satisfy our query.

The preceding matrix is good, but considering the large corpus, it can grow into anything with the entry of 1 and 0. Think of creating a matrix of 500,000 terms of 1 million documents, which will result in a matrix of 500,000 x 1 million dimensions. As shown in the preceding table, the matrix entries will be 0 and 1, so an inverted index is used. It stores terms and lists of documents in the form of a dictionary that looks like the following diagram:

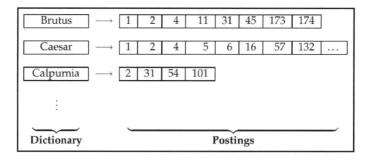

Taken from https://nlp.stanford.edu/IR-book/pdf/01bool.pdf

The documents in the term appears from a list, known as the posting list, and an individual document is known as a posting. To create such a structure, the document is tokenized, and the tokens created are normalized by linguistic preprocessing. Once the normalized tokens are formed, a dictionary and a posting are created. To provide the ranking, the frequency of the term is also stored, as shown in the following diagram:

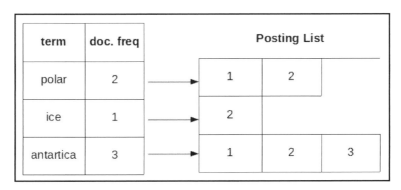

The extra information stored is useful for search engines in a rank retrieval model. The posting list is also sorted for efficient query processing. Using this method, the storage requirement is reduced; recall the *m x n* matrix with 1 and 0. This also helps in processing the Boolean query or retrieval.

Dictionaries and tolerant retrieval

Dictionary data structures store the list term vocabulary, with the list of documents that contain the given term, also as posting.

Dictionary data structures can be stored in two different ways: using hash tables or trees. The naive approach to storing such data structures will lead to performance issues when the corpus grows. Some IR systems use the hash approach, whereas others use the tree approach to make the dictionaries. Both approaches have their pros and cons.

Hash tables store vocabulary terms in the form of integers, which are obtained by hashing. Lookups or searches in hash tables are faster,as it is time constant $O(1)$. If the search is prefix-based search like find text starting with "abc", it will not work if the hash tables are used to store the terms because terms will be hashed. It is not easy to find minor variants. As the terms grow, rehashing is expensive.

A tree base approach uses a tree structure, normally a binary tree, which is very efficient for searching. It handles the prefix base searching efficiently. It is slower, as it takes $O(\log M)$ to search. Each re-balancing of the tree is expensive.

Wildcard queries

Wildcard queries use * to specify what to search for. It can be seen in different places like at the starting of the word or ending of the word. The search term may have a beginning such as *its, which means find words that end with its. Such queries are called suffix queries. The search term may use * at the end, such as its*, which means find words starting with its. Such queries are called prefix queries. In term of trees, prefix queries are easy, as they require us to find terms between its <= t <= itt. Suffix queries require extra trees that maintain terms for backward movement. The next kind, which require more operations, are queries that have * in the middle, such as "fil*er", "se*te", and "pro*cent". To solve such queries, it requires to find "fil*" and "*er", and intersects the result of the two sets. This is an expensive operation, as one needs to traverse in both directions of the tree; this needs a workaround to make it simpler. One approach is to modify the query so that it contains "*" at the end only. The permuterm index approach adds a special character, "$", to words; for example, the term "hello" can be represented as hello$, ello$h, llohe, lohel, or o$hell. Let's assume the query is for hel*o, so it will look for hel and o, ending up in o$hel. It simply rotates the wildcard so that it appears at the end only. It adds all rotations in the B-tree. It also takes up a lot of space. Another approach is to use bigram (k-gram) indexes, which are more efficient than permuterm indexes. In bigram indexes, all k-grams are enumerated. For example, "April is the cruelest month", split into 2-grams (bigrams) will look like the following:

```
$a, ap, pr, ri, il, l$, $i, is, s$, $t, th, he, e$, $c, cr, ru, ue, el,
le, es, st, t$, $m, mo, on, nt, h$
```

$ is used to denote the start or end of the term. It maintains the second index in inverted form for all bigrams, and dictionary terms that contain the bigram. It retrieves all the postings that match the bigrams and intersects the whole list. Now, a query such as hel* is run as $h and he and el. It applies a post filter to filter results that are not relevant. It is fast and space efficient.

Spelling correction

The best example of spelling correction is Google. When we search for something with an incorrect spelling, it suggests the correct spelling, as seen in the following screenshot:

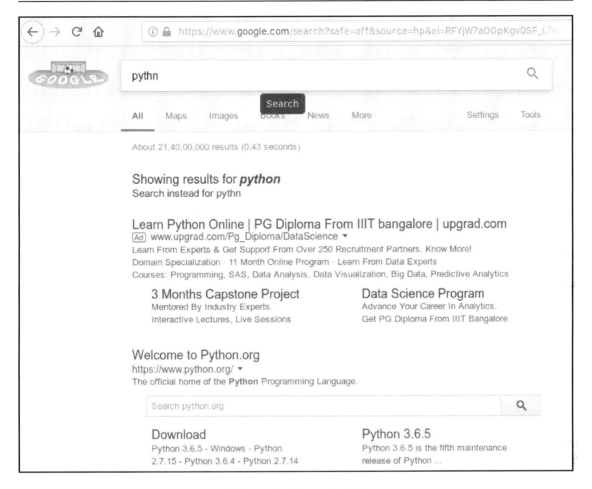

Spelling correction simple example on Google

The two basic principles used by most algorithms for spelling correction are the following:

- To find the nearest match to the wrongly spelled word. This requires us to have proximity measures for terms.
- If two or more words are correct and tied together, use the one that is the most common. The most common word is calculated based on the count of each term in the documents; the highest is selected.

Two specific forms of spelling correction are isolated term correction and context sensitive correction. Isolated term correction deals with spelling mistakes. Basically, it checks each word for misspellings; it does not consider the context of the sentence. For example, if the word "form" is encountered, in place of word "from" it will treat it as correct, as the spelling is correct. Context sensitive correction will look at the surrounding words and can suggest required corrections, so it can suggest "form" instead of "forms." If the given sentence is "We took flight form point A to point B", in this sentence, the word "form" is wrong but the spelling is correct, so isolated term correction will treat it as correct, whereas context sensitive correction will suggest "from" instead of "form."

Soundex

Phonetic correction is required when the misspells arises by a query that sounds like the target term. This mainly occurs in names of people. The idea is to generate a hash for each term to be the same for the words that sound the same. Algorithms perform phonetic hashing so that hashing is same for the similar sounding words is known as the Soundex algorithm. It was invented in 1981 for the US census. The approach is as follows:

1. Turn every term to be indexed into a four-character reduced form. Build an inverted index from these reduced forms to the original terms; call this the Soundex index.
2. Do the same with query terms.
3. When the query calls for a Soundex match, search this Soundex index.

It is a standard algorithm provided by many popular databases. Soundex is not much help for information retrieval, but it has its own application where searching by names of people is important.

Vector space model

Boolean retrieval works fine, but it only gives output in binary; it says the term matches or is not in the document, which works well if there are only a limited number of documents. If the number of documents increases, the results generated are difficult for humans to follow. Consider a search term, X is searched for in 1 million documents, out of which half return positive results. The next phase is to order the documents on some basis, such as rank or some other mechanism, to show the results.

If the rank is required, then the document needs to attach some kind of score, which is given by a search engine. For a normal user, writing a Boolean query itself is a difficult task, where they have to make a query using and, or, and not. In real-time, the queries can be simple as single words query and as complex as a sentence containing lots of words.

The vector space model can be divided into three stages:

- Document indexing, where the terms are extracted from the documents
- Weighing of the indexed terms, so the retrieval system can be enhanced
- Ranking the documents on the basis of query and similarity measures

There is always metadata associated with the document that has various types of information, such as the following:

- Author details
- Creation date
- Format of the document
- Title
- Date of publication
- Abstract (although not always)

This metadata helps in forming queries such as "search for all documents whose author is *xyz* and were published in *2017*" or "search for the document whose title contains the word *AI* and the author is *ABC*." For such queries, a parametric index is maintained, and such queries are called parametric searches. Zones contain the free text, such as title, which is not possible in a parametric index. Normally, for each parameter, a separate parametric index is prepared. Searching for a title or abstract requires a zonal approach. A separate index is prepared for each zone, as shown in the following diagram:

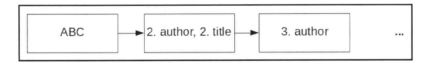

This ensures efficient retrieval and storage of data. It still works well for Boolean queries and retrieval on fields and zones.

A representation of a set of documents as a vector in common vector space is known as a vector space model.

Scoring and term weighting

Term weighting deals with evaluating the importance of a term with respect to a document. A simple way is to think of this is that the term that appears more in the documents is an important term, apart from the stop words. A score from 0-1 can be assigned to each document. A score is a measurement that shows how well the term or query is matched in the document. A score of 0 means that the term does not exist in the document. As the frequency of the term increases in the document, the score moves from 0 toward 1. So, for a given term X, the scores for three documents, *d1*, *d2*, and *d3* are 0.2, 0.3, and 0.5, respectively, which means that the match in *d3* is more important than *d2* and *d1* is least important for the overall score. The same applies for the zones as well. How to assign such a score or weight to the term requires learning from some training set or continuously running and updating the score for terms.

The real-time query will be in the form of free text, and not in the form of a Boolean expression; for example, a Boolean query would be able to answer whether something looks like *A* and *B*, but not *C*, whereas a free text query would check whether *A* is with *B* and *C* is absent. So, in free text, a scoring mechanism is required, where the score of each individual term is summed up and the weight is assigned to the term with respect to the document. The simplest way is to assign a weight equal to the number of times the term appears in the document. This weighting scheme is referred to as term frequency, and is normally written as $tf_{t,d}$, where *tf* is term frequency, *t* is term, and *d* is document.

Inverse document frequency

If we consider all the terms with the same importance for all the queries, it will not work for all queries. If the documents are related to ice, it is obvious that "ice" will be in almost all documents, probably with high frequency. Collection frequency and document frequency are two different terms that need to be explained. A collection contains many documents. The **collection frequency** (**cf**) shows the frequency of **terms** (**t**) in all documents in the collection, whereas the **document frequency** (**df**) shows the frequency of *t* in a single document. So the word "ice" will have a high collection frequency, as it is presumed to appear in all the documents in the collection. A simple idea is to reduce the weight of such terms if they have a high collection frequency. Inverse frequency is defined as follows:

$$idf_t = log\frac{N}{df_t}$$

Here, *N* is the total number of documents in a collection. The *idf* of a frequent term is likely to be low, and that of a rare term will be high.

TF-IDF weighting

TF-IDF combines the approaches of **term frequency (TF)** and **inverse document frequency (IDF)** to generate a weight for each term in a document, and it is done using the following formula:

$$tf - idf_{t,d} = tf_{t,d} \times idf_t$$

In other words, it assigns a weight to term *t* in document *d* as follows:

- If term *t* occurs many times in a few documents, it will be the highest
- If term *t* occurs a small number of times in a document, it will be lower
- If term *t* occurs in all documents, it will be the lowest
- If term *t* occurs in no documents, it will be 0

Evaluation of information retrieval systems

To evaluate an information retrieval system the standard way, a test collection is needed, which should have the following:

- A collection of documents
- Test query set for the required information
- Binary assessment of relevant or not relevant

The documents in collections are classified using two categories, relevant and not relevant. The test document collection should be of a reasonable size, so the test can have reasonable scope to find the average performance. Relevance of output is always assessed relative to information required, and not on the basis of a query. In other words, having a query word in the results does not mean that it is relevant. For example, if the search term or query is for "Python," the results may show the Python programming language or a pet python; both the results contain the query term, but whether it is relevant to the user is the important factor. If the system contains a parameterized index, then it can be tuned for better performance, in which case, a separate test collection is required to test the parameters. It may happen that the weights assigned are different according to parameters also altered by the parameters.

There are some standard test collections available for the evaluation of information retrieval. Some of them are as listed here:

- The Cranfield collection contains 1398 abstracts from aerodynamic journals and 225 queries, as well as exhaustive relevance judgments on all.
- The **Text REtrieval Conference** (**TREC**) has maintained a large IR test series for evaluation since 1992. It consists of 1.89 million documents and relevance judgment for 450 information needs.
- GOV2 has a collection of 25 million web pages.
- NTCIR focuses on test collection focusing on East Asian language and cross-language information retrieval. [http://ntcir.nii.ac.jp/about/]
- REUTERS consists of 806,791 documents.
- 20 newsgroups is another collection used widely for classification.

Two measures that are used to find the effectiveness of a retrieval system are precision and recall. Precision is the fraction of documents that are retrieved and are relevant, and recall is the fraction of relevant document that are found.

Summary

In this chapter, we covered how to find information from unstructured data using various techniques. We covered boolean retrieval, dictionaries and tolerant retrieval. We also covered wild card queries and how it is used. Spelling correction is covered in brief followed by vector space model and TF-IDF weighting and we end with evaluation of information retrieval. In next chapter, Chapter 8, *Classifying Texts and Documents* we will cover how to classify texts and documents.

8
Classifying Texts and Documents

In this chapter, we will demonstrate how to use various **Natural Language Processing (NLP)** APIs to perform text classification. This is not to be confused with text clustering. Clustering is concerned with the identification of text without the use of predefined categories. Classification, in contrast, uses predefined categories. In this chapter, we will focus on text classification, where tags are assigned to text to specify its type.

The general approach that is used to perform text classification starts with the training of a model. The model is validated and then used to classify documents. We will focus on the training and usage stages of this process.

Documents can be classified according to any number of attributes, such as their subject, document type, time of publication, author, language used, and reading level. Some classification approaches require humans to label sample data.

Sentiment analysis is a type of classification. It is concerned with determining what the text is trying to convey to a reader, usually in the form of a positive or negative attitude. We will investigate several techniques that can be used to perform this type of analysis.

We will cover the following topics in this chapter:

- How classification is used
- Understanding sentiment analysis
- Text-classifying techniques
- Using APIs to classify text

How classification is used

Classifying text is used for a number of purposes:

- Spam detection
- Authorship attribution
- Sentiment analysis
- Age and gender identification
- Determining the subject of a document
- Language identification

Spamming is an unfortunate reality for most email users. If an email can be classified as spam, then it can be moved to a spam folder. A text message can be analyzed and certain attributes can be used to designate the email as spam. These attributes can include misspellings, lack of an appropriate email address for the recipients, and a non-standard URL.

Classification has been used to determine the authorship of documents. This has been performed on historical documents, such as *The Federalist Papers* and the book *Primary Colors*, where the authors were identified using classification techniques.

Sentiment analysis is a technique that determines the attitude of a piece of text. Movie reviews have been a popular domain for this kind of analysis, but it can be used for almost any product review. This helps companies better assess how their product is perceived. Often, a negative or positive attribute is assigned to the text. Sentiment analysis is also called opinion extraction/mining and subjectivity analysis. Consumer confidence and the performance of a stock market can be predicted from Twitter feeds and other sources.

Classification can be used to determine the age and gender of a text's author and to provide more insight into its author. Frequently, the number of pronouns, determiners, and noun phrases are used to identify the gender of a writer. Females tend to use more pronouns and males tend to use more determiners.

Determining the subject of pieces of text is useful when we need to organize a large number of documents. Search engines are very much concerned with this activity, but it has also been used simply to place documents in different categories—for example, in tag clouds. A tag cloud is a group of words that reflects the relative frequency of the occurrence of each word.

The following diagram is an example of a tag cloud generated by IBM Word Cloud Generator (`http://www.softpedia.com/get/Office-tools/Other-Office-Tools/IBM-Word-Cloud-Ge nerator.shtml`), and can be found at `http://upload.wikimedia.org/wikipedia/commons/9/9e/Foundation-l_word_cloud_with out_headers_and_quotes.png`:

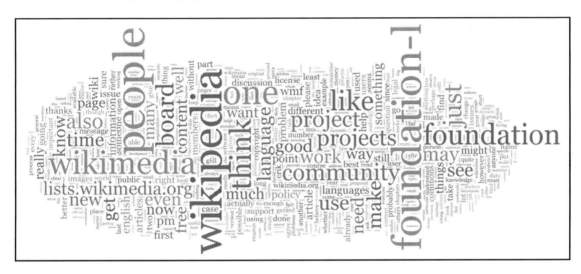

The identification of the language used by a document is supported using classification techniques. This analysis is useful for many NLP problems where we need to apply specific language models to the problem.

Understanding sentiment analysis

With sentiment analysis, we are concerned with who holds what type of feeling about a specific product or topic. This can tell us, for example, that citizens of a particular city hold positive or negative feelings about the performance of a sports team. They may hold a different sentiment about the team's performance than they do about its management.

Sentiment analysis can be useful in automatically determining the sentiment regarding certain aspects, or attributes, of a product and then displaying the results in some meaningful manner.

This is illustrated using a review of the 2014 Camry from the Kelly Blue Book (http://www.kbb.com/toyota/camry/2014-toyota-camry/?r=471659652516861060), as shown in the following screenshot:

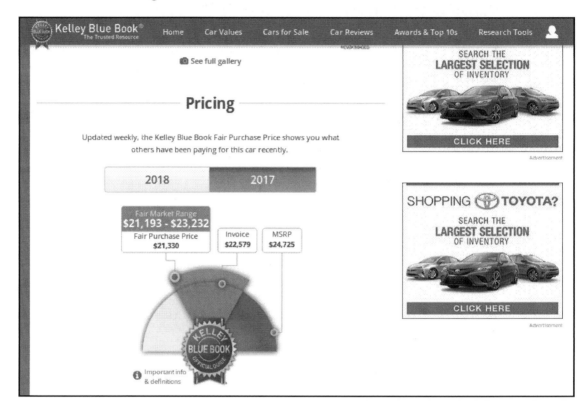

If you scroll down you can find the expert review about the model shown as following:

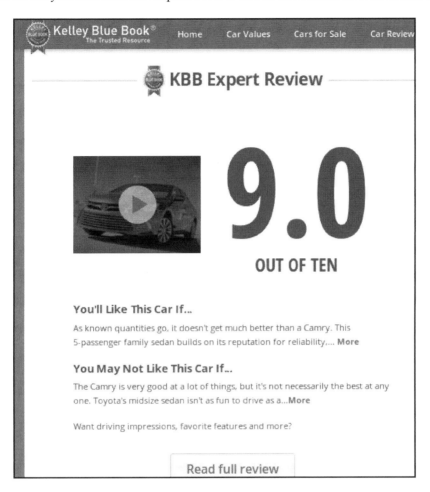

The attributes, such as the overall rating and value, are depicted both as a bar graph and as a numeric value. The calculation of these values can be performed automatically using sentiment analysis.

Sentiment analysis can be applied to a sentence, a clause, or an entire document. Sentiment analysis may be either positive or negative, or it could be a rating using numeric values, such as 1 through 10. More complex attitude types are possible.

Further complicating the process, within a single sentence or document, different sentiments could be expressed against different topics.

How do we know which words have which types of sentiment? This question can be answered using sentiment lexicons. In this context, lexicons are dictionaries that contain the sentiments of different words. The General Inquirer (`http://www.wjh.harvard.edu/~inquirer/`) is one such lexicon. It contains 1,915 words that are considered to be positive. It also contains a list for words denoting other attributes, such as pain, pleasure, strength, and motivation. There are other lexicons that are available for use, such as the MPQA Subjectivity Cues Lexicon (`http://mpqa.cs.pitt.edu/`).

Sometimes, it may be desirable to build a lexicon. This is typically done using semi-supervised learning, where a few labelled examples or rules are used to bootstrap the lexicon-building process. This is useful when the domain of the lexicon being used does not match the domain of the problem area we are working on very well.

Not only are we interested in obtaining a positive or negative sentiment, we are interested in determining the attributes—sometimes called the targets—of the sentiment. Consider the following example:

"The ride was very rough, but the attendants did an excellent job of making us comfortable."

This sentence contains two sentiments: roughness and comfortableness. The first was negative and the second was positive. The target, or attribute, of the positive sentiment was the job and the target of the negative sentiment was the ride.

Text-classifying techniques

Classification is concerned with taking a specific document and determining whether it fits into one of several other document groups. There are two basic techniques for classifying text:

- Rule-based classification
- Supervised machine learning

Rule-based classification uses a combination of words and other attributes that are organized around expert crafted rules. These can be very effective, but creating them is a time-consuming process.

Supervised machine learning (**SML**) takes a collection of annotated training documents to create a model. The model is normally called the classifier. There are many different machine learning techniques, including Naive Bayes, **support vector machine** (**SVM**), and *k*-nearest neighbor.

We are not concerned with how these approaches work, but the interested reader will find innumerable sources that expand upon these and other techniques.

Using APIs to classify text

We will use OpenNLP, Stanford API, and LingPipe to demonstrate the various classification approaches. We will spend more time with LingPipe as it offers several different classification approaches.

Using OpenNLP

The `DocumentCategorizer` interface specifies methods that can be used to support the classification process. The interface is implemented by the `DocumentCategorizerME` class. This class will classify text into predefined categories using a maximum-entropy framework. In this section, we will do the following:

- Demonstrate how to train the model
- Illustrate how the model can be used

Training an OpenNLP classification model

First, we have to train our model because OpenNLP does not have prebuilt models. This process consists of creating a file of training data and then using the `DocumentCategorizerME` model to perform the actual training. The model that is created is typically saved in a file for later use.

The training file format consists of a series of lines where each line represents a document. The first word of the line is the category. The category is followed by text separated by whitespace. Here is an example of the `dog` category:

```
dog The most interesting feature of a dog is its ...
```

To demonstrate the training process, we created the `en-animals.train` file, where we created two categories: cats and dogs. For the training text, we used sections of Wikipedia. For dogs (`http://en.wikipedia.org/wiki/Dog`), we used the *As Pets* section. For cats (`http://en.wikipedia.org/wiki/Cats_and_humans`), we used the *Pet* section plus the first paragraph of the *Domesticated varieties* section. We also removed the numeric references from the sections.

The first part of each line is shown in the following code:

```
dog The most widespread form of interspecies bonding occurs ...
dog There have been two major trends in the changing status of  ...
dog There are a vast range of commodity forms available to  ...
dog An Australian Cattle Dog in reindeer antlers sits on Santa's lap ...
dog A pet dog taking part in Christmas traditions ...
dog The majority of contemporary people with dogs describe their  ...
dog Another study of dogs' roles in families showed many dogs have  ...
dog According to statistics published by the American Pet Products  ...
dog The latest study using Magnetic resonance imaging (MRI) ...
cat Cats are common pets in Europe and North America, and their  ...
cat Although cat ownership has commonly been associated  ...
cat The concept of a cat breed appeared in Britain during ...
cat Cats come in a variety of colors and patterns. These are physical  ...
cat A natural behavior in cats is to hook their front claws periodically
...
cat Although scratching can serve cats to keep their claws from growing
...
```

When creating training data, it is important to use a large enough sample size. The data we used is not sufficient for some kinds of analysis. However, as we will see, it does a pretty good job of identifying the categories correctly.

The `DoccatModel` class supports the categorization and classification of text. A model is trained using the `train` method based on annotated text. The `train` method uses a string denoting the language and an `ObjectStream<DocumentSample>` instance that's holding the training data. The `DocumentSample` instance holds the annotated text and its category.

In the following example, the `en-animal.train` file is used to train the model. Its input stream is used to create a `PlainTextByLineStream` instance, which is then converted to an `ObjectStream<DocumentSample>` instance. The `train` method is then applied. The code is enclosed in a `try-with-resources` block to handle exceptions. We also created an output stream that we will use to persist the model:

```
DoccatModel model = null;
try (InputStream dataIn =
        new FileInputStream("en-animal.train");
```

```
            OutputStream dataOut =
                new FileOutputStream("en-animal.model");) {
        ObjectStream<String> lineStream
            = new PlainTextByLineStream(dataIn, "UTF-8");
        ObjectStream<DocumentSample> sampleStream =
            new DocumentSampleStream(lineStream);
        model = DocumentCategorizerME.train("en", sampleStream);
        ...
    } catch (IOException e) {
    // Handle exceptions
    }
```

The output is as follows, and has been shortened for the sake of brevity:

```
Indexing events using cutoff of 5
  Computing event counts...   done. 12 events
  Indexing...   done.
Sorting and merging events... done. Reduced 12 events to 12.
Done indexing.
Incorporating indexed data for training...
done.
  Number of Event Tokens: 12
      Number of Outcomes: 2
    Number of Predicates: 30
...done.
Computing model parameters ...
Performing 100 iterations.
  1:   ... loglikelihood=-8.317766166719343  0.75
  2:   ... loglikelihood=-7.1439957443937265  0.75
  3:   ... loglikelihood=-6.560690872956419  0.75
  4:   ... loglikelihood=-6.106743124066829  0.75
  5:   ... loglikelihood=-5.721805583104927  0.8333333333333334
  6:   ... loglikelihood=-5.3891508904777785  0.8333333333333334
  7:   ... loglikelihood=-5.098768040466029  0.8333333333333334
  ...
 98:   ... loglikelihood=-1.4117372921765519  1.0
 99:   ... loglikelihood=-1.4052738190352423  1.0
100:   ... loglikelihood=-1.398916120150312  1.0
```

The model is saved using the `serialize` method, as shown in the following code. The model is saved to the `en-animal.model` file, as opened in the previous `try-with-resources` block:

```
OutputStream modelOut = null;
modelOut = new BufferedOutputStream(dataOut);
model.serialize(modelOut);
```

Using DocumentCategorizerME to classify text

Once a model has been created, we can use the `DocumentCategorizerME` class to classify text. We need to read the model, create an instance of the `DocumentCategorizerME` class, and then invoke the `categorize` method to return an array of probabilities that will tell us which category the text best fits.

Since we are reading from a file, exceptions need to be dealt with, as shown here:

```
try (InputStream modelIn =
        new FileInputStream(new File("en-animal.model"));) {
    ...
} catch (IOException ex) {
    // Handle exceptions
}
```

With the `InputStream`, we create instances of the `DoccatModel` and `DocumentCategorizerME` classes, as illustrated here:

```
DoccatModel model = new DoccatModel(modelIn);
DocumentCategorizerME categorizer =
    new DocumentCategorizerME(model);
```

The `categorize` method is called using a string as an argument. This returns an array of double values, with each element having the likelihood that the text belongs to a category. The `DocumentCategorizerME` class's `getNumberOfCategories` method returns the number of categories handled by the model. The `DocumentCategorizerME` class's `getCategory` method returns the given category an index.

We have used these methods in the following code to display each category and its corresponding likelihood:

```
double[] outcomes = categorizer.categorize(inputText);
for (int i = 0; i<categorizer.getNumberOfCategories(); i++) {
    String category = categorizer.getCategory(i);
    System.out.println(category + " - " + outcomes[i]);
}
```

For testing, we used part of the Wikipedia article for Toto, Dorothy's dog, from *The Wizard of Oz* (`http://en.wikipedia.org/wiki/Toto_%28Oz%29`). We used the first sentence of *The classic books* section, as declared here:

```
String toto = "Toto belongs to Dorothy Gale, the heroine of "
        + "the first and many subsequent books. In the first "
        + "book, he never spoke, although other animals, native "
        + "to Oz, did. In subsequent books, other animals "
```

```
        + "gained the ability to speak upon reaching Oz or "
        + "similar lands, but Toto remained speechless.";
```

To test for a cat, we used the first sentence of the *Tortoiseshell and Calico* section of the Wikipedia article at `https://en.wikipedia.org/wiki/Tortoiseshell_cat`, as declared here:

```
String calico = "This cat is also known as a calimanco cat or "
        + "clouded tiger cat, and by the abbreviation 'tortie'. "
        + "In the cat fancy, a tortoiseshell cat is patched "
        + "over with red (or its dilute form, cream) and black "
        + "(or its dilute blue) mottled throughout the coat.";
```

Using the text for `toto`, we get the following output. This suggests that the text should be placed in the `dog` category:

```
        dog - 0.5870711529777994
        cat - 0.41292884702220056
```

Using `calico` instead yields the following results:

```
        dog - 0.28960436044424276
        cat - 0.7103956395557574
```

We could have used the `getBestCategory` method to return only the best category. This method uses the array of outcomes and returns a string. The `getAllResults` method will return all of the results as a string. These two methods are illustrated as follows:

```
System.out.println(categorizer.getBestCategory(outcomes));
System.out.println(categorizer.getAllResults(outcomes));
```

The output will be as follows:

```
cat
dog[0.2896]    cat[0.7104]
```

Using the Stanford API

The Stanford API supports several classifiers. We will examine the use of the `ColumnDataClassifier` class for general classification and the `StanfordCoreNLP` pipeline to perform sentiment analysis. The classifiers supported by the Stanford API can be difficult to use at times. With the `ColumnDataClassifier` class, we will demonstrate how to classify the size of boxes. With the pipeline, we will illustrate how to determine the positive or negative sentiment of short text phrases. The classifier can be downloaded from `http://www-nlp.stanford.edu/wiki/Software/Classifier`.

Using the ColumnDataClassifier class for classification

This classifier uses data with multiple values to describe the data. In this demonstration, we will use a training file to create a classifier. We will then use a test file to assess the performance of the classifier. The class uses a property file to configure the creation process.

We will be creating a classifier that attempts to classify a box based on its dimensions. There are three possible categories: small, medium, and large. The height, width, and length dimensions of a box will be expressed as floating-point numbers. They are used to characterize a box.

The properties file specifies parameter information and supplies data about the training and test files. There are many possible properties that can be specified. For this example, we will use only a few of the more relevant properties.

We will use the following properties file, saved as `box.prop`. The first set of properties deals with the number of features that are contained in the training and test files. Since we used three values, three `realValued` columns are specified. The `trainFile` and `testFile` properties specify the location and names of the respective files:

```
useClassFeature=true
1.realValued=true
2.realValued=true
3.realValued=true
trainFile=.box.train
testFile=.box.test
```

The training and test files use the same format. Each line consists of a category followed by the defining values, each separated by a tab. The `box.train` training file consists of 60 entries and the `box.test` file consists of 30 entries. These files can be downloaded from `https://github.com/PacktPublishing/Natural-Language-Processing-with-Java-Second-Edition/` or from the GitHub repository. The first line of the `box.train` file is shown in the following code. The category is small; its height, width, and length are `2.34`, `1.60`, and `1.50`, respectively:

```
small   2.34   1.60   1.50
```

The code to create the classifier is shown in the following code. An instance of the `ColumnDataClassifier` class is created using the properties file as the constructor's argument. An instance of the `Classifier` interface is returned by the `makeClassifier` method. This interface supports three methods, two of which we will demonstrate. The `readTrainingExamples` method reads the training data from the training file:

```
ColumnDataClassifier cdc =
    new ColumnDataClassifier("box.prop");
Classifier<String, String> classifier =
    cdc.makeClassifier(cdc.readTrainingExamples("box.train"));
```

When executed, we get extensive output. We will discuss the more relevant parts in this section. The first part of the output repeats parts of the property file:

```
3.realValued = true
testFile = .box.test
...
trainFile = .box.train
```

The next part displays the number of datasets, read along with the information regarding various features, as shown here:

```
Reading dataset from box.train ... done [0.1s, 60 items].
numDatums: 60
numLabels: 3 [small, medium, large]
...
AVEIMPROVE     The average improvement / current value
EVALSCORE      The last available eval score
Iter ## evals ## <SCALING> [LINESEARCH] VALUE TIME |GNORM| {RELNORM}
AVEIMPROVE EVALSCORE
```

The classifier then iterates over the data to create the classifier:

```
Iter 1 evals 1 <D> [113M 3.107E-4] 5.985E1 0.00s |3.829E1| {1.959E-1}
0.000E0 -
Iter 2 evals 5 <D> [M 1.000E0] 5.949E1 0.01s |1.862E1| {9.525E-2}
3.058E-3 -
Iter 3 evals 6 <D> [M 1.000E0] 5.923E1 0.01s |1.741E1| {8.904E-2}
3.485E-3 -
...
Iter 21 evals 24 <D> [1M 2.850E-1] 3.306E1 0.02s |4.149E-1| {2.122E-3}
1.775E-4 -
Iter 22 evals 26 <D> [M 1.000E0] 3.306E1 0.02s
QNMinimizer terminated due to average improvement: | newest_val -
previous_val | / |newestVal| < TOL
Total time spent in optimization: 0.07s
```

At this point, the classifier is ready to use. Next, we use the test file to verify the classifier. We start by getting a line from the text file using the `ObjectBank` class's `getLineIterator` method. This class supports the conversion of data that has been read into a more standardized form. The `getLineIterator` method returns one line at a time in a format that can be used by the classifier. The loop for this process is shown here:

```
for (String line :
        ObjectBank.getLineIterator("box.test", "utf-8")) {
    ...
}
```

Within the for-each statement, a `Datum` instance is created from the line and then its `classOf` method is used to return the predicted category, as shown in the following code. The `Datum` interface supports objects that contain features. When used as the argument of the `classOf` method, the category determined by the classifier is returned:

```
Datum<String, String> datum = cdc.makeDatumFromLine(line);
System.out.println("Datum: {"
    + line + "]\tPredicted Category: "
    + classifier.classOf(datum));
```

When this sequence is executed, each line of the test file is processed and the predicted category is displayed, as shown in the following code. Only the first two and last two lines are shown here. The classifier was able to correctly classify all of the test data:

```
Datum: {small  1.33  3.50  5.43]  Predicted Category: medium
Datum: {small  1.18  1.73  3.14]  Predicted Category: small
...
Datum: {large  6.01  9.35  16.64]  Predicted Category: large
Datum: {large  6.76  9.66  15.44]  Predicted Category: large
```

To test an individual entry, we can use the `makeDatumFromStrings` method to create a `Datum` instance. In the following code sequence, a one-dimensional array of strings is created, where each element represents data values for a box. The first entry, the category, is left null. The `Datum` instance is then used as the argument of the `classOf` method to predict its category:

```
String sample[] = {"", "6.90", "9.8", "15.69"};
Datum<String, String> datum =
    cdc.makeDatumFromStrings(sample);
System.out.println("Category: " + classifier.classOf(datum));
```

The output for this sequence is shown here. It correctly classifies the box:

```
Category: large
```

Using the Stanford pipeline to perform sentiment analysis

In this section, we will illustrate how the Stanford API can be used to perform sentiment analysis. We will use the `StanfordCoreNLP` pipeline to perform this analysis on different texts.

We will use three different texts, as defined in the following code. The `review` string is a movie review from Rotten Tomatoes (`http://www.rottentomatoes.com/m/forrest_gump/`) about the movie *Forrest Gump*:

```
String review = "An overly sentimental film with a somewhat "
    + "problematic message, but its sweetness and charm "
    + "are occasionally enough to approximate true depth "
    + "and grace. ";

String sam = "Sam was an odd sort of fellow. Not prone "
    + "to angry and not prone to merriment. Overall, "
    + "an odd fellow.";
String mary = "Mary thought that custard pie was the "
    + "best pie in the world. However, she loathed "
    + "chocolate pie.";
```

To perform this analysis, we need to use a sentiment `annotator`, as shown in the following code. This also requires the use of the `tokenize`, `ssplit`, and `parse` annotators. The `parse` annotator provides more structural information about the text, which will be discussed in more detail in `Chapter 10`, *Using Parsers to Extract Relationships*:

```
Properties props = new Properties();
props.put("annotators", "tokenize, ssplit, parse, sentiment");
StanfordCoreNLP pipeline = new StanfordCoreNLP(props);
```

The text is used to create an `Annotation` instance, which is then used as the argument to the `annotate` method that performs the actual work, as shown here:

```
Annotation annotation = new Annotation(review);
pipeline.annotate(annotation);
```

The following array holds the strings for the different possible sentiments:

```
String[] sentimentText = {"Very Negative", "Negative",
    "Neutral", "Positive", "Very Positive"};
```

The `Annotation` class's `get` method returns an object that implements the `CoreMap` interface. In this case, these objects represent the results of splitting the input text into sentences, as shown in the following code. For each sentence, an instance of a `Tree` object is obtained that represents a tree structure containing a parse of the text for the sentiment. The `getPredictedClass` method returns an index to the `sentimentText` array, reflecting the sentiment of the test:

```
for (CoreMap sentence : annotation.get(
        CoreAnnotations.SentencesAnnotation.class)) {
    Tree tree = sentence.get(
        SentimentCoreAnnotations.AnnotatedTree.class);
    int score = RNNCoreAnnotations.getPredictedClass(tree);
    System.out.println(sentimentText[score]);
}
```

When the code is executed using the `review` string, we get the following output:

```
Positive
```

The text `sam` consists of three sentences. The output for each is as follows, showing the sentiment for each sentence:

```
Neutral
Negative
Neutral
```

The text `mary` consists of two sentences. The output for each is as follows:

```
Positive
Neutral
```

Using LingPipe to classify text

In this section, we will use LingPipe to demonstrate a number of classification tasks, including general text classification using trained models, sentiment analysis, and language identification. We will cover the following classification topics:

- Training text using the `Classified` class
- Training models using other training categories
- Classifying text using LingPipe
- Performing sentiment analysis using LingPipe
- Identifying the language used

Several of the tasks described in this section will use the following declarations. LingPipe comes with training data for several categories. The `categories` array contains the names of the categories packaged with LingPipe:

```
String[] categories = {"soc.religion.christian",
    "talk.religion.misc","alt.atheism","misc.forsale"};
```

The `DynamicLMClassifier` class is used to perform the actual classification. It is created using the `categories` array, giving it the names of the categories to use. The `nGramSize` value specifies the number of contiguous items in a sequence that are used in the model for classification purposes:

```
int nGramSize = 6;
DynamicLMClassifier<NGramProcessLM> classifier =
    DynamicLMClassifier.createNGramProcess(
        categories, nGramSize);
```

Training text using the Classified class

General text classification using LingPipe involves training the `DynamicLMClassifier` class using training files and then using the class to perform the actual classification. LingPipe comes with several training datasets, as found in the LingPipe directory named `demos/data/fourNewsGroups/4news-train`. We will use these datasets to illustrate the training process. This example is a simplified version of the process found at `http://alias-i.com/lingpipe/demos/tutorial/classify/read-me.html`.

We start by declaring the `trainingDirectory`:

```
String directory = ".../demos";
File trainingDirectory = new File(directory
    + "/data/fourNewsGroups/4news-train");
```

In the `trainingDirectory`, there are four subdirectories whose names are listed in the `categories` array. In each subdirectory, there is a series of files with numeric names. These files contain newsgroup (`http://qwone.com/~jason/20Newsgroups/`) data that deals with the name of the subdirectories.

The process of training the model involves using each file and category with the `DynamicLMClassifier` class's `handle` method. The method will use the file to create a training instance for the category and then augment the model with this instance. The process uses nested `for` loops.

The outer `for` loop creates a `File` object using the directory's name and then applies the `list` method against it. The `list` method returns a list of the files in the directory. The names of these files are stored in the `trainingFiles` array, which will be used in the inner `for` loop:

```
for (int i = 0; i < categories.length; ++i) {
    File classDir =
        new File(trainingDirectory, categories[i]);
    String[] trainingFiles = classDir.list();
    // Inner for-loop
}
```

The inner `for` loop, as shown in the following code, will open each file and read the text from the file. The `Classification` class represents a classification with a specified category. It is used with the text to create a `Classified` instance. The `DynamicLMClassifier` class's `handle` method updates the model with the new information:

```
for (int j = 0; j < trainingFiles.length; ++j) {
    try {
        File file = new File(classDir, trainingFiles[j]);
        String text = Files.readFromFile(file, "ISO-8859-1");
        Classification classification =
            new Classification(categories[i]);
        Classified<CharSequence> classified =
            new Classified<>(text, classification);
        classifier.handle(classified);
    } catch (IOException ex) {
        // Handle exceptions
    }
}
```

 You can alternatively use the `com.aliasi.util.Files` class instead in `java.io.File`; otherwise, the `readFromFile` method will not be available.

The classifier can be serialized for later use, as shown in the following code. The `AbstractExternalizable` class is a utility class that supports the serialization of objects. It has a static `compileTo` method that accepts a `Compilable` instance and a `File` object. It writes the object to the file, as follows:

```
try {
    AbstractExternalizable.compileTo( (Compilable) classifier,
        new File("classifier.model"));
```

```
} catch (IOException ex) {
    // Handle exceptions
}
```

The loading of the classifier will be illustrated in the *Classifying text using LingPipe* section later in this chapter.

Using other training categories

Other newsgroup data can be found at `http://qwone.com/~jason/20Newsgroups/`. These collections of data can be used to train other models, as listed in the following table. Although there are only 20 categories, they can be useful training models. Three different downloads are available. Some have been sorted, and in others, duplicate data has been removed:

Newsgroups	
comp.graphics	sci.crypt
comp.os.ms-windows.misc	sci.electronics
comp.sys.ibm.pc.hardware	sci.med
comp.sys.mac.hardware	sci.space
comp.windows.x	misc.forsale
rec.autos	talk.politics.misc
rec.motoXrcycles	talk.politics.guns
rec.sport.baseball	talk.politics.mideast
rec.sport.hockey	talk.religion.misc
alt.atheism	

Classifying text using LingPipe

To classify text, we will use the `DynamicLMClassifier` class's `classify` method. We will demonstrate its use with two different text sequences:

- `forSale`: This is from `http://www.homes.com/for-sale/`, where we use the first complete sentence
- `martinLuther`: This is from `http://en.wikipedia.org/wiki/Martin_Luther`, where we use the first sentence of the second paragraph

These strings are declared here:

```
String forSale =
    "Finding a home for sale has never been "
    + "easier. With Homes.com, you can search new "
    + "homes, foreclosures, multi-family homes, "
    + "as well as condos and townhouses for sale. "
    + "You can even search our real estate agent "
    + "directory to work with a professional "
    + "Realtor and find your perfect home.";
String martinLuther =
    "Luther taught that salvation and subsequently "
    + "eternity in heaven is not earned by good deeds "
    + "but is received only as a free gift of God's "
    + "grace through faith in Jesus Christ as redeemer "
    + "from sin and subsequently eternity in Hell.";
```

To reuse the classifier that is serialized in the previous section, use the `AbstractExternalizable` class's `readObject` method, as shown in the following code. We will use the `LMClassifier` class instead of the `DynamicLMClassifier` class. They both support the `classify` method, but the `DynamicLMClassifier` class is not readily serializable:

```
LMClassifier classifier = null;
try {
    classifier = (LMClassifier)
        AbstractExternalizable.readObject(
            new File("classifier.model"));
} catch (IOException | ClassNotFoundException ex) {
    // Handle exceptions
}
```

In the following code sequence, we will apply the `LMClassifier` class's `classify` method. This returns a `JointClassification` instance, which we use to determine the best match:

```
JointClassification classification =
    classifier.classify(text);
System.out.println("Text: " + text);
String bestCategory = classification.bestCategory();
System.out.println("Best Category: " + bestCategory);
```

For the `forSale` text, we get the following output:

```
    Text: Finding a home for sale has never been easier. With Homes.com,
you can search new homes, foreclosures, multi-family homes, as well as
condos and townhouses for sale. You can even search our real estate agent
directory to work with a professional Realtor and find your perfect home.
    Best Category: misc.forsale
```

For the `martinLuther` text, we get the following output:

```
    Text: Luther taught that salvation and subsequently eternity in heaven
is not earned by good deeds but is received only as a free gift of God's
grace through faith in Jesus Christ as redeemer from sin and subsequently
eternity in Hell.
    Best Category: soc.religion.christian
```

They both correctly classified the text.

Sentiment analysis using LingPipe

Sentiment analysis is performed in a very similar manner to that of general text classification. One difference is that it uses only two categories: positive and negative.

We need to use data files to train our model. We will use a simplified version of the sentiment analysis performed at `http://alias-i.com/lingpipe/demos/tutorial/sentiment/read-me.html` by using sentiment data that was developed for movies (`http://www.cs.cornell.edu/people/pabo/movie-review-data/review_polarity.tar.gz`). This data was developed from 1,000 positive and 1,000 negative reviews of movies that are in IMDb's movie archives.

These reviews need to be downloaded and extracted. A `txt_sentoken` directory will be extracted along with its two subdirectories: `neg` and `pos`. Both of these subdirectories contain movie reviews. Although some of these files can be held in reserve to evaluate the model that was created, we will use all of them to simplify the explanation.

We will start with the reinitialization of variables declared in the *Using LingPipe to classify text* section. The `categories` array is set to a two-element array to hold the two categories. The `classifier` variable is assigned a new `DynamicLMClassifier` instance using the new category array and a `nGramSize` of size 8:

```
categories = new String[2];
categories[0] = "neg";
categories[1] = "pos";
```

```
nGramSize = 8;
classifier = DynamicLMClassifier.createNGramProcess(
    categories, nGramSize);
```

As we did earlier, we will create a series of instances based on the content found in the training files. We will not examine the following code in detail as it is very similar to the one found in the *Training text using the Classified class* section. The main difference is that there are only two categories to process:

```
String directory = "...";
File trainingDirectory = new File(directory, "txt_sentoken");
for (int i = 0; i < categories.length; ++i) {
    Classification classification =
        new Classification(categories[i]);
    File file = new File(trainingDirectory, categories[i]);
    File[] trainingFiles = file.listFiles();
    for (int j = 0; j < trainingFiles.length; ++j) {
        try {
            String review = Files.readFromFile(
                trainingFiles[j], "ISO-8859-1");
            Classified<CharSequence> classified =
                new Classified<>(review, classification);
            classifier.handle(classified);
        } catch (IOException ex) {
            ex.printStackTrace();
        }
    }
}
```

The model is now ready to be used. We will use the review for the movie *Forrest Gump*:

```
String review = "An overly sentimental film with a somewhat "
    + "problematic message, but its sweetness and charm "
    + "are occasionally enough to approximate true depth "
    + "and grace. ";
```

We use the `classify` method to perform the actual work. It returns a `Classification` instance whose `bestCategory` method returns the best category, as shown here:

```
Classification classification = classifier.classify(review);
String bestCategory = classification.bestCategory();
System.out.println("Best Category: " + bestCategory);
```

When executed, we get the following output:

```
Best Category: pos
```

This approach will also work well for other categories of text.

Language identification using LingPipe

LingPipe comes with a model called `langid-leipzig.classifier`, which is trained for several languages and is found in the `demos/models` directory. The following table contains a list of supported languages. This model was developed using training data derived from the Leipzig Corpora Collection (`http://corpora.uni-leipzig.de/`). Another good tool can be found at `http://code.google.com/p/language-detection/`:

Language	Abbreviation	Language	Abbreviation
Catalan	cat	Italian	it
Danish	dk	Japanese	jp
English	en	Korean	kr
Estonian	ee	Norwegian	no
Finnish	fi	Sorbian	sorb
French	fr	Swedish	se
German	de	Turkish	tr

To use this model, we use essentially the same code that we used in the *Classifying text using LingPipe* section earlier in this chapter. We start with the same movie review of *Forrest Gump*:

```
String text = "An overly sentimental film with a somewhat "
    + "problematic message, but its sweetness and charm "
    + "are occasionally enough to approximate true depth "
    + "and grace. ";
System.out.println("Text: " + text);
```

The `LMClassifier` instance is created using the `langid-leipzig.classifier` file:

```
LMClassifier classifier = null;
try {
    classifier = (LMClassifier)
        AbstractExternalizable.readObject(
            new File(".../langid-leipzig.classifier"));
} catch (IOException | ClassNotFoundException ex) {
    // Handle exceptions
}
```

The `classify` method is used, followed by the application of the `bestCategory` method, to obtain the best language fit, as shown here:

```
Classification classification = classifier.classify(text);
String bestCategory = classification.bestCategory();
System.out.println("Best Language: " + bestCategory);
```

The output is as follows, with English being chosen as the language:

```
    Text: An overly sentimental film with a somewhat problematic message,
but its sweetness and charm are occasionally enough to approximate true
depth and grace.
    Best Language: en
```

The following code example uses the first sentence of the Swedish Wikipedia entry in Swedish (`http://sv.wikipedia.org/wiki/Svenska`) for the text:

```
text = "Svenska är ett östnordiskt språk som talas av cirka "
    + "tio miljoner personer[1], främst i Finland "
    + "och Sverige.";
```

The output, as shown here, correctly selects the Swedish language:

```
    Text: Svenska är ett östnordiskt språk som talas av cirka tio miljoner
personer[1], främst i Finland och Sverige.
    Best Language: se
```

Training can be conducted using the same method that we used for the previous LingPipe models. Another consideration when performing language identification is that the text may be written in multiple languages. This can complicate the language detection process.

Summary

In this chapter, we discussed the issues surrounding the classification of text and examined several approaches to perform this process. The classification of text is useful for many activities, such as detecting email spam, determining who the author of a document may be, performing gender identification, and performing language identification.

We also demonstrated how to perform sentiment analysis. This analysis is concerned with determining whether a piece of text is positive or negative in nature. It is also possible to assess other sentiment attributes using this process.

Most of the approaches we used required us to first create a model based on training data. Normally, this model needs to be validated using a set of test data. Once the model has been created, it is usually easy to use.

In the next chapter, Chapter 9, *Topic Modeling* we will investigate the parsing process and how it contributes to extracting relationships from text.

9
Topic Modeling

In this chapter, we will learn about the basics of topic modeling using a document that contains some text. The idea here is to get the topic from the text using certain available methods. This process falls under the category of text mining, and plays an important role in searching as well as clustering and organizing text. Today, it is used by many sites for recommendation purposes, such as when news sites recommend articles based on the topic of the article that is currently being read by the reader. This chapter covers the basics of topic modeling, including the basic concept of **Latent Dirichlet Allocation** (**LDA**). It will also show you how to use the MALLET package for topic modeling.

We will cover the following topics in this chapter:

- What is topic modeling?
- The basics of LDA
- Topic modeling with MALLET

What is topic modeling?

In very simple terms, topic modeling is a technique by which the computer programs try and extract a topic from the text. The text is usually unstructured data, such as a blog, email, article, a chapter from a book, or something similar. It is a text-mining approach, but should not be confused with rule-based text mining. In a machine learning scenario, topic modeling falls under the category of unsupervised learning, where the machine or computer program tries to find the topic by observing a bunch of words in the last collection of text. A good model should result in the words "program", "programmer", "IT", "computer", "software", and "hardware" when given the topic of "IT industry". It helps in making sense of large text, and plays a vital role in the operation of search engines.

Topic modeling can be used with methods to organize, categorize, understand, and summarize large collections of textual information. It enables us to discover hidden patterns in collections and annotation using topics. It finds the group of words from the collection of documents that best represents the collection.

There are many different ways to do topic modeling, but the most popular is LDA. The next section will look at the basics of LDA.

The basics of LDA

LDA is the most popular method among the different methods of topic modeling. It is a form of text data mining and machine learning, where backtracking is performed to figure out the topic for the document. It also involves the use of probability, as it is a generative probabilistic model.

LDA represents the documents as a mixture of topics that will give a topic based on probability.

Any given document has a greater or lesser chance of having a certain word as its underlying topic; for example, given a document about sports, the probability of the word "cricket" occurring is higher than the probability of the word "Android One Phone". If the document is about mobile technology, then the probability of the word "Android One Phone" will be higher than the word "cricket". Using a sampling method, some words are selected from a document as a topic using Dirichlet distribution in a semi random manner. These randomly selected topics may not be the best suited as the potential topic of the document, so for each document, one need to go through the words and compute probability of word from document. Let *p(topic|document)* be the probability of a word from document *d* assigned to topic *t*—and *p(word|topic)* is the probability of the topic *t* from all documents that comes from the word *w*. This helps in finding the proportion of each word that constitutes the topics. It finds the relevance of each word across the topic and the relevance of the topic across the document. Now, reassign the word *w* with a new topic—let's call it *topic'*—using *p(topic' | document) * p(word | topic')*. Repeat this process until you reach the point where the topic assignments are finalized.

To accomplish this, LDA uses a document–term matrix and converts it into a document–topic matrix and a topic–term matrix. LDA uses sampling techniques in order to improve the matrices. Let's say that there are *N* documents labeled *d1, d2, d3 .... dn*. There are *M* terms labeled *t1, t2, t3 .... tm*, so the document–term matrix will represent the count of the terms in the documents and represent them as follows:

	t1	t2	t3	tm
d1	0	3	1	2
d2	0	5	4	1
d3	1	0	3	2
dn	0	1	1	2

Let *k* be the number of topics we want LDA to suggest. It divides the document–term matrix into a dimension–topic matrix and a topic–term matrix:

	topic-1	topic-2	topic-k
d1	1	0	1
d2	1	1	0
d3	1	0	1
dn	1	0	1

Document–topic matrix [*N* x *k*]

	t1	t2	t3	tm
topic-1	0	1	1	0
topic-2	1	1	0	0
topic-k	1	0	1	0

Topic–term matrix [*k* x *m*]

To see how LDA works, visit `https://lettier.com/projects/lda-topic-modeling/`. This is a good web page, where you can add documents, decide the number of topics, and tweak the alpha and beta parameters to get topics.

Topic modeling with MALLET

MALLET is a well-known library in topic modeling. It also supports document classification and sequence tagging. More about MALLET can be found at `http://mallet.cs.umass.edu/index.php`. To download MALLET, visit `http://mallet.cs.umass.edu/download.php` (the latest version is 2.0.6). Once downloaded, extract MALLET in the directory. It contains the sample data in `.txt` format in the `sample-data/web/en` path of the MALLET directory.

The first step is to import the files into MALLET's internal format. To do this, open the Command Prompt or Terminal, move to the `mallet` directory, and execute the following command:

```
mallet-2.0.6$ bin/mallet import-dir --input sample-data/web/en --output
tutorial.mallet --keep-sequence --remove-stopwords
```

This command will generate the `tutorial.mallet` file.

Training

The next step is to use `train-topics` to build a topic model and save the `output-state`, `topic-keys`, and `topics` using the `train-topics` command:

```
mallet-2.0.6$ bin/mallet train-topics --input tutorial.mallet --num-topics
20 --output-state topic-state.gz --output-topic-keys tutorial_keys.txt --
output-doc-topics tutorial_compostion.txt
```

This will train for 20 topics, and will create a ZIP file for every word in your corpus of materials, and the topic they belong to. All `topic-keys` will be stored in `tutorial_key.txt`. The topicwise proposition for files will be stored in `tutorial_composition.txt`.

Evaluation

A `tutorial_key.txt` is a simple text file, and the content will look similar to the following screenshot:

```
 1 0     2.5   australian century general rulers greek run don wadia organs marsupials intensive island commonly largest sa moral william
         plate brothel
 2 1     2.5   battle union army day confederates tennessee men maj launched beauregard april pittsburg evening buell continental called
         centuries block hopes
 3 2     2.5   death year father online bbc biggest heroine common sentenced reformers moll procuress forest caused commercialism
         concentrate committee publisher caulfield
 4 3     2.5   including gunnhild life norway parks king generally husband saga figure orkney erik dogs miocene highest founding peers
         discord industrialization
 5 4     2.5   rings dust number uranus moons narrow uranian relative system particles dark found march discovered psychology criminal
         wales make lost
 6 5     2.5   time grant gen northern line position fighting reported numerous addition shiloh league boyfriend alvida lead living factors
         times industry
 7 6     2.5   years yard wilderness needham park career ring states movement effects treatment fashionable house notorious establish led
         princeton graduated group
 8 7     2.5   test cricket hill filmfare acted involved ended innings batsman critical performer kabhi romance fiction mammals wolves
         officially contributory encouraged
 9 8     2.5   record england naa marsupial thylacinus independent ness running reproductive evolution tigers member dog genuine greeting
         bawd masterpieces writer sterling
10 9     2.5   standards performances daily east civil whig punjab markets portrayal veer consecutive se preity external sightings resulted
         publicize stephen worked
11 10    2.5   average equipartition system london opera forced stars classical heat motion original debut thick human severe exclusive
         portraits hackabout educate
12 11    2.5   sullivan gilbert thespis died society theatre stage cinema degree protective convergent hemisphere habitat bounties
         cynocephalus pronounced stand eventually recorded
```

It contains all the topics, as we have asked for 20 topics. The lines in the file can be seen in three ways. The first is by using the number starting from 0 onward, denoting the topic number. The second number is the Dirichlet parameter, with a default of 2.5, and the third way is by looking at the paragraph showing possible topics.

The tutorial_compostion.txt file contains a percentage breakdown of each topic with each original text file. The tutorial_compostion.txt file can be opened in Excel or LibreOffice so that you can understand it more easily. It shows the filename followed by the topic and proportion for all words in the topic:

	B	C	D	E	F	G	H	I	J
#doc	source	topic	proportion	...					
0	sample-data/web/en/hawes.txt	19	0.43809524178505	17	0.12380952388048	1	0.09523809701204	7	0.05714285746217
1	sample-data/web/en/uranus.txt	4	0.5420560836792	6	0.06542056053877	15	0.04672897234559	5	0.04672897234559
2	sample-data/web/en/equipartition_theorem.t	10	0.36458334326744	12	0.30208334326744	17	0.05208333209157	9	0.05208333209157
3	sample-data/web/en/sunderland_echo.txt	16	0.33333334326744	18			0.125	14	0.09375	9	0.0625
4	sample-data/web/en/thespis.txt	11	0.24210526049137	17	0.08421052992344	15	0.07368420809507	0	0.07368420809507
5	sample-data/web/en/gunnhild.txt	3	0.39759036898613	14	0.12048193067312	17	0.08433734625578	18	0.07228915393353
6	sample-data/web/en/shiloh.txt	1	0.37931033968926	5	0.24827586114407	9	0.05517241358757	17	0.04827586188912
7	sample-data/web/en/hill.txt	7	0.31313130259514	8	0.10101009905338	2	0.10101009905338	0	0.09090909361839
8	sample-data/web/en/yard.txt	6	0.21621622145176	14	0.14414414763451	3	0.17117114365101	12	0.07207207381725
9	sample-data/web/en/elizabeth_needham.txt	11	0.16666667163372	6	0.12962962687016	10	0.11111111938953	0	0.09259258955717
10	sample-data/web/en/thylacine.txt	13	0.40769231319428	8	0.0846153870225	0	0.0846153870225	17	0.07692307978868
11	sample-data/web/en/zinta.txt	15	0.39568346738815	18	0.12230215966702	14	0.05755395814776	9	0.05755395814776

The first file is hawes.txt and topic 19 has a proportion of 0.438 %.

Let's try this using custom data. Create a `mydata` folder in the `mallet` directory with four text files with the names `1.txt`, `2.txt`, `3.txt`, and `4.txt`. The following is the content of the file:

Filename	Content
`1.txt`	I love eating bananas.
`2.txt`	I have a dog. He also loves to eat bananas.
`3.txt`	Banana is a fruit, rich in nutrients.
`4.txt`	Eating bananas in the morning is a healthy habit.

Let's train and evaluate the model. Execute the following two commands:

```
mallet-2.0.6$ bin/mallet import-dir --input mydata/ --output
mytutorial.mallet --keep-sequence --remove-stopwords

mallet-2.0.6$ bin/mallet train-topics  --input mytutorial.mallet --num-
topics 2 --output-state mytopic-state.gz --output-topic-keys
mytutorial_keys.txt --output-doc-topics mytutorial_compostion.txt
```

As mentioned previously, it will create three files, which we will now look at in detail.

The first file is `mytopic-state.gz`. Extract and open the file. This will display all the words that are used, and in which topic they are set:

```
 1 #doc source pos typeindex type topic
 2 #alpha : 25.0 25.0
 3 #beta : 0.01
 4 0 mydata/3.txt 0 0 banana 0
 5 0 mydata/3.txt 1 1 fruit 1
 6 0 mydata/3.txt 2 2 rich 1
 7 0 mydata/3.txt 3 3 nutrients 0
 8 1 mydata/2.txt 0 4 dog 1
 9 1 mydata/2.txt 1 5 love 0
10 1 mydata/2.txt 2 6 eat 0
11 1 mydata/2.txt 3 7 bananas 0
12 2 mydata/1.txt 0 5 love 0
13 2 mydata/1.txt 1 8 eating 1
14 2 mydata/1.txt 2 7 bananas 1
15 3 mydata/4.txt 0 8 eating 1
16 3 mydata/4.txt 1 7 bananas 0
17 3 mydata/4.txt 2 9 morning 1
18 3 mydata/4.txt 3 10 healthy 0
19 3 mydata/4.txt 4 11 habit 0
```

The next file is `mytutorial_key.txt`, which, when opened, will display the topic terms. As we have asked for two topics, it will have two lines:

```
1 0     25    bananas love habit healthy eat nutrients banana
2 1     25    eating morning bananas dog rich fruit
```

The last file is `mytutorial_composition.txt`, which we will open in Excel or LibreOffice. It will display `doc`, `topic`, and `proportion`:

	A	B	C	D	E	F
1	#doc	source	topic	proportion	...	
2	0	mydata/3.txt	0	0.75	1	0.25
3	1	mydata/2.txt	0	0.75	1	0.25
4	2	mydata/1.txt	1	0.666666686534882	0	0.333333343267441
5	3	mydata/4.txt	1	0.600000023841858	0	0.400000005960465
6						

It can be seen that for the `3.txt` file, which contains "`Banana is a fruit, rich in nutrients.`", topic `0` is more in proportion to topic `1`. From the first file, we can see that topic `0` contains the topics `banana`, `nutrients`, `love`, and `healthy`.

Summary

In this chapter, we learned why we should do topic modeling and how it is important in a world of ever-increasing data. We also looked at the concept of LDA and its use in deciding how topics are selected from a given corpus. We also looked at the use of the MALLET tool for topic modeling on sample data and creating our own custom data. We also learned about the different files that are generated and how to interpret them.

In the next chapter, `Chapter 10`, *Using Parser to Extract Relationships*, we will see how to use the parser to extract relationships.

10
Using Parsers to Extract Relationships

Parsing is the process of creating a parse tree for a textual unit. This unit may be for a line of code or a sentence. It is easy to do for computer languages, since they were designed to make this task easy. However, this has made it harder to write code. Natural language parsing is considerably more difficult, and this is due to the ambiguity found in natural languages. This ambiguity makes a language difficult to learn but offers great flexibility and expressive power. Here, we are not interested in parsing computer languages, but rather natural languages.

A parse tree is a hierarchical data structure that represents the syntactic structure of a sentence. Often, this is presented as a tree graph with a root, as we will illustrate shortly. We will use the parse tree to help identify relationships between entities in the tree.

Parsing is used for many tasks, including the following:

- Machine translation of languages
- Synthesizing speech from text
- Speech recognition
- Grammar checking
- Information extraction

Coreference resolution is the condition where two or more expressions in text refer to the same individual or thing. Take this sentence, for example:

"Ted went to the party where he made an utter fool of himself."

The words *Ted*, *he*, and *himself* refer to the same entity, *Ted*. This is important in determining the correct interpretation of text and in determining the relative importance of text sections. We will demonstrate how the Stanford API addresses this problem.

Extracting relationships and information from text is an important NLP task. Relationships may exist between entities, such as the subject of a sentence and either its object, other entities, or perhaps its behavior. We may also want to identify relationships and present them in a structured form. We can use this information either to present the results for immediate use by people or to format relationships so that they can be better utilized for a downstream task.

In this chapter, we will examine the parsing process and see how the parse tree is used. We will examine the relationship extraction process and investigate relationship types, use extracted relationships, and learn to use NLP APIs.

We will cover the following topics in this chapter:

- Relationship types
- Understanding parse trees
- Using extracted relationships
- Extracting relationships
- Using NLP APIs
- Extracting relationships for a question-answer system

Relationship types

There are many possible relationship types. A few categories and examples of relationships are found in the following table. An interesting site that contains a multitude of relationships is Freebase (https://www.freebase.com/). It is a database of people, places, and things organized by categories. The WordNet thesaurus (http://wordnet.princeton.edu/) contains a number of relationships:

Relationship	Example
Personal	father-of, sister-of, girlfriend-of
Organizational	subsidiary-of, subcommittee-of
Spatial	near-to, northeast-of, under
Physical	part-of, composed-of
Interactions	bonds-with, associates-with, reacts-with

Named Entity Recognition (NER) is a low-level type of NLP classification that was covered in Chapter 4, *Finding People and Things*. However, many applications need to go beyond this and identify different types of relationships. For example, when NER is applied to identify individuals, then knowing that we are dealing with a person can further refine the relationships that are present.

Once these entities have been identified, then links can be created to their containing documents or used as indexes. For question answering applications, named entities are often used for answers. When a sentiment of text is determined, it needs to be attributed to some entity.

For example, consider the following input:

```
He was the last person to see Fred.
```

Using OpenNLP NER as input with the preceding sentence, as we did in Chapter 4, *Finding People and Things*, we get the following output:

```
Span: [7..9) person
Entity: Fred
```

Using the OpenNLP parser, we get a lot more information about the sentence:

```
    (TOP (S (NP (PRP He)) (VP (VBD was) (NP (NP (DT the) (JJ last) (NN
person)) (SBAR (S (VP (TO to) (VP (VB see))))))) (. Fred.)))
```

Consider the following input:

```
The cow jumped over the moon.
```

For the preceding sentence, the parser returns this:

```
    (TOP (S (NP (DT The) (NN cow)) (VP (VBD jumped) (PP (IN over) (NP (DT
the) (NN moon))))))
```

There are two types of parsing:

- **Dependency**: This focuses on the relationship between words
- **Phrase structure**: This deals with phrases and their recursive structure

Dependencies can use labels such as subject, determiner, and prepositions to find relationships. Parsing techniques include shift-reduce, spanning tree, and cascaded chunking. We are not concerned about these differences here, but will focus on the use and outcome of various parsers.

Understanding parse trees

Parse trees represent hierarchical relationships between elements of text. For example, a dependency tree shows the relationship between the grammatical elements of a sentence. Let's reconsider the following sentence:

```
The cow jumped over the moon.
```

A parse tree for the preceding sentence is shown here. It was generated using the techniques that will be found in the *Using the LexicalizedParser class* section later in this chapter:

```
(ROOT
  (S
    (NP (DT The)  (NN cow))
    (VP (VBD jumped)
      (PP (IN over)
        (NP (DT the)  (NN moon))))
    (. .)))
```

This sentence can be graphically depicted, as shown in the following diagram. It was generated using the application found at http://nlpviz.bpodgursky.com/. Another editor that allows you to examine text in a graphical manner is GrammarScope (http://grammarscope.sourceforge.net/). This is a Stanford supported tool that uses a Swing-based GUI to generate a parse tree, a grammatical structure, typed dependencies, and a semantic graph of text:

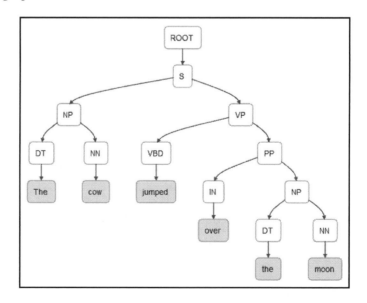

However, there may be more than one way of parsing a sentence. Parsing is difficult because it is necessary to handle a wide range of text where many ambiguities may exist. The following output illustrates other possible dependency trees for the previous example sentence. The tree was generated using OpenNLP, as will be demonstrated in the *Using OpenNLP* section later in this chapter:

```
        (TOP (S (NP (DT The) (NN cow)) (VP (VBD jumped) (PP (IN over) (NP (DT
the) (NN moon))))))
        (TOP (S (NP (DT The) (NN cow)) (VP (VP (VBD jumped) (PRT (RP over)))
(NP (DT the) (NN moon)))))
        (TOP (S (NP (DT The) (NNS cow)) (VP (VBD jumped) (PP (IN over) (NP (DT
the) (NN moon))))))
```

Each of these represents a slightly different parse of the same sentence. The most likely parse is shown first.

Using extracted relationships

Extracted relationships can be used for a number of purposes, including:

- Building knowledge bases
- Creating directories
- Product searches
- Patent analysis
- Stock analysis
- Intelligence analysis

An example of how relationships can be presented is illustrated by Wikipedia's infobox, as shown in the following screenshot. This infobox is for the entry Oklahoma and contains relationship types such as **Official language**, **Capital**, and details about its area:

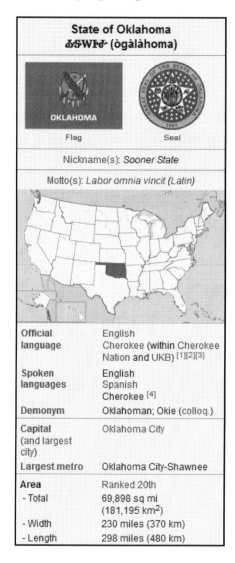

There are many databases built using Wikipedia that extract relationships and information, such as:

- **Resource Description Framework (RDF)**: This uses triples such as Yosemite-location-California, where the location is the relation. This can be found at `http://www.w3.org/RDF/`.
- **DBpedia**: This holds over one billion triples and is an example of a knowledge base created from Wikipedia. This can be found at `https://wiki.dbpedia.org/about`.

Another simple but interesting example is the infobox that is presented when a Google search of `planet mercury` is made. As shown in the following screenshot, not only do we get a list of links for the query but we also see a list of relations and images for **Mercury** displayed on the right-hand side of the page:

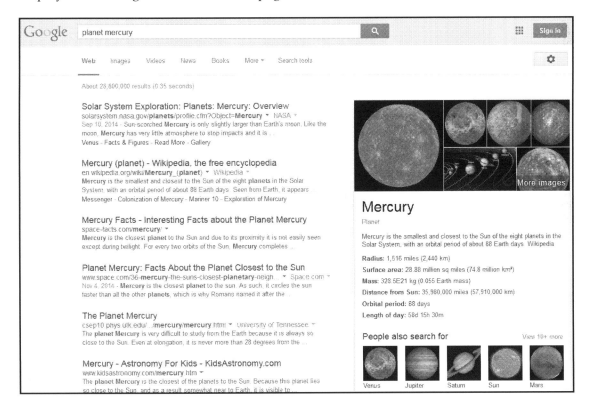

Information extraction is also used to create web indexes. These indexes are developed for a site to allow a user to navigate through the site. An example of a web index for the U.S. Census Bureau (`http://www.census.gov/main/www/a2z`) is shown in the following screenshot:

ALL A B C D E F G H I J K L M N O P Q R S T U V W X Y Z
American
American Community Survey (ACS) Home page
American Housing Survey (AHS)
American Indians and Alaska Natives (AIAN) - see Race
American National Standards Institute (ANSI) Codes (formerly FIPS)
American Samoa - see Puerto Rico and the U.S. Island Areas
Ancestry
Annual
Annual Capital Expenditures Survey (ACES)
Annual Retail Trade Survey
Annual Service Survey
Annual Survey of Manufactures (ASM)
Monthly & Annual Wholesale Trade Survey
ANSI (American National Standards Institute) Codes (formerly FIPS)
Application Program Interface (API)

Extracting relationships

There are a number of techniques available to extract relationships. These can be grouped as follows:

- Hand-built patterns
- Supervised methods
- Semi-supervised or unsupervised methods
- Bootstrapping methods
- Distant supervision methods
- Unsupervised methods

Hand-built models are used when we have no training data. This can occur with new business domains or entirely new types of projects. These often require the use of rules. A rule might be:

"If the word "actor" or "actress" is used and not the word "movie" or "commercial", then the text should be classified as a play."

However, this approach takes a lot of effort and needs to be adjusted for the actual text in-hand.

If only a little training data is amiable, then the Naive Bayes classifier is a good choice. When more data is available, then techniques such as **support vector machine** (**SVM**), regularized logistic regression, and random forest can be used.

Although it is useful to understand these techniques in more detail, we will not cover them here as our focus is on the use of these techniques.

Using NLP APIs

We will use the OpenNLP and Stanford APIs to demonstrate parsing and the extraction of relation information. LingPipe can also be used, but will not be discussed here. An example of how LingPipe is used to parse biomedical literature can be found at `http://alias-i.com/lingpipe-3.9.3/demos/tutorial/medline/read-me.html`.

Using OpenNLP

Parsing text is simple using the `ParserTool` class. Its static `parseLine` method accepts three arguments and returns a `Parser` instance. These arguments are as follows:

- A string containing the text to be parsed
- A `Parser` instance
- An integer specifying how many parses are to be returned

The `Parser` instance holds the elements of the parse. The parses are returned in order of their probability. To create a `Parser` instance, we will use the `ParserFactory` class' `create` method. This method uses a `ParserModel` instance that we will create using the `en-parser-chunking.bin` file.

This process is shown here, in which an input stream for the model file is created using a try-with-resources block. The `ParserModel` instance is created, followed by a `Parser` instance:

```
String fileLocation = getModelDir() +
    "/en-parser-chunking.bin";
try (InputStream modelInputStream =
        new FileInputStream(fileLocation);) {
    ParserModel model = new ParserModel(modelInputStream);
    Parser parser = ParserFactory.create(model);
```

```
      . . .
} catch (IOException ex) {
    // Handle exceptions
}
```

We will use a simple sentence to demonstrate the parsing process. In the following code sequence, the `parseLine` method is invoked using a value of 3 for the third argument. This will return the top three parses:

```
String sentence = "The cow jumped over the moon";
Parse parses[] = ParserTool.parseLine(sentence, parser, 3);
```

Next, these parses are displayed along with their probabilities, as shown here:

```
for(Parse parse : parses) {
    parse.show();
    System.out.println("Probability: " + parse.getProb());
}
```

The output is as follows:

```
    (TOP (S (NP (DT The) (NN cow)) (VP (VBD jumped) (PP (IN over) (NP (DT
the) (NN moon))))))
    Probability: -1.043506016751117
    (TOP (S (NP (DT The) (NN cow)) (VP (VP (VBD jumped) (PRT (RP over)))
(NP (DT the) (NN moon)))))
    Probability: -4.248553665013661
    (TOP (S (NP (DT The) (NNS cow)) (VP (VBD jumped) (PP (IN over) (NP (DT
the) (NN moon))))))
    Probability: -4.761071294573854
```

Notice that each parse produces a slightly different order and assignment of tags. The following output shows the first parse formatted to make it easier to read:

```
(TOP
    (S
        (NP
            (DT The)
            (NN cow)
        )
        (VP
            (VBD jumped)
            (PP
                (IN over)
                (NP
                    (DT the)
                    (NN moon)
                )
```

```
                                  )
                          )
                  )
          )
```

The `showCodeTree` method can be used instead to display parent-child relationships:

```
parse.showCodeTree();
```

The output for the first parse is shown here. The first part of each line shows the element levels enclosed in brackets. The tag is displayed next, followed by two hash values separated by `->`. The first number is for the element and the second number is for its parent. For example, in the third line, it shows the proper noun, `The`, to have a parent of the noun phrase, `The cow`:

```
[0] S -929208263 -> -929208263 TOP The cow jumped over the moon
[0.0] NP -929237012 -> -929208263 S The cow
[0.0.0] DT -929242488 -> -929237012 NP The
[0.0.0.0] TK -929242488 -> -929242488 DT The
[0.0.1] NN -929034400 -> -929237012 NP cow
[0.0.1.0] TK -929034400 -> -929034400 NN cow
[0.1] VP -928803039 -> -929208263 S jumped over the moon
[0.1.0] VBD -928822205 -> -928803039 VP jumped
[0.1.0.0] TK -928822205 -> -928822205 VBD jumped
[0.1.1] PP -928448468 -> -928803039 VP over the moon
[0.1.1.0] IN -928460789 -> -928448468 PP over
[0.1.1.0.0] TK -928460789 -> -928460789 IN over
[0.1.1.1] NP -928195203 -> -928448468 PP the moon
[0.1.1.1.0] DT -928202048 -> -928195203 NP the
[0.1.1.1.0.0] TK -928202048 -> -928202048 DT the
[0.1.1.1.1] NN -927992591 -> -928195203 NP moon
[0.1.1.1.1.0] TK -927992591 -> -927992591 NN moon
```

Another way of accessing the elements of the parse is through the `getChildren` method. This method returns an array of the `Parse` objects, each representing an element of the parse. Using various `Parse` methods, we can get each element's text, tag, and labels. This is illustrated here:

```
Parse children[] = parse.getChildren();
for (Parse parseElement : children) {
    System.out.println(parseElement.getText());
    System.out.println(parseElement.getType());
    Parse tags[] = parseElement.getTagNodes();
    System.out.println("Tags");
    for (Parse tag : tags) {
        System.out.println("[" + tag + "]"
            + " type: " + tag.getType()
```

```
                    + "  Probability: " + tag.getProb()
                    + "  Label: " + tag.getLabel());
        }
    }
```

The output of this sequence is as follows:

```
The cow jumped over the moon
S
Tags
[The] type: DT  Probability: 0.9380626549164167  Label: null
[cow] type: NN  Probability: 0.9574993337971017  Label: null
[jumped] type: VBD  Probability: 0.9652983971550483  Label: S-VP
[over] type: IN  Probability: 0.7990638213315913  Label: S-PP
[the] type: DT  Probability: 0.9848023215770413  Label: null
[moon] type: NN  Probability: 0.9942338356992393  Label: null
```

Using the Stanford API

There are several approaches to parsing available in the Stanford NLP API. First, we will demonstrate a general purposes parser, that is, the LexicalizedParser class. Then, we will illustrate how the result of the parser can be displayed using the TreePrint class. This will be followed by a demonstration of how to determine word dependencies using the GrammaticalStructure class.

Using the LexicalizedParser class

The LexicalizedParser class is a lexicalized PCFG parser. It can use various models to perform the parsing process. The apply method is used with a List instance of the CoreLabel objects to create a parse tree.

In the following code sequence, the parser is instantiated using the englishPCFG.ser.gz model:

```
String parserModel = ".../models/lexparser/englishPCFG.ser.gz";
LexicalizedParser lexicalizedParser =
    LexicalizedParser.loadModel(parserModel);
```

The `list` instance of the `CoreLabel` objects is created using the `Sentence` class' `toCoreLabelList` method. The `CoreLabel` objects contain a word and other information. There are no tags or labels for these words. The words in the array have been effectively tokenized:

```
String[] senetenceArray = {"The", "cow", "jumped", "over",
    "the", "moon", "."};
List<CoreLabel> words =
    Sentence.toCoreLabelList(senetenceArray);
```

The `apply` method can now be invoked:

```
Tree parseTree = lexicalizedParser.apply(words);
```

One simple approach to display the result of the parse is to use the `pennPrint` method, which displays the `parseTree` in the same way as the Penn TreeBank does (http://www.sfs.uni-tuebingen.de/~dm/07/autumn/795.10/ptb-annotation-guide/root.html):

```
parseTree.pennPrint();
```

The output is as follows:

```
(ROOT
  (S
    (NP (DT The)  (NN cow))
    (VP (VBD jumped)
      (PP (IN over)
        (NP (DT the)  (NN moon))))
    (. .)))
```

The `Tree` class provides numerous methods for working with parse trees.

Using the TreePrint class

The `TreePrint` class provides a simple way to display the tree. An instance of the class is created using a string describing the display format to be used. An array of valid output formats can be obtained using the static `outputTreeFormats` variable and are listed in the following table:

	Tree format strings	
penn	dependencies	collocations
oneline	typedDependencies	semanticGraph
rootSymbolOnly	typedDependenciesCollapsed	conllStyleDependencies

words	latexTree	conll2007
wordsAndTags	xmlTree	

Stanford uses type dependencies to describe the grammatical relationships that exist within a sentence. These are detailed in the *Stanford typed dependencies manual* (http://nlp.stanford.edu/software/dependencies_manual.pdf).

The following code example illustrates how the TreePrint class can be used. The printTree method performs the actual display operation.

In this case, the TreePrint object is created, showing "typedDependenciesCollapsed":

```
TreePrint treePrint =
    new TreePrint("typedDependenciesCollapsed");
treePrint.printTree(parseTree);
```

The output of this sequence is as follows, where the number reflects its position within the sentence:

```
det(cow-2, The-1)
nsubj(jumped-3, cow-2)
root(ROOT-0, jumped-3)
det(moon-6, the-5)
prep_over(jumped-3, moon-6)
```

Using the penn string to create the object results in the following output:

```
(ROOT (S (NP (DT The) (NN cow)) (VP (VBD jumped) (PP (IN over) (NP (DT
the) (NN moon)))) (. .)))
```

The dependencies string produces a simple list of dependencies:

```
dep(cow-2,The-1)
dep(jumped-3,cow-2)
dep(null-0,jumped-3,root)
dep(jumped-3,over-4)
dep(moon-6,the-5)
dep(over-4,moon-6)
```

The formats can be combined using commas. The following example will result in both the penn style and the typedDependenciesCollapsed formats being used for the display:

```
"penn,typedDependenciesCollapsed"
```

Finding word dependencies using the GrammaticalStructure class

Another approach to parsing text is to use the `LexicalizedParser` object that we created in the previous section in conjunction with the `TreebankLanguagePack` interface. A Treebank is a text corpus that has been annotated with syntactic or semantic information, providing information about a sentence's structure. The first major Treebank was the Penn TreeBank (`http://www.cis.upenn.edu/~treebank/`). Treebanks can be created manually or semi-automatically.

The following example illustrates how a simple string can be formatted using the parser. A `TokenizerFactory` creates a tokenizer.

The `CoreLabel` class that we discussed in the *Using the LexicalizedParser class* section is used here:

```
String sentence = "The cow jumped over the moon.";
TokenizerFactory<CoreLabel> tokenizerFactory =
    PTBTokenizer.factory(new CoreLabelTokenFactory(), "");
Tokenizer<CoreLabel> tokenizer =
    tokenizerFactory.getTokenizer(new StringReader(sentence));
List<CoreLabel> wordList = tokenizer.tokenize();
parseTree = lexicalizedParser.apply(wordList);
```

The `TreebankLanguagePack` interface specifies methods for working with a Treebank. In the following code, a series of objects are created that culminate with the creation of a `TypedDependency` instance, which is used to obtain dependency information about elements of a sentence. An instance of a `GrammaticalStructureFactory` object is created and used to create an instance of a `GrammaticalStructure` class.

As this class' name implies, it stores grammatical information between elements in the tree:

```
TreebankLanguagePack tlp =
    lexicalizedParser.treebankLanguagePack;
GrammaticalStructureFactory gsf =
    tlp.grammaticalStructureFactory();
GrammaticalStructure gs =
    gsf.newGrammaticalStructure(parseTree);
List<TypedDependency> tdl = gs.typedDependenciesCCprocessed();
```

We can simply display the list, as shown here:

```
System.out.println(tdl);
```

The output is as follows:

```
[det(cow-2, The-1), nsubj(jumped-3, cow-2), root(ROOT-0, jumped-3),
det(moon-6, the-5), prep_over(jumped-3, moon-6)]
```

This information can also be extracted using the `gov`, `reln`, and `dep` methods, which return the governor word, the relationship, and the dependent element, respectively, as illustrated here:

```
for(TypedDependency dependency : tdl) {
    System.out.println("Governor Word: [" + dependency.gov()
        + "] Relation: [" + dependency.reln().getLongName()
        + "] Dependent Word: [" + dependency.dep() + "]");
}
```

The output is as follows:

```
Governor Word: [cow/NN] Relation: [determiner] Dependent Word: [The/DT]
Governor Word: [jumped/VBD] Relation: [nominal subject] Dependent Word:
[cow/NN]
Governor Word: [ROOT] Relation: [root] Dependent Word: [jumped/VBD]
Governor Word: [moon/NN] Relation: [determiner] Dependent Word:
[the/DT]
Governor Word: [jumped/VBD] Relation: [prep_collapsed] Dependent Word:
[moon/NN]
```

From this, we can gleam the relationships within a sentence and the elements of the relationship.

Finding coreference resolution entities

Coreference resolution refers to the occurrence of two or more expressions in text that refer to the same person or entity. Consider the following sentence:

"He took his cash and she took her change and together they bought their lunch."

There are several coreferences in this sentence. The word *his* refers to *He* and the word *her* refers to *she*. In addition, *they* refers to both *He* and *she*.

An **endophora** is a coreference of an expression that either precedes it or follows it. Endophoras can be classified as anaphors or cataphors. In the following sentence, the word *It* is the anaphor that refers to its antecedent, *the earthquake*:

"Mary felt the earthquake. It shook the entire building."

In the next sentence, *she* is a cataphor, as it points to the postcedent, *Mary*:

"As she sat there, Mary felt the earthquake."

The Stanford API supports coreference resolution with the `StanfordCoreNLP` class using a `dcoref` annotation. We will demonstrate the use of this class with the previous sentence.

We will start with the creation of the pipeline and the use of the `annotate` method, as shown here:

```
String sentence = "He took his cash and she took her change "
    + "and together they bought their lunch.";
Properties props = new Properties();
props.put("annotators",
    "tokenize, ssplit, pos, lemma, ner, parse, dcoref");
StanfordCoreNLP pipeline = new StanfordCoreNLP(props);
Annotation annotation = new Annotation(sentence);
pipeline.annotate(annotation);
```

The `Annotation` class' `get` method, when used with an argument of `CorefChainAnnotation.class`, will return a `Map` instance of the `CorefChain` objects, as shown here. These objects contain information about the coreferences found in the sentence:

```
Map<Integer, CorefChain> corefChainMap =
    annotation.get(CorefChainAnnotation.class);
```

The set of `CorefChain` objects are indexed using integers. We can iterate over these objects, as shown in the following code. The key set is obtained and then each `CorefChain` object is displayed:

```
Set<Integer> set = corefChainMap.keySet();
Iterator<Integer> setIterator = set.iterator();
while(setIterator.hasNext()) {
    CorefChain corefChain =
        corefChainMap.get(setIterator.next());
    System.out.println("CorefChain: " + corefChain);
}
```

The following output is generated:

```
CorefChain: CHAIN1-["He" in sentence 1, "his" in sentence 1]
CorefChain: CHAIN2-["his cash" in sentence 1]
CorefChain: CHAIN4-["she" in sentence 1, "her" in sentence 1]
CorefChain: CHAIN5-["her change" in sentence 1]
CorefChain: CHAIN7-["they" in sentence 1, "their" in sentence 1]
CorefChain: CHAIN8-["their lunch" in sentence 1]
```

We get more detailed information using methods of the `CorefChain` and `CorefMention` classes. The latter class contains information about a specific coreference found in the sentence.

Add the following code sequence to the body of the previous `while` loop to obtain and display this information. The `startIndex` and `endIndex` fields of the class refer to the position of the words in the sentence:

```
System.out.print("ClusterId: " + corefChain.getChainID());
CorefMention mention = corefChain.getRepresentativeMention();
System.out.println(" CorefMention: " + mention
    + " Span: [" + mention.mentionSpan + "]");

List<CorefMention> mentionList =
    corefChain.getMentionsInTextualOrder();
Iterator<CorefMention> mentionIterator =
    mentionList.iterator();
while(mentionIterator.hasNext()) {
    CorefMention cfm = mentionIterator.next();
    System.out.println("\tMention: " + cfm
        + " Span: [" + mention.mentionSpan + "]");
    System.out.print("\tMention Mention Type: "
        + cfm.mentionType + " Gender: " + cfm.gender);
    System.out.println(" Start: " + cfm.startIndex
        + " End: " + cfm.endIndex);
}
System.out.println();
```

The output is as follows. Only the first and last mentions are displayed to conserve space:

```
CorefChain: CHAIN1-["He" in sentence 1, "his" in sentence 1]
ClusterId: 1 CorefMention: "He" in sentence 1 Span: [He]
  Mention: "He" in sentence 1 Span: [He]
  Mention Type: PRONOMINAL Gender: MALE Start: 1 End: 2
  Mention: "his" in sentence 1 Span: [He]
  Mention Type: PRONOMINAL Gender: MALE Start: 3 End: 4
...
CorefChain: CHAIN8-["their lunch" in sentence 1]
ClusterId: 8 CorefMention: "their lunch" in sentence 1 Span: [their
lunch]
    Mention: "their lunch" in sentence 1 Span: [their lunch]
    Mention Type: NOMINAL Gender: UNKNOWN Start: 14 End: 16
```

Extracting relationships for a question-answer system

In this section, we will examine an approach for extracting relationships that can be useful for answering queries. Possible/candidate queries include the following:

- Who is/was the 14th president of the United States?
- What is the first president's home town?
- When was Herbert Hoover president?

The process of answering these types of questions is not easy. We will demonstrate one approach to answer certain types of questions, but we will simplify many aspects of this process. Even with these restrictions, we will find that the system responds well to the queries.

This process consists of several steps:

1. Finding word dependencies
2. Identifying the type of questions
3. Extracting its relevant components
4. Searching for the answer
5. Presenting the answer

We will show the general framework to identify whether a question is of the types who, what, when, or where. Next, we will investigate some of the issues required to answer the *who* type questions.

To keep this example simple, we will restrict the questions to those relating to presidents of the U.S. A simple database of presidential facts will be used to look up the answer to a question.

Finding the word dependencies

The question is stored as a simple string:

```
String question =
    "Who is the 32nd president of the United States?";
```

We will use the `LexicalizedParser` class, as developed in the *Finding word dependencies using the GrammaticalStructure class* section. The relevant code is duplicated here for your convenience:

```
String parserModel = ".../englishPCFG.ser.gz";
LexicalizedParser lexicalizedParser =
    LexicalizedParser.loadModel(parserModel);

TokenizerFactory<CoreLabel> tokenizerFactory =
    PTBTokenizer.factory(new CoreLabelTokenFactory(), "");
Tokenizer<CoreLabel> tokenizer =
    tokenizerFactory.getTokenizer(new StringReader(question));
List<CoreLabel> wordList = tokenizer.tokenize();
Tree parseTree = lexicalizedParser.apply(wordList);

TreebankLanguagePack tlp =
    lexicalizedParser.treebankLanguagePack();
GrammaticalStructureFactory gsf =
    tlp.grammaticalStructureFactory();
GrammaticalStructure gs =
    gsf.newGrammaticalStructure(parseTree);
List<TypedDependency> tdl = gs.typedDependenciesCCprocessed();
System.out.println(tdl);
for (TypedDependency dependency : tdl) {
    System.out.println("Governor Word: [" + dependency.gov()
        + "] Relation: [" + dependency.reln().getLongName()
        + "] Dependent Word: [" + dependency.dep() + "]");
}
```

When executed with the question, we get the following output:

```
    [root(ROOT-0, Who-1), cop(Who-1, is-2), det(president-5, the-3),
amod(president-5, 32nd-4), nsubj(Who-1, president-5), det(States-9, the-7),
nn(States-9, United-8), prep_of(president-5, States-9)]
    Governor Word: [ROOT] Relation: [root] Dependent Word: [Who/WP]
    Governor Word: [Who/WP] Relation: [copula] Dependent Word: [is/VBZ]
    Governor Word: [president/NN] Relation: [determiner] Dependent Word:
[the/DT]
    Governor Word: [president/NN] Relation: [adjectival modifier] Dependent
Word: [32nd/JJ]
    Governor Word: [Who/WP] Relation: [nominal subject] Dependent Word:
[president/NN]
    Governor Word: [States/NNPS] Relation: [determiner] Dependent Word:
[the/DT]
    Governor Word: [States/NNPS] Relation: [nn modifier] Dependent Word:
[United/NNP]
    Governor Word: [president/NN] Relation: [prep_collapsed] Dependent
Word: [States/NNPS]
```

This information provides the foundation to determine the type of question.

Determining the question type

The relationships detected suggest ways to detect different types of questions. For example, to determine whether it is a *who* type question, we can check whether the relationship is a `nominal subject` and that the governor is `who`.

In the following code, we iterate over the question type dependencies to determine whether it matches this combination, and if so, call the `processWhoQuestion` method to process the question:

```
for (TypedDependency dependency : tdl) {
    if ("nominal subject".equals( dependency.reln().getLongName())
        && "who".equalsIgnoreCase( dependency.gov().originalText())) {
        processWhoQuestion(tdl);
    }
}
```

This simple distinction worked reasonably well. It will correctly identify all of the following variations to the same question:

```
Who is the 32nd president of the United States?
Who was the 32nd president of the United States?
The 32nd president of the United States was who?
The 32nd president is who of the United States?
```

We can also determine other question types using different selection criteria. The following questions typify other question types:

```
What was the 3rd President's party?
When was the 12th president inaugurated?
Where is the 30th president's home town?
```

We can determine the question type using the relations that are suggested in the following table:

Question type	Relation	Governor	Dependent
What	Nominal subject	What	NA
When	Adverbial modifier	NA	When
Where	Adverbial modifier	NA	Where

This approach does require hardcoding `relationships.createPresidentList`.

Searching for the answer

Once we know the type of question, we can use the relations found in the text to answer the question. To illustrate this process, we will develop the `processWhoQuestion` method. This method uses the `TypedDependency` list to garner the information needed to answer a *who* type question about presidents. Specifically, we need to know which president they are interested in, based on the president's ordinal rank.

We will also need a list of presidents to search for relevant information. The `createPresidentList` method was developed to perform this task. It reads a file, `PresidentList`, containing the president's name, inauguration year, and last year in office. This file uses the following format, and can be downloaded from `https://github.com/PacktPublishing/Natural-Language-Processing-with-Java-Second-Edition`:

```
George Washington    (1789-1797)
```

The following `createPresidentList` method demonstrates the use of OpenNLP's `SimpleTokenizer` class to tokenize each line. A variable number of tokens make up a president's name. Once that is determined, the dates are easily extracted:

```java
public List<President> createPresidentList() {
    ArrayList<President> list = new ArrayList<>();
    String line = null;
    try (FileReader reader = new FileReader("PresidentList");
            BufferedReader br = new BufferedReader(reader)) {
        while ((line = br.readLine()) != null) {
            SimpleTokenizer simpleTokenizer =
                SimpleTokenizer.INSTANCE;
            String tokens[] = simpleTokenizer.tokenize(line);
            String name = "";
            String start = "";
            String end = "";
            int i = 0;
            while (!"(".equals(tokens[i])) {
                name += tokens[i] + " ";
                i++;
            }
            start = tokens[i + 1];
            end = tokens[i + 3];
            if (end.equalsIgnoreCase("present")) {
                end = start;
            }
            list.add(new President(name,
                Integer.parseInt(start),
                Integer.parseInt(end)));
        }
```

```
        } catch (IOException ex) {
            // Handle exceptions
        }
        return list;
    }
```

The `President` class holds presidential information, as shown here. The getter methods have been left out:

```
public class President {
    private String name;
    private int start;
    private int end;

    public President(String name, int start, int end) {
        this.name = name;
        this.start = start;
        this.end = end;
    }
    ...
}
```

The `processWhoQuestion` method follows. We use type dependencies again to extract the ordinal value of the question. If the governor is `president` and the `adjectival modifier` is the relation, then the dependent word is the ordinal.

This string is passed to the `getOrder` method, which returns the ordinal as an integer. We add 1 to it since the list of presidents also started at one:

```
public void processWhoQuestion(List<TypedDependency> tdl) {
    List<President> list = createPresidentList();
    for (TypedDependency dependency : tdl) {
        if ("president".equalsIgnoreCase(
                dependency.gov().originalText())
                && "adjectival modifier".equals(
                    dependency.reln().getLongName())) {
            String positionText =
                dependency.dep().originalText();
            int position = getOrder(positionText)-1;
            System.out.println("The president is "
                + list.get(position).getName());
        }
    }
}
```

The `getOrder` method is as follows and simply takes the first numeric characters and converts them to an integer. A more sophisticated version would look at other variations, including words such as "first" and "sixteenth":

```
private static int getOrder(String position) {
    String tmp = "";
    int i = 0;
    while (Character.isDigit(position.charAt(i))) {
        tmp += position.charAt(i++);
    }
    return Integer.parseInt(tmp);
}
```

When executed, we get the following output:

```
The president is Franklin D . Roosevelt
```

This implementation is a simple example of how information can be extracted from a sentence and used to answer questions. The other types of questions can be implemented in a similar fashion and are left as an exercise for the reader.

Summary

We have discussed the parsing process and how it can be used to extract relationships from text. It can be used for a number of purposes, including grammar checking and machine translation of text. There are numerous possible text relations. These include such relationships as father of, near to, and under. They are concerned with how elements of text are related to each other.

Parsing the text will return relationships that exist within the text. These relationships can be used to extract information of interest. We demonstrated a number of techniques using the OpenNLP and Stanford APIs to parse text.

We also explained how the Stanford API can be used to find coreference resolutions within text. This occurs when two or more expressions, such as *he* or *they*, refer to the same person.

We concluded with an example of how a parser is used to extract relations from a sentence. These relations were used to extract information to answer simple *who* type queries about U.S. presidents.

In the next chapter, `Chapter 11`, The *Combined Pipeline,* we will investigate how the techniques developed in this and the previous chapters can be used to solve more complicated problems.

11
Combined Pipeline

In this chapter, we will address several issues surrounding the use of combinations of techniques to solve NLP problems. We will start with a brief introduction to the process of preparing data. This is followed by a discussion on pipelines and their construction. A pipeline is nothing more than a sequence of tasks integrated to solve some problems. The chief advantage of a pipeline is the ability to insert and remove various elements of the pipeline to solve a problem in a slightly different manner.

The Stanford API supports a good pipeline architecture, which we have used repeatedly in this book. We will expand upon the details of this approach and then show how OpenNLP can be used to construct a pipeline. Preparing data for processing is an important first step in solving many NLP problems. We introduced the data preparation process in Chapter 1, *Introduction to NLP*, and then discussed the normalization process in Chapter 2, *Finding Parts of Text*. In this chapter, we will focus on extracting text from different data sources, such as HTML, Word, and PDF documents. The Stanford StanfordCoreNLP class is a good example of a pipeline that is easily used. In a sense, it is preconstructed. The actual tasks performed are dependent on the annotations added. This works well for many types of problems. However, other NLP APIs do not support pipeline architecture as directly as Stanford APIs; while more difficult to construct, these approaches can be more flexible for many applications. We will demonstrate this construction process using OpenNLP.

We will cover the following topics in this chapter:

- Preparing data
- Using boilerpipe to extract text from HTML
- Using POI to extract text from Word documents
- Using PDFBox to extract text from PDF documents
- Using Apache Tika for content analysis and extraction
- Pipelines
- Using the Stanford pipeline
- Using multiple cores with the Stanford pipeline
- Creating a pipeline to search text

Preparing data

Text extraction is the primary phase for any NLP tasks you want to undertake. If given a blog post, we want to extract the content of the blog and want to find the title of the post, author of the post, date when the post is published, text or content of the post, media-like images, videos in the post, and links to other posts, if any. Text extraction includes the following:

- Structuring so as to identify different fields, blocks of contents, and so on
- Determining the language of the document
- Finding the sentences, paragraphs, phrases, and quotes
- Breaking the text in tokens so as to process it further
- Normalization and tagging
- Lemmatization and stemming so as to reduce the variations and come close to root words

It also helps in topic modeling, which we have covered in Chapter 9, *Topic Modeling*. Here, we will quickly cover how text extraction can be performed for HTML, Word, and PDF documents. Although there are several APIs that support these tasks, we will use the following:

- Boilerpipe (https://code.google.com/p/boilerpipe/) for HTML
- Apache POI (http://poi.apache.org/index.html) for Word
- Apache PDFBox (http://pdfbox.apache.org/) for PDF

Some APIs support the use of XML for input and output. For example, the Stanford XMLUtils class provides support for reading XML files and manipulating XML data. The LingPipe's XMLParser class will parse XML text. Organizations store their data in many forms and frequently it is not in simple text files. Presentations are stored in PowerPoint slides, specifications are created using Word documents, and companies provide marketing and other materials in PDF documents. Most organizations have an internet presence, which means that much useful information is found in HTML documents. Due to the widespread nature of these data sources, we need to use tools to extract their text for processing.

Using boilerpipe to extract text from HTML

There are several libraries available for extracting text from HTML documents. We will demonstrate how to use boilerpipe (https://code.google.com/p/boilerpipe/) to perform this operation. This is a flexible API that not only extracts the entire text of an HTML document but can also extract selected parts of an HTML document, such as its title and individual text blocks. We will use the HTML page at http://en.wikipedia.org/wiki/Berlin to illustrate the use of boilerpipe. Part of this page is shown in the following screenshot:

In order to use boilerpipe, you will need to download the binary for the Xerces Parser, which can be found at http://xerces.apache.org/index.html.

We start by creating a URL object that represents this page. We will use two classes to extract text. The first is the HTMLDocument class that represents the HTML document. The second is the TextDocument class that represents the text within an HTML document. It consists of one or more TextBlock objects that can be accessed individually if needed. We will create a HTMLDocument instance for the Berlin page. The BoilerpipeSAXInput class uses this input source to create a TextDocument instance. It then uses the TextDocument class' getText method to retrieve the text. This method uses two arguments. The first argument specifies whether to include the TextBlock instances marked as content. The second argument specifies whether non-content TextBlock instances should be included. In this example, both types of TextBlock instances are included. The following is the working code:

```
try{
            URL url = new URL("https://en.wikipedia.org/wiki/Berlin");
            HTMLDocument htmldoc = HTMLFetcher.fetch(url);
            InputSource is = htmldoc.toInputSource();
            TextDocument document = new
BoilerpipeSAXInput(is).getTextDocument();
            System.out.println(document.getText(true, true));
        } catch (MalformedURLException ex) {
            System.out.println(ex);
        } catch (IOException ex) {
            System.out.println(ex);
        } catch (SAXException | BoilerpipeProcessingException ex) {
            System.out.println(ex);
        }
```

The output is lengthy, but a few lines are shown here:

```
Berlin
From Wikipedia, the free encyclopedia
Jump to navigation Jump to search
This article is about the capital of Germany. For other uses, see Berlin
(disambiguation) .
State of Germany in Germany
Berlin
State of Germany
From top: Skyline including the TV Tower ,
City West skyline with Kaiser Wilhelm Memorial Church , Brandenburg Gate ,
East Side Gallery ( Berlin Wall ),
Oberbaum Bridge over the Spree ,
Reichstag building ( Bundestag )
. . . . . . .
This page was last edited on 18 June 2018, at 11:18 (UTC).
Text is available under the Creative Commons Attribution-ShareAlike License
; additional terms may apply.  By using this site, you agree to the Terms
```

```
of Use and Privacy Policy . Wikipedia® is a registered trademark of the
Wikimedia Foundation, Inc. , a non-profit organization.
Privacy policy
About Wikipedia
Disclaimers
Contact Wikipedia
Developers
Cookie statement
Mobile view
```

Using POI to extract text from Word documents

The Apache POI project (`http://poi.apache.org/index.html`) is an API used to extract information from Microsoft Office products. It is an extensive library that allows information extraction from Word documents and other office products, such as Excel and Outlook. When downloading the API for POI, you will also need to use XMLBeans (`http://xmlbeans.apache.org/`), which supports POI. The binaries for XMLBeans can be downloaded from `http://www.java2s.com/Code/Jar/x/Downloadxmlbeans524jar.htm`. Our interest is in demonstrating how to use POI to extract text from word documents.

To demonstrate this, we will use a file called `TestDocument.docx`, with some text, tables, and other stuff, as shown in the following screenshot (we have taken the English home page of Wikipedia):

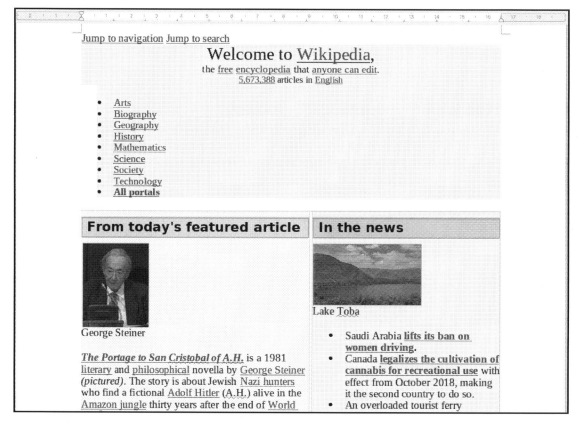

There are several different file formats used by different versions of Word. To simplify the selection of which text extraction class to use, we will use the `ExtractorFactory` factory class. Although the POI's capabilities are considerable, the process of extracting text is simple. As shown here, a `FileInputStream` object representing the file, `TestDocument.docx`, is used by the `ExtractorFactory` class' `createExtractor` method to select the appropriate `POITextExtractor` instance. This is the base class for several different extractors. The `getText` method is applied to the extractor to get the text:

```
private static String getResourcePath(){
        File currDir = new File(".");
        String path = currDir .getAbsolutePath();
        path = path.substring(0, path.length()-2);
        String resourcePath = path + File.separator  +
```

```
"src/chapter11/TestDocument.docx";
        return resourcePath;
    }
    public static void main(String args[]){
        try {
            FileInputStream fis = new FileInputStream(getResourcePath());
            POITextExtractor textExtractor =
ExtractorFactory.createExtractor(fis);
            System.out.println(textExtractor.getText());
        } catch (FileNotFoundException ex) {
Logger.getLogger(WordDocExtractor.class.getName()).log(Level.SEVERE, null,
ex);
        } catch (IOException ex) {
            System.out.println(ex);
        } catch (OpenXML4JException ex) {
            System.out.println(ex);
        } catch (XmlException ex) {
            System.out.println(ex);
        }
    }
}
```

The output is as follows:

```
Jump to navigation Jump to search
Welcome to Wikipedia,
the free encyclopedia that anyone can edit.
5,673,388 articles in English
Arts
Biography
Geography
History
Mathematics
Science
Society
Technology
All portals
From today's featured article George Steiner The Portage to San Cristobal
of A.H. is a 1981 literary and philosophical novella by George Steiner
(pictured). The story is about Jewish Nazi hunters who find a fictional
Adolf Hitler (A.H.) alive in the Amazon jungle thirty years after the end
of World War II. The book was controversial, particularly among reviewers
and Jewish scholars, because the author allows Hitler to defend himself
when he is put on trial in the jungle by his captors. There Hitler
maintains that Israel owes its existence to the Holocaust and that he is
the "benefactor of the Jews". A central theme of The Portage is the nature
of language, and revolves around Steiner's lifelong work on the subject and
his fascination in the power and terror of human speech. Other themes
include the philosophical and moral analysis of history, justice, guilt and
```

revenge. Despite the controversy, it was a 1983 finalist in the
PEN/Faulkner Award for Fiction. It was adapted for the theatre by British
playwright Christopher Hampton. (Full article...) Recently featured: Monroe
Edwards C. R. M. F. Cruttwell Russulaceae Archive By email More featured
articles Did you know... Maria Bengtsson ... that a reviewer found Maria
Bengtsson (pictured) believable and expressive when she first performed the
title role of Arabella by Strauss? ... that the 2018 Osaka earthquake
disrupted train services during the morning rush hour, forcing passengers
to walk between the tracks? ... that funding for Celia Brackenridge's
research into child protection in football was ended because the sport "was
not ready for a gay former lacrosse international rummaging through its
dirty linen"? ... that the multi-armed Heliaster helianthus sheds several
of its arms when attacked by the six-armed predatory starfish Meyenaster
gelatinosus? ... that if elected, Democratic candidate Deb Haaland would be
the first Native American woman to become a member of the United States
House of Representatives? ... that 145 Vietnamese civilians were killed
during the 1967 Thuy Bo massacre? ... that Velvl Greene, a University of
Minnesota professor of public health, taught more than 30,000 students? ...
that a group of Fijians placed a newspaper ad to recruit skiers for Fiji at
the 2002 Olympic Games after discussing it at a New Year's Eve party?
Archive Start a new article Nominate an article In the news Lake Toba Saudi
Arabia lifts its ban on women driving. Canada legalizes the cultivation of
cannabis for recreational use with effect from October 2018, making it the
second country to do so. An overloaded tourist ferry capsizes in Lake Toba
(pictured), Indonesia, killing at least 3 people and leaving 193 others
missing. In golf, Brooks Koepka wins the U.S. Open at the Shinnecock Hills
Golf Club. Ongoing: FIFA World Cup Recent deaths: Joe Jackson Richard
Harrison Yan Jizhou John Mack Nominate an article On this day June 28:
Vidovdan in Serbia Anna Pavlova as Giselle 1776 — American Revolutionary
War: South Carolina militia repelled a British attack on Charleston. 1841 —
Giselle (Anna Pavlova pictured in the title role), a ballet by French
composer Adolphe Adam, was first performed at the Théâtre de l'Académie
Royale de Musique in Paris. 1911 — The first meteorite to suggest signs of
aqueous processes on Mars fell to Earth in Abu Hummus, Egypt. 1978 — In
Regents of the Univ. of Cal. v. Bakke, the U.S. Supreme Court barred quota
systems in college admissions but declared that affirmative action programs
giving advantage to minorities are constitutional. 2016 — Gunmen attacked
Istanbul's Atatürk Airport, killing 45 people and injuring more than 230
others. Primož Trubar (d. 1586) · Paul Broca (b. 1824) · Yvonne Sylvain (b.
1907) More anniversaries: June 27 June 28 June 29 Archive By email List of
historical anniversaries

Today's featured picture
    Henry VIII of England (1491–1547) was King of England from 1509 until
his death. Henry was the second Tudor monarch, succeeding his father, Henry
VII. Perhaps best known for his six marriages, his disagreement with the
Pope on the question of annulment led Henry to initiate the English
Reformation, separating the Church of England from papal authority and

making the English monarch the Supreme Head of the Church of England. He also instituted radical changes to the English Constitution, expanded royal power, dissolved monasteries, and united England and Wales. In this, he spent lavishly and frequently quelled unrest using charges of treason and heresy. Painting: Workshop of Hans Holbein the Younger Recently featured: Lion of Al-lāt Sagittarius Japanese destroyer Yamakaze (1936) Archive More featured pictures

Other areas of Wikipedia
Community portal – Bulletin board, projects, resources and activities covering a wide range of Wikipedia areas.
Help desk – Ask questions about using Wikipedia.

Furthermore, metadata about the document can also be extracted using `metaExtractor`, as shown in the following code:

```
POITextExtractor metaExtractor = textExtractor.getMetadataTextExtractor();
        System.out.println(metaExtractor.getText());
```

It will generate the following output:

```
Created = Thu Jun 28 06:36:00 UTC 2018
CreatedString = 2018-06-28T06:36:00Z
Creator = Ashish
LastModifiedBy = Ashish
LastPrintedString =
Modified = Thu Jun 28 06:37:00 UTC 2018
ModifiedString = 2018-06-28T06:37:00Z
Revision = 1
Application = Microsoft Office Word
AppVersion = 12.0000
Characters = 26588
CharactersWithSpaces = 31190
Company =
HyperlinksChanged = false
Lines = 221
LinksUpToDate = false
Pages = 8
Paragraphs = 62
Template = Normal.dotm
TotalTime = 1
```

The other approach is to create an instance of the `POIXMLPropertiesTextExtractor` class using `XWPFDocument`, which can be used for `CoreProperties` and `ExtendedProperties`, as shown in the following code:

```
fis = new FileInputStream(getResourcePath());
          POIXMLPropertiesTextExtractor properties = new
POIXMLPropertiesTextExtractor(new XWPFDocument(fis));
          CoreProperties coreProperties = properties.getCoreProperties();
          System.out.println(properties.getCorePropertiesText());

          ExtendedProperties extendedProperties =
properties.getExtendedProperties();
          System.out.println(properties.getExtendedPropertiesText());
```

The output is as follows:

```
Created = Thu Jun 28 06:36:00 UTC 2018
CreatedString = 2018-06-28T06:36:00Z
Creator = Ashish
LastModifiedBy = Ashish
LastPrintedString =
Modified = Thu Jun 28 06:37:00 UTC 2018
ModifiedString = 2018-06-28T06:37:00Z
Revision = 1

Application = Microsoft Office Word
AppVersion = 12.0000
Characters = 26588
CharactersWithSpaces = 31190
Company =
HyperlinksChanged = false
Lines = 221
LinksUpToDate = false
Pages = 8
Paragraphs = 62
Template = Normal.dotm
TotalTime = 1
```

Using PDFBox to extract text from PDF documents

The Apache PDFBox (http://pdfbox.apache.org/) project is an API for processing PDF documents. It supports the extraction of text and other tasks, such as document merging, form filling, and PDF creation. We will only illustrate the text extraction process. To demonstrate the use of POI, we will use a file called TestDocument.pdf. This file was saved as a PDF document using the TestDocument.docx file, as shown in the *Using POI to extract text from Word documents* section. The process is straightforward. A File object is created for the PDF document. The PDDocument class represents the document and the PDFTextStripper class performs the actual text extraction using the getText method, as shown here:

```
File file = new File(getResourcePath());
PDDocument pd = PDDocument.load(file);
PDFTextStripper stripper = new PDFTextStripper();
String text= stripper.getText(pd);
System.out.println(text);
```

The output is as follows:

```
Jump to navigation Jump to search
Welcome to Wikipedia,
the free encyclopedia that anyone can edit.
5,673,388 articles in English
 Arts
 Biography
 Geography
 History
 Mathematics
 Science
 Society
 Technology
 All portals
From today's featured article

George Steiner
The Portage to San Cristobal of A.H. is a 1981
literary and philosophical novella by George Steiner
(pictured). The story is about Jewish Nazi hunters
who find a fictional Adolf Hitler (A.H.) alive in the
Amazon jungle thirty years after the end of World
War II. The book was controversial, particularly
among reviewers and Jewish scholars, because the
author allows Hitler to defend himself when he is
```

```
put on trial in the jungle by his captors. There Hitler
maintains that Israel owes its existence to the
Holocaust and that he is the "benefactor of the
Jews". A central theme of The Portage is the nature
of language, and revolves around Steiner's lifelong
work on the subject and his fascination in the power
and terror of human speech. Other themes include
the philosophical and moral analysis of history,
justice, guilt and revenge. Despite the controversy, it
was a 1983 finalist in the PEN/Faulkner Award for
Fiction. It was adapted for the theatre by British

In the news

Lake Toba
 Saudi Arabia lifts its ban on
women driving.
 Canada legalizes the cultivation of
cannabis for recreational use
with effect from October 2018,
making it the second country to do
so.
 An overloaded tourist ferry
capsizes in Lake Toba (pictured),
Indonesia, killing at least 3 people
and leaving 193 others missing.
 In golf, Brooks Koepka wins the
U.S. Open at the Shinnecock Hills
Golf Club.
Ongoing:
 FIFA World Cup
 .....
```

Using Apache Tika for content analysis and extraction

Apache Tika is capable of detecting and extracting metadata and text from thousands of different type of files, such as `.doc`, `.docx`, `.ppt`, `.pdf`, `.xls`, and so on. It can be used for various file formats, which makes it useful for search engines, indexing, content analysis, translation, and so on. It can be downloaded from `https://tika.apache.org/download.html`. This section will explore how Tika can be used for text extraction for various formats. We will use `Testdocument.docx` and `TestDocument.pdf` only.

Using Tika is very straightforward, as shown in the following code:

```
File file = new File("TestDocument.pdf");
Tika tika = new Tika();
String filetype = tika.detect(file);
System.out.println(filetype);
System.out.println(tika.parseToString(file));
```

Simply create an instance of `Tika` and use the `detect` and `parseToString` methods to get the following output:

```
application/pdf
Jump to navigation Jump to search

Welcome to Wikipedia,
the free encyclopedia that anyone can edit.

5,673,388 articles in English

 Arts

 Biography

 Geography

 History

 Mathematics

 Science

 Society

 Technology

 All portals

From today's featured article


George Steiner

The Portage to San Cristobal of A.H. is a 1981

literary and philosophical novella by George Steiner

(pictured). The story is about Jewish Nazi hunters
```

```
who find a fictional Adolf Hitler (A.H.) alive in the

Amazon jungle thirty years after the end of World

War II. The book was controversial, particularly
....
```

Internally, Tika will first detect the type of the document, select the appropriate parser, and then it will perform text extraction from the document. Tika also provides the parser interface and classes to parse the documents. We can also use `AutoDetectParser` or `CompositeParser` of Tika to achieve the same thing. Using the parser, it is possible to get the metadata of the document. More on Tika can be explored at `https://tika.apache.org/`.

Pipelines

A pipeline is nothing more than a sequence of operations where the output of one operation is used as the input to another operation. We have seen it used in several examples in previous chapters but they have been relatively short. In particular, we saw how the Stanford `StanfordCoreNLP` class, with its use of annotators objects, supports the concept of pipelines nicely. We will discuss this approach in the next section. One of the advantages of a pipeline, if structured properly, is that it allows the easy addition and removal of processing elements. For example, if one step of the pipeline converts a token to lowercase, then it is easy to simply remove this step, with the remaining elements of the pipeline left untouched. However, some pipelines are not always this flexible. One step may require a previous step in order to work properly. In a pipeline, such as the one supported by the `StanfordCoreNLP` class, the following set of annotators is needed to support POS processing:

```
props.put("annotators", "tokenize, ssplit, pos");
```

If we leave out the `ssplit` annotator, the following exception is generated:

```
java.lang.IllegalArgumentException: annotator "pos" requires   annotator
"ssplit"
```

Although the Stanford pipeline does not require a lot of effort to set up, other pipelines may. We will demonstrate the latter approach in the *Creating a pipeline to search text* section later in this chapter.

Using the Stanford pipeline

In this section, we will discuss the Stanford pipeline in more detail. Although we have used it in several examples in this book, we have not fully explored its capabilities. Having used this pipeline before, you are now in a better position to understand how it can be used. Upon reading this section, you will be able to better assess its capabilities and applicability to your needs. The `edu.stanford.nlp.pipeline` package holds the **StanfordCoreNLP** and annotator classes. The general approach uses the following code sequence where the text string is processed. The `Properties` class holds the annotation names, and the **Annotation** class represents the text to be processed. The **StanfordCoreNLP** class's **Annotate** method will apply annotation specified in the properties list. The **CoreMap** interface is a basic interface of all annotable objects. It uses key and value pairs. A hierarchy of the classes and interfaces is shown in the following diagram:

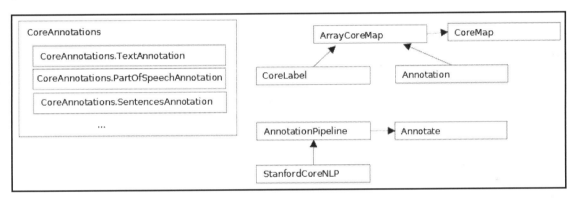

It is a simplified version of the relationship between classes and interfaces. The **CoreLabel** class implements the **CoreMap** interface. It represents a single word with annotation information attached to it. The information attached depends on the properties set when the pipeline is created. However, there will always be positional information available, such as its beginning and ending positions or the whitespace before and after the entity. The `get` method for either **CoreMap** or **CoreLabel** returns information specific to its argument. The `get` method is overloaded and returns a value that's dependent on the type of its argument. The **CoreLabel** class has been used to access individual words in a sentence.

We will use the `keyset` method that returns a set of all of the annotation keys currently held by the `Annotation` object. The keys are displayed before and after the `annotate` method is applied. The full working code is shown here:

```
String text = "The robber took the cash and ran";
        Properties props = new Properties();
```

```
        props.put("annotators", "tokenize, ssplit, pos, lemma, ner, parse,
dcoref");
        StanfordCoreNLP pipeline = new StanfordCoreNLP(props);
        Annotation annotation = new Annotation(text);
        System.out.println("Before annotate method executed ");
        Set<Class<?>> annotationSet = annotation.keySet();
        for(Class c : annotationSet) {
            System.out.println("\tClass: " + c.getName());
        }

        pipeline.annotate(annotation);

        System.out.println("After annotate method executed ");
        annotationSet = annotation.keySet();
        for(Class c : annotationSet) {
            System.out.println("\tClass: " + c.getName());
        }
        List<CoreMap> sentences =
annotation.get(SentencesAnnotation.class);
        for (CoreMap sentence : sentences) {
            for (CoreLabel token: sentence.get(TokensAnnotation.class)) {
                String word = token.get(TextAnnotation.class);
                String pos = token.get(PartOfSpeechAnnotation.class);
                System.out.println(word);
                System.out.println(pos);
            }
        }
```

The following output shows the before and after call as well as words and POS:

```
Before annotate method executed
    Class: edu.stanford.nlp.ling.CoreAnnotations$TextAnnotation
After annotate method executed
    Class: edu.stanford.nlp.ling.CoreAnnotations$TextAnnotation
    Class: edu.stanford.nlp.ling.CoreAnnotations$TokensAnnotation
    Class: edu.stanford.nlp.ling.CoreAnnotations$SentencesAnnotation
    Class: edu.stanford.nlp.ling.CoreAnnotations$MentionsAnnotation
    Class:
edu.stanford.nlp.coref.CorefCoreAnnotations$CorefMentionsAnnotation
    Class:
edu.stanford.nlp.ling.CoreAnnotations$CorefMentionToEntityMentionMappingAnn
otation
    Class:
edu.stanford.nlp.ling.CoreAnnotations$EntityMentionToCorefMentionMappingAnn
otation
    Class: edu.stanford.nlp.coref.CorefCoreAnnotations$CorefChainAnnotation
The
DT
```

```
robber
NN
took
VBD
the
DT
cash
NN
and
CC
ran
VBD
```

Using multiple cores with the Stanford pipeline

The `annotate` method can also take advantage of multiple cores. It is an overloaded method where one version uses an instance of an `Iterable<Annotation>` as its parameter. It will process each `Annotation` instance using the processors available. We will use the previously defined `pipeline` object to demonstrate this version of the `annotate` method.

First, we create four `Annotation` objects based on four short sentences, as shown here. To take full advantage of the technique, it would be better to use a larger set of data. The following is the working code snippet:

```
Annotation annotation1 = new Annotation("The robber took the cash and
ran.");
Annotation annotation2 = new Annotation("The policeman chased him down the
street.");
Annotation annotation3 = new Annotation("A passerby, watching the action,
tripped the thief "
            + "as he passed by.");
Annotation annotation4 = new Annotation("They all lived happily ever after,
except for the thief "
            + "of course.");
ArrayList<Annotation> list = new ArrayList();
list.add(annotation1);
list.add(annotation2);
list.add(annotation3);
list.add(annotation4);
Iterable<Annotation> iterable = list;
pipeline.annotate(iterable);
List<CoreMap> sentences1 = annotation2.get(SentencesAnnotation.class);
```

```
for (CoreMap sentence : sentences1) {
    for (CoreLabel token : sentence.get(TokensAnnotation.class)) {
            String word = token.get(TextAnnotation.class);
            String pos = token.get(PartOfSpeechAnnotation.class);
            System.out.println("Word: " + word + " POS Tag: " + pos);
        }
    }
```

The output is as follows:

```
Word: The POS Tag: DT
Word: policeman POS Tag: NN
Word: chased POS Tag: VBD
Word: him POS Tag: PRP
Word: down POS Tag: RP
Word: the POS Tag: DT
Word: street POS Tag: NN
Word: . POS Tag:
```

Creating a pipeline to search text

Searching is a rich and complex topic. There are many different types of searches and approaches to perform a search. The intent here is to demonstrate how various NLP techniques can be applied to support this effort. A single text document can be processed at one time in a reasonable time period on most machines. However, when multiple large documents need to be searched, then creating an index is a common approach to support searches. This results in a search process that completes in a reasonable period of time. We will demonstrate one approach to create an index and then search using the index. Although the text we will use is not that large, it is sufficient to demonstrate the process. We need to do the following:

- Read the text from the file
- Tokenize and find sentence boundaries
- Remove stop words
- Accumulate the index statistics
- Write out the index file

There are several factors that influence the contents of an index file, including:

- Removal of stop words
- Case-sensitive searches
- Finding synonyms

- Using stemming and lemmatization
- Allowing searches across sentence boundaries

We will use OpenNLP to demonstrate this process. The intent of this example is to demonstrate how to combine NLP techniques in a pipeline process to solve a search-type problem. This is not a comprehensive solution and we will ignore some techniques, such as stemming. In addition, the actual creation of an index file will not be presented but rather left as an exercise for the reader. Here, we will focus on how NLP techniques can be used. Specifically, we will do the following:

- Split the book into sentences
- Convert the sentences to lowercase
- Remove stop words
- Create an internal index data structure

We will develop two classes to support the index data structure: `Word` and `Positions`. We will also augment the `StopWords` class, developed in `Chapter 2`, *Finding Parts of Text*, to support an overloaded version of the `removeStopWords` method. The new version will provide a more convenient method for removing stop words. We start with a try-with-resources block to open streams for the sentence model, `en-sent.bin`, and a file containing the contents of *Twenty Thousand Leagues Under the Sea*, by Jules Verne. The book was downloaded from `http://www.gutenberg.org/ebooks/164`. The following code shows a working example of the search:

```
try {
            InputStream is = new FileInputStream(new File(getResourcePath()
+ "en-sent.bin"));
            FileReader fr = new FileReader(getResourcePath() +
"pg164.txt");
            BufferedReader br = new BufferedReader(fr);
            System.out.println(getResourcePath() + "en-sent.bin");
            SentenceModel model = new SentenceModel(is);
            SentenceDetectorME detector = new SentenceDetectorME(model);
            String line;
            StringBuilder sb = new StringBuilder();
            while((line = br.readLine())!=null){
                sb.append(line + " ");
            }
            String sentences[] = detector.sentDetect(sb.toString());
            for (int i = 0; i < sentences.length; i++) {
                sentences[i] = sentences[i].toLowerCase();
            }
//          StopWords stopWords = new StopWords("stop-
words_english_2_en.txt");
```

```
//                  for (int i = 0; i < sentences.length; i++) {
//                      sentences[i] = stopWords.removeStopWords(sentences[i]);
//                  }
            HashMap<String, Word> wordMap = new HashMap();
            for (int sentenceIndex = 0; sentenceIndex < sentences.length;
sentenceIndex++) {
            String words[] =
WhitespaceTokenizer.INSTANCE.tokenize(sentences[sentenceIndex]);
            Word word;
            for (int wordIndex = 0;
                    wordIndex < words.length; wordIndex++) {
                String newWord = words[wordIndex];
                if (wordMap.containsKey(newWord)) {
                    word = wordMap.remove(newWord);
                } else {
                    word = new Word();
                }
                word.addWord(newWord, sentenceIndex, wordIndex);
                wordMap.put(newWord, word);
            }

            Word sword = wordMap.get("sea");
            ArrayList<Positions> positions = sword.getPositions();
            for (Positions position : positions) {
                System.out.println(sword.getWord() + " is found at line "
                    + position.sentence + ", word "
                    + position.position);
            }
        }

        } catch (FileNotFoundException ex) {
            Logger.getLogger(SearchText.class.getName()).log(Level.SEVERE,
null, ex);
        } catch (IOException ex) {
            Logger.getLogger(SearchText.class.getName()).log(Level.SEVERE,
null, ex);
        }

class Positions {
    int sentence;
    int position;

    Positions(int sentence, int position) {
        this.sentence = sentence;
        this.position = position;
    }
}
```

```
public class Word {
    private String word;
    private final ArrayList<Positions> positions;

    public Word() {
        this.positions = new ArrayList();
    }

    public void addWord(String word, int sentence,
            int position) {
        this.word = word;
        Positions counts = new Positions(sentence, position);
        positions.add(counts);
    }

    public ArrayList<Positions> getPositions() {
        return positions;
    }

    public String getWord() {
        return word;
    }
}
```

Let's break up the code to understand it. The `SentenceModel` is used to create an instance of the `SentenceDetectorME` class, as shown here:

```
SentenceModel model = new SentenceModel(is);
SentenceDetectorME detector = new SentenceDetectorME(model);
```

Next, we will create a string using a `StringBuilder` instance to support the detection of sentence boundaries. The book's file is read and added to the `StringBuilder` instance. The `sentDetect` method is then applied to create an array of sentences, and we used the `toLowerCase` method to convert the text to lowercase. This was done to ensure that when stop words are removed, the method will catch all of them, as shown here:

```
String line;
StringBuilder sb = new StringBuilder();
while((line = br.readLine())!=null){
    sb.append(line + " ");
}
String sentences[] = detector.sentDetect(sb.toString());
for (int i = 0; i < sentences.length; i++) {
    sentences[i] = sentences[i].toLowerCase();
}
```

The next step will be to create an index-like data structure based on the processed text. This structure will use the `Word` and `Positions` class. The `Word` class consists of fields for the word and an `ArrayList` of `Positions` objects. Since a word may appear more than once in a document, the list is used to maintain its position within the document. The `Positions` class contains a field for the sentence number, `sentence`, and for the position of the word within the sentence, `position`. Both of these classes are defined here:

```
class Positions {
    int sentence;
    int position;

    Positions(int sentence, int position) {
        this.sentence = sentence;
        this.position = position;
    }
}


public class Word {
    private String word;
    private final ArrayList<Positions> positions;

    public Word() {
        this.positions = new ArrayList();
    }

    public void addWord(String word, int sentence,
            int position) {
        this.word = word;
        Positions counts = new Positions(sentence, position);
        positions.add(counts);
    }

    public ArrayList<Positions> getPositions() {
        return positions;
    }

    public String getWord() {
        return word;
    }
}
```

To use these classes, we create a `HashMap` instance to hold positional information about each word in the file. The creation of the word entries in the map is shown in the following code. Each sentence is tokenized and then each token is checked to see if it exists in the map. The word is used as the key to the hash map. The `containsKey` method determines whether the word has already been added. If it has, then the `Word` instance is removed. If the word has not been added before, a new `Word` instance is created. Regardless, the new positional information is added to the `Word` instance and then it is added to the map, as shown here:

```
HashMap<String, Word> wordMap = new HashMap();
        for (int sentenceIndex = 0; sentenceIndex < sentences.length;
sentenceIndex++) {
        String words[] =
WhitespaceTokenizer.INSTANCE.tokenize(sentences[sentenceIndex]);
        Word word;
        for (int wordIndex = 0;
            wordIndex < words.length; wordIndex++) {
            String newWord = words[wordIndex];
            if (wordMap.containsKey(newWord)) {
                word = wordMap.remove(newWord);
            } else {
                word = new Word();
            }
            word.addWord(newWord, sentenceIndex, wordIndex);
            wordMap.put(newWord, word);
        }
}
```

To demonstrate the actual lookup process, we use the `get` method to return an instance of the `Word` object for the word "reef". The list of the positions is returned with the `getPositions` method and then each position is displayed, as shown here:

```
Word sword = wordMap.get("sea");
        ArrayList<Positions> positions = sword.getPositions();
        for (Positions position : positions) {
            System.out.println(sword.getWord() + " is found at line "
                + position.sentence + ", word "
                + position.position);
        }
```

The output is as follows:

```
sea is found at line 0, word 7
sea is found at line 2, word 6
sea is found at line 2, word 37
sea is found at line 3, word 5
sea is found at line 20, word 11
```

```
sea is found at line 39,  word 3
sea is found at line 46,  word 6
sea is found at line 57,  word 4
sea is found at line 133, word 2
sea is found at line 229, word 3
sea is found at line 281, word 14
sea is found at line 292, word 12
sea is found at line 320, word 22
sea is found at line 328, word 21
sea is found at line 355, word 22
sea is found at line 363, word 1
sea is found at line 391, word 13
sea is found at line 395, word 6
sea is found at line 450, word 12
sea is found at line 460, word 6
. . . . .
```

This implementation is relatively simple but does demonstrate how to combine various NLP techniques to create and use an index data structure that can be saved as an index file. Other enhancements are possible, including the following:

- Other filter operations
- Storing document information in the `Positions` class
- Storing chapter information in the `Positions` class
- Providing search options, such as:
  - Case-sensitive searches
  - Exact text searches
  - Better exception handling

These are left as exercises for the reader.

Summary

In this chapter, we addressed the process of preparing data and discussed pipelines. We illustrated several techniques for extracting text from HTML, Word, and PDF documents. We also saw how Apache Tika can be used easily with any kind of document for extraction. We showed that a pipeline is nothing more than a sequence of tasks integrated to solve some problem. We can insert and remove various elements of the pipeline as needed. The Stanford pipeline architecture was discussed in detail. We examined the various annotators that can be used. The details of this pipeline were explored, along with how it can be used with multiple processors. In next chapter, Chapter 12, *Creating a Chatbot* we will work on creating a simple chat bot to demonstrate use of NLP we have seen so far.

12
Creating a Chatbot

Chatbots have become popular in the last few years, and are used by many businesses to help customers to perform routine tasks through the web. Social media and messenger platforms have added to the growth of chatbots more than anything. Recently, Facebook messenger hit 100,000 bots on its messenger platform. Along with chatbots, voicebots are also gaining a lot of traction nowadays, and Alexa by Amazon is a prime example of a voicebot. Chatbots have now penetrated deep into customer markets so that the customer gets a prompt reply and doesn't have to wait for information. With time, the evolution of machine learning has evolved chatbots from being simply conversational to action-oriented, where they can now help customers book appointments, get product details, and even take user's inputs, bookings and reservations, and orders online. The healthcare industry is seeing that the use of chatbots can help with ever-growing number of patients.

You can also understand the importance and expected growth of chatbots, as many of the heads of big companies have heavily invested in chatbots or bought chatbot-based companies. You can name any giant organization—say, Google, Microsoft, Facebook, or IBM—all are active in providing chatbot platforms and APIs. We have all used Siri, or Google Assistant, or Alexa, which are nothing but bots.

The following diagram shows the landscape of chatbots in 2017:

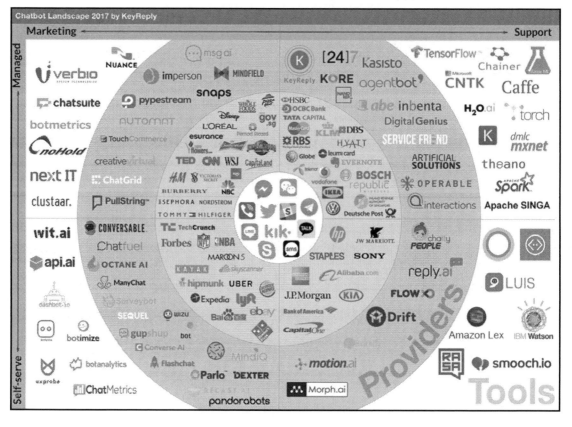

Source – https://blog.keyreply.com/the-chatbot-landscape-2017-edition-ff2e3d2a0bdb

The concentric circles, starting from the inner circle, show platforms, brands, providers, and tools.

In this chapter, we will be looking at different types of chatbots, and we will be developing a simple appointment-booking chatbot too.

The following topics are going to be covered in this chapter:

- Chatbot architecture
- Artificial Linguistic Internet Computer Entity

Chatbot architecture

A chatbot is nothing but a computer program that can chat with a user and perform certain levels of tasks on behalf of the user. Chatbots seem to have a direct connection between the user's problem and the solution. The main aspects of chatbots are as follows:

- **Simple chatbot**: Regarding this type of chatbot, the user will type some text, mostly in the form of questions, and the bot will respond with an appropriate reply in the form of text.
- **Conversational chatbot**: This type of chatbot is aware of the context of the conversation and maintains the state. The response to user text is in the form of a conversation according to the user.
- **AI chatbot**: This type of chatbot learns from the training data provided to it, which is prepared from many different scenarios or from a long log of conversations from the past.

The main aspect of a chatbot is to generate a proper or appropriate response to the user's text using some predefined library or database, or using machine learning models to generate a response. A machine learning algorithm allows training bots with lots of examples of data or conversations to pick a pattern. It uses intent classification and entities to generate a response. To find the intents and entities, it uses the concept of **Natural Language Understanding (NLU)**:

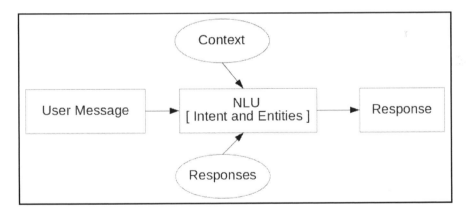

Using machine learning for chatbots requires a great understanding of machine learning algorithms, which is out of the scope of this book.

We will be looking into an option where machine learning is not involved, and such a model is called a **retrieval-based model**, where the response is generated from some predefined logic and context. It is easy to build and reliable, but not 100% accurate in response generation. It is widely used, and several APIs and algorithms are available for such models. It generates a response on the basis of an `if...else` condition, which is known as pattern base response generation:

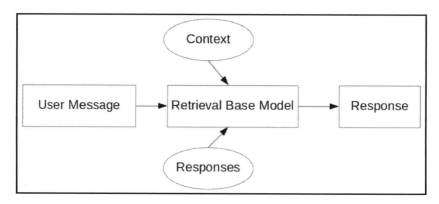

It relies on **Artificial Intelligence Markup Language** (**AIML**) to record patterns and responses. This will be discussed in the next section.

Artificial Linguistic Internet Computer Entity

The **Artificial Linguistic Internet Computer Entity** (**ALICE**) is a free software chatbot that was created in AIML. It's a NLP chatbot, which can engage in conversation with humans using some heuristical pattern matching rules. It has won the Loebner Prize three times, which is awarded to accomplished talking robots. It failed the Turing test, but it can still be used for normal chats and can be customized.

Understanding AIML

In this section, we will be using AIML. AIML is an XML-based markup language used in developing AI applications, especially for software agents. It contains the rules or responses for user requests, which are used by NLU units internally. In simple terms, the more rules we add in AIML, the more intelligent and accurate our chatbot will be.

As AIML is an XML-based markup language; it starts with the root tag `<aiml>`, so a typical AIML file will look like this:

```
<?xml version="1.0" encoding="UTF-8"?>
<aiml>
</aiml>
```

To add questions and answers or responses for possible queries, the `<category>` tag is used. It is a base unit for the knowledge base of a chatbot. In simple words, `<category>` accepts the input and returns the output. All AIML elements must be enclosed in the `<category>` element. The `<pattern>` tag is used to match the user's input, and the `<template>` tag is the response to the user's input. Adding this to the previous code, the code should now look like the following:

```
<?xml version="1.0" encoding="UTF-8"?>
<aiml>
    <category>
        <pattern>Hello</pattern>
        <template> Hello, How are you ? </template>
    </category>
</aiml>
```

So, whenever a user inputs the word `Hello`, the bot will respond with `Hello, How are you ?`.

A `*` is used as a wild card character in the `<pattern>` tag to specify that anything can be put in place of star, and a `<star>` tag is used in the `<template>` tag to form the response, as shown here:

```
<?xml version="1.0" encoding="UTF-8"?>
<aiml>
    <category>
        <pattern>I like *.</pattern>
        <template>Ok, so you like <star/></template>
    </category>
</aiml>
```

Now, when the user says, "I like Mangoes", the response from the bot will be "Ok so you like mangoes". We can also use more than one *, as follows:

```
<?xml version="1.0" encoding="UTF-8"?>
<aiml>
    <category>
    <pattern>I like * and *</pattern>
        <template> Ok, so you like <star index="1"/> and <star
index="2"/></template>
    </category>
</aiml>
```

Now, when the user says, "I like Mangoes and Bananas", the response from the bot will be "Ok so you like mangoes and bananas".

Next is the `<srai>` tag, which is used for different patterns in order to generate same template, as follows:

```
<?xml version="1.0" encoding="UTF-8"?>
<aiml>
    <category>
        <pattern>I WANT TO BOOK AN APPOINTMENT</pattern>
        <template>Are you sure</template>
    </category>
    <category>
        <pattern>Can I *</pattern>
        <template><srai>I want to <star/></srai></template>
    </category>
    <category>
        <pattern>May I * </pattern>
        <template>
            <srai>I want to <star/></srai>
        </template>
    </category>
</aiml>
```

The first category has a pattern of "I WANT TO BOOK AN APPOINTMENT" for which the response is "Are you sure". In the next category, if the user asks "Can I book an appointment" or "May I book an appointment", the response will be the same: "Are you sure".

The <srai> tag is used for many purposes like we saw here, and it can also be used for synonyms and keyword resolution.

For more tags, refer to http://callmom.pandorabots.com/static/reference/#aiml-2-0-reference.

Developing a chatbot using ALICE and AIML

To develop a chatbot, we need an AIML interpreter or reference implementation of the AIML. One such tool for this is Program AB, which can be found at https://code.google.com/archive/p/program-ab/. In the download section, the ZIP file is available for Program AB. Extract the file, which will have the following directories:

- bots: Contains the super folder to show the name of the bot
- data: Contains sample text
- lib: Contains Ab.jar
- out: Contains a class file

In the super subdirectory of the bots directory, we can see the directory names aiml, aimlf, config, data, maps, and sets. These are standard directories that are needed for creating a chatbot using AIML and ALICE. Let's test the chatbot. Open a new Terminal and move to the program-ab folder that we extracted and execute the following command:

```
program-ab-0.0.4.3$ java -cp lib/Ab.jar Main bot = test action=chat
trace=false
```

It will load all the files and will present you with a prompt, as follows:

```
Human :
```

Try to chat with some text and you will soon realize that it works, but not always and not for all queries. The following is a demo chat:

```
Human: Hello
Robot: Hi! It's delightful to see you.
Human: My name is ashish
AIMLMap get ASHISH=M
Robot: Hi there Ashish
Human: Date
CalendarUtils.date: June 28, 2018
Robot: Today is June 28, 2018
Human: Time
CalendarUtils.date: 4:02 PM
Robot: The time is 4:02 PM
Human: What is your name
Robot: I am
SUPER.
Human: How old are you
CalendarUtils.date: June 28, 2018
CalendarUtils.date: June 28, 2018
Robot: I am 5 years old.
Human: Where do you live
Robot: I'm inside your phone.
Human: Oh great
Robot: Uh. How old are you?
Human: I am same
Robot: That sounds interesting.   Tell me more
Human: What you want to know
Robot: Yo, back at you.
Human: ok
Robot: Um.
```

Now, let's create out own chatbot for appointment scheduling. The first step is to create an AIML file.

Create the following folder structure in your new NetBeans project and add `Ab.jar` in your project library:

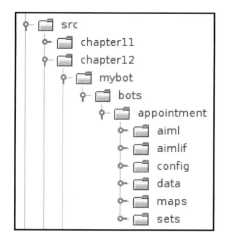

In the `aiml` directory, let's create an AIML file with the following content:

```
<?xml version="1.0" encoding="UTF-8"?>
<aiml>
<!--   -->
<category><pattern>I WANT TO BOOK AN APPOINTMENT</pattern>
<template>Are you sure you want to book an appointment</template>
</category>
<category><pattern>YES</pattern><that>ARE YOU SURE YOU WANT TO BOOK AN
APPOINTMENT</that>
<template>Can you tell me date and time</template>
</category>
<category><pattern>NO</pattern><that>ARE YOU SURE YOU WANT TO BOOK AN
APPOINTMENT</that>
<template>No Worries.</template>
</category>
<category><pattern>DATE * TIME *</pattern><that>CAN YOU TELL ME DATE AND
TIME</that>
<template>You want appointment on <set name="udate"><star index="1"/>
</set> and time <set name="utime"><star index="2"/></set>. Should i
confirm.</template>
</category>
<category><pattern>YES</pattern><that>SHOULD I CONFIRM</that>
<template><get name="username"/>, your appointment is confirmed for <get
name="udate"/> : <get name="utime"/></template>
</category>
<category><pattern>I AM *</pattern>
<template>Hello <set name="username"> <star/>! </set></template>
</category>
<category><pattern>BYE</pattern>
<template>Bye <get name="username"/> Thanks for the
conversation!</template>
</category>
</aiml>
```

Let's explore the AIML file. Using the `set` and `get` tags, the context can be saved in variables and retrieved when required:

```
<category><pattern>I AM *</pattern>
<template>Hello <set name="username"> <star/>! </set></template>
</category>
```

This shows the use of the `set` property, so when the user inputs "`I am ashish`", it is saved in the variable `name` and the response is "`Hello Ashish !`". Now, this can be used anywhere in AIML by using `get` to print the username. So, this means that using the `set` and `get` tag context can be maintained.

The next part is to create an appointment. When the user asks for an appointment, the response will ask for confirmation, as follows:

```
<category><pattern>I WANT TO BOOK AN APPOINTMENT</pattern>
<template>Are you sure you want to book an appointment</template>
</category>
```

Now, the expected request from the user will be yes or no, according to which the next response is generated. To continue the conversation in context with the last question, the tag is used, as follows:

```
<category><pattern>YES</pattern><that>ARE YOU SURE YOU WANT TO BOOK AN
APPOINTMENT</that>
<template>Can you tell me date and time</template>
</category>
<category><pattern>NO</pattern><that>ARE YOU SURE YOU WANT TO BOOK AN
APPOINTMENT</that>
<template>No Worries.</template>
</category>
```

If the user says "YES", the chatbot will ask for the date and time, which again is saved, and confirmation is asked as to whether the user wants to book an appointment on the stated date and time, as follows:

```
<category><pattern>DATE * TIME *</pattern><that>CAN YOU TELL ME DATE AND
TIME</that>
<template>You want appointment on <set name="udate"><star index="1"/>
</set> and time <set name="utime"><star index="2"/></set>. Should i
confirm.</template>
</category>
<category><pattern>YES</pattern><that>SHOULD I CONFIRM</that>
<template><get name="username"/>, your appointment is confirmed for <get
name="udate"/> : <get name="utime"/></template>
</category>
```

A sample chat output is as follows:

```
Robot : Hello, I am your appointment scheduler May i know your name
Human :
I am ashish
Robot : Hello ashish!
Human :
I want to book an appointment
Robot : Are you sure you want to book an appointment
Human :
yes
Robot : Can you tell me date and time
Human :
```

```
Date 24/06/2018 time 4 pm
Robot : You want appointment on 24/06/2018 and time 4 pm. Should i confirm.
Human :
yes
Robot : ashish!, your appointment is confirmed for 24/06/2018 : 4 pm
```

Save this AIML file as `myaiml.aiml` in the `aiml` directory. The next step is to create the AIML intermediate format CSV files. Create a Java file named `GenerateAIML.java` and add the following code:

```java
public class GenerateAIML {
        private static final boolean TRACE_MODE = false;
        static String botName = "appointment";

    public static void main(String[] args) {
        try {

            String resourcesPath = getResourcesPath();
            System.out.println(resourcesPath);
            MagicBooleans.trace_mode = TRACE_MODE;
            Bot bot = new Bot("appointment", resourcesPath);
            bot.writeAIMLFiles();

        } catch (Exception e) {
            e.printStackTrace();
        }
    }

    private static String getResourcesPath(){
        File currDir = new File(".");
        String path = currDir .getAbsolutePath();
        path = path.substring(0, path.length()-2);
        System.out.println(path);
        String resourcePath = path + File.separator  +
"src/chapter12/mybot";
        return resourcePath;
    }
}
```

Execute this file. It will generate `myaiml.aiml.csv` in the `aimlif` directory.

Change the `ResourcePath` variable according to your package in NetBeans. In this case, `chapter12` is the package name, and `mybot` is the directory inside the package.

Create another Java file to test the bot, follows:

```
public class Mychatbotdemo {
    private static final boolean TRACE_MODE = false;
    static String botName = "appointment";
    private static String getResourcePath(){
        File currDir = new File(".");
        String path = currDir .getAbsolutePath();
        path = path.substring(0, path.length()-2);
        System.out.println(path);
            String resourcePath = path + File.separator  +
"src/chapter12/mybot";
        return resourcePath;
    }
    public static void main(String args[]){
        try
        {
            String resourcePath = getResourcePath();
            System.out.println(resourcePath);
            MagicBooleans.trace_mode = TRACE_MODE;
            Bot bot = new Bot(botName, resourcePath);
            Chat chatSession = new Chat(bot);
            bot.brain.nodeStats();
            String textLine = "";
            System.out.println("Robot : Hello, I am your appointment
scheduler May i know your name");
            while(true){
                System.out.println("Human : ");
                textLine = IOUtils.readInputTextLine();
                if ((textLine==null) || (textLine.length()<1)){
                    textLine = MagicStrings.null_input;
                }
                if(textLine.equals("q")){
                    System.exit(0);
                } else if (textLine.equals("wq")){
                    bot.writeQuit();
                } else {
                    String request = textLine;
                    if(MagicBooleans.trace_mode)
                        System.out.println("STATE=" + request + ":THAT" +
((History)chatSession.thatHistory.get(0)).get(0) + ": Topic" +
chatSession.predicates.get("topic"));
                    String response =
chatSession.multisentenceRespond(request);
                    while(response.contains("&lt;"))
                        response = response.replace("&lt;", "<");
                    while(response.contains("&gt;"))
                        response = response.replace("&gt;", ">");
```

```
                    System.out.println("Robot : " + response);
                }
            }
        }
        catch(Exception e){
            e.printStackTrace();
        }
    }
}
```

Execute the Java code and you will see the prompt saying `Human:`, and it will wait for an input. Pressing *Q* will end the program. As per our AIML file, our dialogue is limited as we have only asked for basic information. We can integrate it with the `super` folder and add our AIML file in the `super` directory so that we can use all the available conversations by default and our custom conversation for appointments.

Summary

In this chapter, we saw the importance of chatbots and where they are heading. We also showed you the different chatbot architectures. We started with understanding ALICE and AIML, and using AIML, we created a demo chatbot for appointment scheduling to show the concept of chatbots using ALICE and AIML.

Other Books You May Enjoy

If you enjoyed this book, you may be interested in these other books by Packt:

Java Deep Learning Projects
Md. Rezaul Karim

ISBN: 978-1-78899-745-4

- Master deep learning and neural network architectures
- Build real-life applications covering image classification, object detection, online trading, transfer learning, and multimedia analytics using DL4J and open-source APIs
- Train ML agents to learn from data using deep reinforcement learning
- Use factorization machines for advanced movie recommendations
- Train DL models on distributed GPUs for faster deep learning with Spark and DL4J
- Ease your learning experience through 69 FAQs

Hands-On Natural Language Processing with Python
Rajesh Arumugam, Rajalingappaa Shanmugamani

ISBN: 978-1-78913-949-5

- Implement semantic embedding of words to classify and find entities
- Convert words to vectors by training in order to perform arithmetic operations
- Train a deep learning model to detect classification of tweets and news
- Implement a question-answer model with search and RNN models
- Train models for various text classification datasets using CNN
- Implement WaveNet a deep generative model for producing a natural-sounding voice
- Convert voice-to-text and text-to-voice
- Train a model to convert speech-to-text using DeepSpeech

Leave a review - let other readers know what you think

Please share your thoughts on this book with others by leaving a review on the site that you bought it from. If you purchased the book from Amazon, please leave us an honest review on this book's Amazon page. This is vital so that other potential readers can see and use your unbiased opinion to make purchasing decisions, we can understand what our customers think about our products, and our authors can see your feedback on the title that they have worked with Packt to create. It will only take a few minutes of your time, but is valuable to other potential customers, our authors, and Packt. Thank you!

Index

Made in the USA
Middletown, DE
07 September 2018